DATE DUE

OCT 1 5 1996	
DEC 0 5 1996	
MAR 1 0 1997	
Mar 25	
April 8 OCT 3 1 1997	
FEB - 6 1998	
APR - 9 1998	
MAR 1 9 1999	
FEB 2 8 2000	
MAR 2 9 2000	
MAR 2 5 2001	

BRODART.   Cat. No. 23-221

Illness and Power

Illness and Power

Women's Mental Disorders
and the Battle between
the Sexes

Brant Wenegrat

New York University Press
New York and London

New York University Press
New York and London
Copyright © 1995 by New York University
All rights reserved

New York University Press books are printed on acid-free paper,
and their binding materials are chosen for strength and durability.

Library of Congress Cataloging-in-Publication Data
Wenegrat, Brant.
Illness and power : women's mental disorders and the battle
between the sexes / Brant Wenegrat.
p.   cm.
Includes bibliographical references and index.
ISBN 0-8147-9282-0
1. Women—Mental health—Sociological aspects. 2. Social
isolation. 3. Women—Social conditions. I. Title.
RC451.4.W6W46   1995
616.89'0082—dc20   94-40877
                          CIP
Manufactured in the United States of America
10 9 8 7 6 5 4 3 2 1

Contents

Acknowledgments

Numerous friends and colleagues contributed to the writing of this book. Adolf Pfefferbaum and Bert Kopell maintained the institutional arrangements that made it possible for me to study and write. Over the years, Walton T. Roth consistently helped me to refine my thinking on many of the topics discussed in later chapters, as did many of the psychiatry residents with whom I have been privileged to work. Linda Garfield, Annette Hollander, Robert Ornstein, Margaret Nesse, Randolph Nesse, and others read this manuscript at various stages and offered important suggestions. Robert Ornstein and Kitty Moore provided invaluable help in finding a publisher. Niko Pfund, of New York University Press, provided important advice and shepherded this book through the publication process.

I am especially indebted to my wife, Anne O'Reilly, and to my son, Jacob O'Reilly Wenegrat. Both supported me during the writing process. As a clinical psychologist, Anne also contributed to many of the ideas and arguments in this book.

Of course, I am solely responsible for any errors, whether in fact or in reasoning, found in the following pages.

Introduction: Explaining Women's Disorders

Since ancient times, physicians have believed that women are especially vulnerable to certain mental illnesses. Modern-day research studies confirm that women are more susceptible than men to anxiety, depression, multiple personality, eating disorders, and several forms of what used to be called hysteria.[1] Women's excess risk of these disorders is real; it cannot be accounted for by use of different diagnostic criteria in men and women, by greater willingness of women to admit psychological symptoms, or by help-seeking behavior by women patients. This study tries to explain why these disorders are more common in women.

The thesis of this book is that mental disorders that are more common in women are partly caused by lack of social power and that women's higher risk of these mental disorders results from their relative powerlessness in many societies. Social power is the ability to provide for one's needs and security and the needs and security of loved ones, to stand up for oneself in conflicts with others, and to make life decisions based on one's own desires. To explain women's relative lack of social power and to understand its psychological meaning, I will review women's powerlessness from an evolutionary, cross-cultural perspective. Although men in most societies have much more power than women, women in some societies do have sufficient power to provide for their needs and security, to stand up for their interests, and to make life decisions. Men's power advantage results from differences in men's and women's strategies pertaining to reproduction. The allocation of power in particular societies is determined by diverse factors, the most important of which is women's control of resources. Societies in which women produce more material goods are those in which women control the greatest resources and thus wield more social power.

An important corollary point is that mental disorders can be understood only when their larger social settings have been given more attention than is often the case. Not only personal circumstances but also general conditions—sociological, economic, and cultural—shape and define the symptoms and signs of these disorders and determine their course and incidence. This point is illustrated by many of the illnesses discussed in later chapters. For example, in the late nineteenth century, Jean-Martin Charcot, the great neurological pioneer in charge of the Salpêtrière, the Parisian women's asylum, failed miserably to understand grand hysteria, the disorder that most intrigued him, because he was insufficiently attentive to his patients' sociological and economic handicaps.[2] Charcot's student, Pierre Janet, working just twenty years later, first understood how hysteria could serve an adaptive function for disadvantaged patients. By talking to patients about their lives, Janet founded the modern practice of psychotherapy. Charcot and Janet are discussed in chapter 3.

Some feminist authors, of course, have already argued that women's social conditions and especially their lack of power damages their mental health. Betty Friedan expressed this view in *The Feminine Mystique,* the 1963 classic credited by some with starting the modern women's movement.[3] Friedan claimed that women's depression and suicidality results from their exclusion from work and public life.[4] She argued that work and activities outside the home are essential to women's health and emotional well-being, and that the housewife role produces psychopathology. In chapter 2, I cite evidence to support this thesis. In 1976, Jean Baker Miller, a psychiatrist and psychoanalyst, observed that much of what was then believed to be women's psychology, including many of their psychological problems, is actually the psychology of a subordinate class.[5] This differs from that of the dominant class both because of realities of subordinates' lives and because ideology demands that a difference be found, in order to justify the fact of repression itself. Although some feminist therapists have further developed these viewpoints, the major therapy "schools" have for the most part ignored them.[6] Interpersonal theorists are virtually the only nonfeminist, mainstream authors who even discuss the notion that women's gender roles are bad for mental health.[7] Interpersonal theorists' interest in social relationships has perhaps called their attention to the drawbacks of women's roles. On the other hand, therapists trained in schools of thought that emphasize psychodynamic, familial, behavioral, or biological causes of mental illness, and that take gender roles and social arrangements for granted, may be less attentive to sociocultural factors affecting mental health.

Finally, it is important to emphasize that this book does not aim to offer a complete account of women's mental disorders. Women's disorders are no doubt caused by multiple factors, many or all of which also cause mental disorders in men. I devote little or no attention to the psychodynamic, familial, behavioral, or biological issues that interest most therapists and that are no doubt crucial in treating particular patients. Instead, I attempt to account for the excess numbers of women with certain disorders. Rather than try to explain mental illness in any complete sense, I ask the (possibly) simpler question: What additional factor(s) operate in women to cause excess numbers of women to fall ill?[8]

Evolutionary Politics

The argument here goes beyond those of previous clinical authors in looking at the reasons for women's lack of power. In looking at women's power, I will cite modern theories of behavioral evolution. These theories clarify factors affecting the balance of power between men and women. The latter information can be used to improve public health and in the treatment of individual patients. These theories also clarify women's response to their relative lack of social power. As I show in a later chapter, regardless of the claims made by social conservatives and by some psychological theorists, women cannot have evolved so as to be happy when powerless. Lack of social power is a threat and a stress to women, just as it is to men. That is why it is pathogenic, as I argue in later chapters.

Many feminist authors have strongly condemned the theories I will cite in this book. They mistakenly claim that theories of behavioral evolution undermine women's rights, promote rigid sex roles, and justify male repression. To cite just a few instances, Robin Morgan, a well-known feminist writer and editor of *Ms.* magazine, excoriated what she called the "we-can't-change propaganda inherent in the pseudo-science of sociobiology."[9] Gerda Lerner, a feminist historian whose study of ancient society is described in chapter 5, thought it necessary to dismiss sociobiology before going on to document the importance of cultural factors in determining gender roles.[10] Sociobiology, according to Lerner, is circular, ahistorical, lacking in evidence, and based on unsound assumptions. Cynthia Fuchs Epstein, a feminist sociologist, devoted six pages of her treatise on gender roles to sociobiology, which she claims trades in "anthropomorphism and speculative conclusions."[11] According to Epstein, "the sociobiologists regard human male dominance as ordained by nature." She asserts that sociobiological theories were used to help defeat the Equal Rights Amendment. Sandra Lipsitz Bem, a feminist expert on gender roles, claims that evolutionists "naturalize" inequalities based on stereotypes.[12]

Sociobiologists have even appeared as villains in women's literature. A sociobiologist helped found "The Sons of Jacob," the right-wing organization that took away women's rights in Margaret Atwood's novel *The Handmaid's Tale.*[13]

Some of these attacks are based on misconceptions or superficial readings. Lerner and Epstein, for instance, seem to think that evolutionists believe in group selection, the doctrine that behavior evolved to serve social groups.[14] As Epstein observes, this would imply that women accept subordinate roles for the good of their groups, not because they are forced to. Epstein's remarks echo Betty Friedan's earlier critique of "functionalism," a movement then in vogue in sociology, which Friedan thought was too melioristic about women's roles.[15] In fact, though, evolutionists believe that human behavior evolved to serve the interests of individuals. This viewpoint implies that people will not choose disadvantageous roles unless they have been coerced to do so or have been misled into believing that these disadvantageous roles are really advantageous. This is a critical issue in relation to women's response to their relative lack of power (see chapter 5). In criticizing the evolutionary theory of mating behavior, Bem fails to mention the hypothesized role of ecology and resource distribution in determining relations between men and women. Thus, she misleads her readers into thinking that the theory is insensitive to the environment.

As I will show in chapter 5, evolutionary theories of human behavior do in fact predict that males will try to dominate women and each other, as many feminists fear, but they do not predict an unvarying pattern of domination. Instead, these theories suggest that men's power advantage is contingent on resource control. When men can control resources needed for rearing children, as they do in most societies, they generally dominate women. Women resist domination, and the two sexes engage in an ongoing "battle." However, when resources needed for children are widely distributed, men and women should be more or less equally powerful, and the battle between men and women should be temporarily stilled. Although there are no societies in which women dominate men, there are, in fact, many societies in which women wield sufficient power to meet their needs. Data cited in chapter 5 support the critical role played by resource distribution in determining men's and women's relative social power.

Do Women's Mental Disorders Really Exist?

Some feminists claim that women are not really more prone to mental disorders than men. Instead, they see psychiatry as an instrument for social control of women, who, like the former Soviet dissidents, are labeled mentally ill whenever they challenge society. According to this view, the large number of women diagnosed with these disorders manifests an organized plot against female dissidents, rather than an increased rate of real pathology. Jane Ussher, for instance, summarized the so-called deconstructionist feminist view of mental disorders.[16] According to Ussher, from the fourteenth through the seventeenth centuries, women who posed threats to the social order were labeled witches and burned at the stake. When witchcraft lost credibility as an anathematizing label, physicians invented hysteria and other women's disorders to threaten and stigmatize women who stepped out of line. Women called mentally ill, like those called witches before them, are more likely rebels and heroines than victims of ill health. The physicians' purpose, likewise, is more akin to thought reform than to genuine healing. Ussher herself was so convinced by this argument that she gave up clinical practice of psychology, although she later rejected the pure deconstructionist viewpoint. Phyllis Chesler, a clinical psychologist and a founder of the Association for Women in Psychology, illustrated this argument by citing Elizabeth Packard, a nineteenth-century woman who dared to disagree with her clergyman husband on a theological issue and who, in another era, would certainly have burned at the stake.[17] Her husband, according to Chesler, kidnapped her against her will (although he was within his legal rights to do so) and removed her to an asylum at Jacksonville, Illinois. He forbade her children, whose ages ranged from eighteen months to eighteen years, to communicate with or talk about her. He kept her own (inherited) income from her. He deprived her of her clothes, books, and personal papers and misrepresented her situation to her parents. Dr. MacFarland, the psychiatrist-director of the asylum, remaindered her outgoing mail and seized her few books and smuggled-in writing paper. Despite these events, Mrs. Packard never lost her "wits." She always referred to the asylum as a "prison"—and never as a "hospital." She began a secret diary of asylum events and ministered to the other inmates, most of whom she regarded as sister victims of the patriarchy. . . . [Mrs. Packard] "forgave" Dr. MacFarland his "sins"—until, in a moment of fury, he nearly strangled her normally docile roommate, Bridget (Bridget had refused to do some domestic dirty work for him, and the Doctor became enraged).[18]

According to Chesler, Elizabeth Packard was the first to liken asylum psychiatry to the Inquisition.

Chesler cited other similar cases, including Zelda Fitzgerald, whose husband, F. Scott Fitzgerald, objected to her dancing lessons and to her writing career, and Sylvia Plath, the poet and writer who killed herself in 1963. Zelda, who wanted her independence from Scott and something other than a career as a mother, was hospitalized for fifteen months. According to Chesler, Zelda's male psychiatrists treated her ambitions as if they were delusions. She was said to be suffering from an "inferiority complex" directed toward her husband. In spite of her great talents, Plath worked in isolation and without the recognition afforded to male poets. A full-time mother and housewife, she rose in the early mornings to find some time to write. Many of her poems have a strongly feminist message. The heroine of *The Bell Jar*, Plath's autobiographical novel, is treated by male psychiatrists who try to make her "normal" but do not understand her.

This same critique of psychiatry has been picked up by feminist novelists and widely read theoreticians, thus reaching a much larger audience than authors like Ussher and Chesler have reached. For example, Connie Ramos, the protagonist of Marge Piercy's *Woman on the Edge of Time,* is a fictional analogue of Elizabeth Packard.[19] Connie's troubles start when she tries to stop a pimp from forcing her niece to have an unsafe abortion. The pimp beats Connie savagely and takes her to Bellevue hospital, where she has a record as a mental patient. Her brother, the *paterfamilias,* consigns Connie to a state hospital, where she is treated brutally and forced to have neurosurgery. To make the point yet more obvious, Connie is in contact with nonsexist future beings, who give voice to the view that psychiatry is barbaric. In another novel, *Small Changes,* Piercy has a character liken mental hospitals to jails, with the difference that in jails men learn "survival skills" while in hospitals women are drugged to forget why they stepped out of line.[20] Here Piercy portrays psychiatrists as agents of male control, to whom men send their wives when they need adjustment.

Marilyn French shows the same negative view of psychiatry and skeptical view of women's mental disorders in *The Women's Room.*[21] One character, Lily, has been locked away in a mental hospital by her husband, Carl, for failing to do the housework. There she finds other women whose husbands no longer want them. French has a character muse that the brutal electric shock treatments described to her by Lily are intended to silence women who try to speak the truth.

As for the theoreticians, Kate Millett, who has had her own unpleasant encounters with psychiatry, seems to deny that any mental illness is real. In *The Loony Bin Trip,* Millett claims that mental disorders are merely pejorative labels used to punish people—more often women than men—who threaten the status quo by somehow being different and that these labels often act as self-fulfilling prophecies.[22] According to Millett, psychotropic drugs cause, rather than cure, paranoia, delusions, and hallucinations, and electroshock therapy is merely a form of torture. She pleads for an end to what she calls psychiatry's "savage methods." Mary

Daly calls psychotherapy "mind rape," which peddles a view of normalcy based on misogynist thinking.[23]

Although it fails to account for data, some of which is cited in later chapters, that women are in fact ill more often than men and that the illnesses they develop are more than just social inventions designed to control their behavior, deconstructionism does highlight some issues important in this context. First, in viewing illness labels as instruments of control, the deconstructionist argument raises the issue of normalcy in societies structured so as to promote ill health. If people are forced to live in unhealthy conditions, those who respond most sanely, like Lily in French's novel, may well be considered crazy. As I and others have argued elsewhere, this is especially the case when the regnant psychology promotes a tabula rasa view of human nature.[24] If normalcy is wholly defined by societal norms, then deviance is insanity almost by definition. Without a concept of mental health independent of social norms, there is no alternative to acceptance of social functionalism like that condemned by Friedan. If, as I argue here, societies that severely limit women's power cause women to be unhealthy, then the healthiest women may be those who are in some respects deviant. Second, as is described in chapters 3 and 4, some mental disorders are in fact social constructions used for "political" purposes, but the purposes served are likely to be the patient's as well as the physician's. That is, several of the disorders described in chapters 3 and 4 help patients protest conditions that they otherwise cannot change, to obtain needed assistance that is otherwise not forthcoming, and to control other persons who are otherwise not controllable. This is not to deny that clinicians' needs are served by these diagnoses, but only to emphasize that clinicians collude with patients in making these diagnoses. They do not impose diagnoses on wholly unwilling patients. Finally, many psychiatrists, men and women alike, are in fact insensitive to the real-life situations of their women patients. I have already cited the theoretical biases that blind many clinicians to sociological factors contributing to ill health. But regardless of their theories, psychiatrists, being professionals, are unlikely to experience firsthand many of the stresses affecting most women patients. Some of the most important stresses affecting women seem to be due to economic dependency. It is hard to be fully attentive to the effects of stresses one has never experienced.

An Outline of This Book

The plan of this book is as follows: The next three chapters show how various forms of psychopathology that are thought to be more common in women are caused, in part, by lack of social power. Women's increased risk of these disorders may be due to their lack of power in comparison with men. Chapter 2 is devoted to anxiety and depression. Both epidemiological and clinical studies show that women are at greatly increased risk for these disorders. Modern-day theories of their etiology suggest that both anxiety and depressive disorders are caused in part by powerlessness, or at least the perception of powerlessness, either in general or in specific situations. Epidemiological studies of these disorders confirm that their incidence in women varies with factors related to social power, such as marital status, maternity, and employment outside the home.

Chapter 3 addresses nineteenth-century women's disorders, in order to lay the groundwork for discussing more contemporary illnesses. The florid forms of hysteria seen in the nineteenth century are rarely seen today, at least in Europe and North America, but Briquet's hysteria has survived in the form of somatization disorder, a modern-day diagnostic entity. These nineteenth-century illnesses were diagnosed only in women, and the majority of patients with somatization disorder today are also women. The nineteenth-century hysterias are most readily understood as illness roles. Social-psychological research has shown that people take on roles suggested to them by others, if these offer hope of meeting unmet needs. Not only behavior, but also beliefs and feelings are altered in response to subtle role expectations. Some roles, called illness roles, dictate abnormal behavior and/or somatic complaints. People take on illness roles if they are unable to otherwise meet their needs. As I show in chapter 3, nineteenth-century women with hysterical illnesses in fact lacked social power to meet their needs more directly than by falling ill.

Chapter 4 applies the conceptual framework developed in chapter 3 to multiple personality disorder, which has been becoming increasingly common in women. Most, and perhaps even all, cases of multiple personality disorder can be understood as illness role behavior. In all likelihood, women who take on this illness role have been abused or maltreated or are otherwise disadvantaged. Like nineteenth-century hysterics, they cannot meet their needs through more normal channels. Eating disorders are also discussed in chapter 4. These can be understood partly in terms of role demands placed upon women. These role demands reflect women's lack of power, and consequent lack of options, even in modern society.

Chapter 5 addresses women's social power. If lack of social power contributes to women's disorders, then women's relative power should be a matter of greater concern and interest on the part of mental health professionals. Modern-day evolutionary studies of human behavior call attention to factors that increase or decrease women's relative power. Women's control of resources useful for rearing children seems to be the leading, though not the exclusive, factor promoting increased power. Although essentially all societies have been or are male dominated, considerable variation has been found in women's power. As I noted above, women in some societies wield sufficient power to provide for their needs and security, to protect their interests, and to make life decisions. In other societies, women are so without power that all these acts are impossible. Relative power is also subject to historic change. For example, evidence suggests that women lost status and power coincident with the rise of ancient Mesopotamia. This change followed closely on technological and social innovations that had the effect of stripping women of resource control. We are currently in the midst of another historic shift, this time, of course, in the other direction. In the last one hundred years, women in some societies have gained significant powers previously denied to them. Women in the future will no doubt have still greater control over useful resources.

Chapter 6 sums up material and ideas presented in earlier chapters and addresses some of their implications for the future and for research and treatment. As women come to control their share of useful resources, major changes may take place in the behavior of men and women and in relations between them. These will affect sexuality, courtship, child rearing, and many other facets of daily life. Disorders that are more common in women today should become equally common in the two sexes. With regard to research and treatment, more emphasis should be placed on social power, and especially on resource control, as a factor affecting mental health. Also, clinicians must be aware that patients without social power are attracted to illness roles. Clinicians should avoid promoting or reinforcing such roles, but instead, they should try to address the personal circumstances that make these roles so attractive. For example, a clinician treating the typical patient with multiple personality disorder should devote at least as much attention to the patient's present-day social world as to past traumas and recovery of memories, and in any event the clinician should not encourage the patient to develop yet more personalities. Finally, the viewpoint developed here implies that women prone to disorders discussed in the following chapters should avoid becoming trapped in traditional women's roles. Proneness to such disorders can be identified on the basis of family or social histories, or past episodes of illness. Insofar as traditional roles deprive such women of power, they may increase the chance of future morbidity.

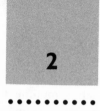

Depression and Anxiety: Responses to Lack of Power

Women are at excess risk for both depression and anxiety disorders. In this chapter, I will argue that these excess risks result from women's relative lack of social power, which is defined here as the ability to provide for one's own needs and security and the needs and security of loved ones, to stand up for oneself in conflicts with others, and to make life decisions based on one's own desires. Several important theories of depression and anxiety, discussed below, directly or indirectly attribute these disorders to factors akin to perceived lack of social power. With one exception, these theories imply that perceived lack of power is most often unrealistic. However, data reviewed in this chapter show that women actually do lack power and resource control in the social settings in which they are at risk; hence, perceived lack of power may be perfectly realistic for many depressed women. The data also show that women who have the least control over needed resources are at the greatest risk for depressive disorders, while women who control all the resources they need may have no greater risk of depressive disorders than men. The relation between resource control and anxiety symptoms has not been sufficiently studied for us to know whether the same pattern would be found. Not surprisingly, the one theory of depressive disorder that gives sufficient weight to real social power is based on concepts derived from observations of hierarchical social structures in nonhuman primate species (see below).

Depression

Both studies of treated cases and community surveys show that depression affects more women than men. In her comprehensive review of this issue, Susan Nolen-Hoeksema, a Stanford University psychologist, cited eight studies of the sex of treated depressives conducted in the United States.[1] These studies showed women at increased risk for dysthymia, which is a chronic form of depression, major depressive disorder, which is a more acute form, and psychotic depression, in which the sad mood is accompanied by delusions or hallucinations. Manic-depressive, or bipolar, disorder appears to be equally common in men and women.[2] The average female-to-male ratio found in the studies cited by Nolen-Hoeksema was 1.95:1. There were three exceptions to the findings of excess numbers of women, only one of which could not be explained away methodologically. This was a study conducted at the University of Washington, which found that although women students were more likely to be dysthymic, male students were more likely to have major depression.[3] Eight methodologically strong studies of treated cases conducted in Denmark, Scotland, England, Wales, Australia, Canada, Iceland, and Israel showed the same broad pattern as the American studies. The average female-to-male ratio found among depressed patients in these countries was 2.39:1. No study found an excess number of male depressives. According to Nolen-Hoeksema, some studies from underdeveloped countries do show excess numbers of men diagnosed with depression, but these are vitiated by gender-related differences in access to health care.

Nolen-Hoeksema identified eleven community surveys conducted in the United States that were designed to find untreated depressives. Although these studies used different rating measures for depressive symptoms and employed different cutoff points for identifying cases, they show a pattern similar to studies of treated cases. Thus, the average female-to-male ratio among the identified cases of depressive illness was 1.62:1. Women outnumbered men for both dysthymic disorder and major depressive disorder. Several exceptions appeared that deserve some comment. Egeland and her coworkers found that men and women from old-order Amish communities were equally likely to report depressive symptoms.[4] This finding has been cited as evidence for one hypothesis about gender-related differences in depressive illness (see below). However, as Nolen-Hoeksema notes, the low rates of depression Egeland and her coworkers discovered in Amish women may indicate that their methods of inquiry failed to detect symptoms in this population. Hammen and Padesky surveyed university students and found no difference between men and women in risk of depressive symptoms.[5] This finding may complement that noted above from the University of Washington, for treated cases. Finally, studies of elderly subjects and of recently bereaved subjects failed to find much difference in gender-related risk. I will discuss these studies and the university findings in a later section. Twelve community surveys conducted outside the United States show findings similar to those of American studies, according to Nolen-Hoeksema. The average female-to-male ratio in identified cases in these latter studies was 2.08:1, and only two studies, conducted in rural areas, found no gender difference.

A number of authors have argued that sex-related differences in rates of depressive illness are artifactual and do not reflect vulnerability to a pathological process. For example, I have already discussed those feminist authors who argue that psychiatric diagnoses are really invidious labels used to control women. According to these authors, the psychiatric establishment labels women as depressed, and therefore mentally ill, when the only thing wrong with them is that they are oppressed. However, women are either depressed by oppression or they are not depressed by it. I doubt that these feminist authors really mean to claim that women are not depressed by oppression, or that most of their readers would believe them if they did. But if women are depressed, then their depression is real, and to claim that it is oppression is to confuse cause with effect. The issue these authors would like to address, perhaps, is the lack of attention to social factors in clinical work, which makes depression always appear as a personal matter, without societal causes. Insofar as some cases of depression have societal causes, then societal change is required, rather than personal change. Jane Ussher made a similar point, in cautioning that a purely deconstructionist view of women's mental disorders ignores the real suffering resulting from women's conditions.[6] She cited some of the same factors as I cite below as contributing causes for women's depressive disorders.

More serious attempts to explain away gender-related differences in risk of depression are noted by Nolen-Hoeksema. Socioeconomic status is inversely related to rates of depressive illness. Hence, women might be more depressed because of their lower incomes and levels of education. Although this theory may be partly correct, in that poverty-stricken women may incur special risks, it nonetheless falsely implies that adequate family income can protect women from illness. The data cited below suggest that traditional gender roles pose a risk to women, regardless of family income. Some theorists claim that women suffer more adverse events—such as losses and failures—than men and that these events cause their excess risk of depression, but a recent study suggests this too is not the case.[7] Considerable sex differences in rates of minor depression remain even after controlling for adverse events. Women might be more willing to seek help for depression, thus accounting for their majority among treated patients. However, the community surveys cited in previous paragraphs show the same sex ratios among untreated subjects. Furthermore, studies of response biases fail to show sex differences in willingness to admit the same levels of distress, especially if such admissions are made in a private setting.[8] Most community surveys were private and confidential. Finally, depression may manifest itself differently in men and women, taking a more disguised course in men. Men in our society are often loath to talk about their feelings and at the same time are more prone than women to act them out through violent behavior or drug abuse. Antisocial and alcoholic men, in particular, have sometimes been thought to ward off their feelings of depression with criminal acts and drinking. The study noted above, conducted among the Amish, is pertinent to this hypothesis.[9] Antisocial behavior and alcoholism are almost unknown among Amish men. Amish men and women, unlike men and women in the general population, were found to be equally likely to complain of depressive symptoms. Possibly, the men who would be criminals or alcoholics in other populations were merely depressed in the Amish. However, as I noted, there are methodological problems with the Amish study. Furthermore, to explain the gender imbalance in depressive illness by treating antisocial behavior or alcoholism as disguised depression creates another question even as it solves one. Why are men living in our society, and in societies like ours, more willing to drink or commit crimes than to discuss their feelings? If there is no difference in the incidence of depression, then why is there one in its expression? What functions are served by lack of male expressiveness?

Taking the view that it is real, researchers and clinicians have offered several theories to account for the higher incidence of depressive disorders in women. Especially well-known psychological theories include the classical Freudian account of women's development, the newer object-relations views of gender differences, theories that point to conflicts inherent in feminine roles, and interpersonal theories. Freud thought that penis envy and repression of clitoral in favor of vaginal sexuality caused women to be more susceptible than men to several mental disorders, including depressive neuroses.[10] However, Karen Horney and other later psychoanalysts cogently criticized the theory of penis envy, which is part of what has been called Freud's "phallocentric" psychology. As for repression of clitoral in favor of vaginal sexuality, Freud's understanding of sexual physiology is now known to be incorrect, and his theory of repression of clitoral sexuality is consequently outmoded. As Nolen-Hoeksema notes, newer psychodynamic theories of women's depression are hardly more supportable than Freud's original theory. Each of these postulates differences between men's and women's psychology that find scant support from empirical studies.[11] Some sex-role theorists observe that women today are exposed to conflicting role demands, such that they are expected to be alternately passive, supportive, and nurturant, and competitive and independent, depending upon the setting in which they happen to find themselves.[12] Conflicting demands cause stress, thus promoting depression. But there is little evidence that the women becoming depressed are those exposed to these conflicting demands. As I will show later, dual roles—at work and at home, for instance—may actually protect women from depression. Interpersonal theories and learned helplessness models will be discussed below. Full accounts of these viewpoints are beyond the scope of this study but can be found in references cited in the Notes.

Biological theorists attribute women's increased risk of depression to female reproductive hormones or to other aspects of female physiology.[13] Thus, depression is a recognized side effect of oral contraceptives, which contain synthetic analogues of naturally occurring female hormones, and mood disorders occur at times of hormonal changes in women not taking medicines. However, the contraceptives with the most effects on mood seem to be those that deliver supraphysiological doses of sex hormones, and the incidence of mood disorders with hormone changes seems to have been overstated. So-called involutional melancholia, or depression during the menopause, was dropped from the American Psychiatric Association's *Diagnostic and Statistical Manual* when it became clear that it is not a distinctive disorder. Most women with menopausal depressions also have depressions at other times of life.

Likewise, postpartum depressive syndromes now are known to be transient, with just a few exceptions. Women who remain depressed several weeks after childbirth are likely to have been depressed while they were still pregnant, ruling out a hormonal explanation for their depression. The changes in hormone levels associated with childbirth occur immediately prior to parturition. Although large numbers of women claim to be tense or depressed before their menstrual periods, the severity of mood changes before the menstrual period may be overstated in retrospective accounts. Actual concurrent ratings of premenstrual moods reveal less extreme cyclical fluctuations.

Biological theorists have recently gained strong support from a series of studies conducted by Kenneth Kendler and his colleagues at the Medical College of Virginia.[14] By studying over one thousand identical or fraternal female twin pairs identified from birth registries, Kendler was able to show that women's depression is much more dependent on genetic factors than was hitherto realized. Twins were sent questionnaires and interviewed on two occasions more than a year apart. As in other twin studies, both identical and fraternal twin pairs were presumed to share early environmental risk factors. Statistical analysis of the risk of depression at different times in the study suggested that genes are the strongest predictors of major depression. Unidentified short-acting environmental factors appear to precipitate specific illness episodes, but even these may be less important than they appeared, since measurement error inflated the apparent effect of these factors. The effect of genes held up when depression was diagnosed according to different criteria.

The aspect of Kendler's studies that militates so strongly in favor of a biological view of women's increased risk is not his finding that depression is partly genetic, but his failure to find an effect of either enduring or shared environmental factors. Of necessity, nonphysiological theories attribute women's excess risk for depression to long-term environmental processes, such as the way women are raised or their social role. Twins reared together should be more alike with regard to some of these processes than children from different families. Kendler found no indication that either long-term or shared environmental factors—which presumably would have varied to some extent between twin pairs—affect the risk of depression. This seems to contradict findings, described below, that marital status, maternity, and economic class, all of which should have appeared as long-term and/or shared environmental factors in Kendler's study, predict women's depression. Indeed, it seems to preclude any effort to relate women's depression to the enduring circumstances of women's lives.

I assume, for my purposes here, that depression is partly genetic and hence physiologically caused in both men and women, but that biological psychiatry is not quite as triumphant as Kendler's study suggests. I assume that enduring aspects of the environment are important and that some of these would be shared by children raised together. Kendler's statistical methods are elegant but complex. They involve many hidden assumptions, one or more of which might have masked environmental effects. Kendler's findings, moreover, are inferences drawn from morbidity risks of twin pairs at different times. Kendler never directly tested effects of some factors others believe are important. Insofar as long-term or shared environmental factors are in fact etiologically significant in women's depression, the way is open for theories that attribute male-female differences in risk to other than physiological differences between men and women.

Anxiety Disorders

Women are also at greatly increased risk for agoraphobia and/or panic disorder.[15] Certain simple phobias, such as of insects and animals, are also more common in women but will not be dealt with here. As of the date of this writing, too little work has been done on these specific phobias to meaningfully discuss them in the present context. The higher female prevalence of simple phobias may be secondary to normative gender roles. Social phobias are probably equally common in men and women. The Epidemiologic Catchment Area (ECA) study provides illustrative data regarding agoraphobia and panic disorder.[16] Women surveyed at the five ECA study sites endorsed typical agoraphobic fears—such as fear of leaving the house alone, being alone, being in a crowd, or being on public transportation—far more frequently than men at the ECA sites. The one-month, six-month, and one-year prevalence rates for definite agoraphobia were 4.42, 5.29, and 5.88 percent for women and 1.56, 1.82, and 2.08 percent for men. The one-year prevalence ratio for female to male cases was nearly three to one. Women were two-and-a-half times as likely as men to be agoraphobic at the time of the survey. Prevalence data for panic disorder without avoidance showed similar ratios in the ECA study.

Women's higher risk for panic and agoraphobia may be related to their greater risk of depression. Panic and agoraphobic disorders frequently coexist with depressive illness. For example, Raskin and coworkers found that fifteen of seventeen patients with panic disorder had experienced major depressions, and all but one of these patients had been depressed before developing panic.[17] Breier, Charney, and Heninger found that forty-one of sixty agoraphobics had at one time had a major depressive episode.[18] In twenty patients, major depressive episodes antedated anxiety by an average of three years. Women agoraphobics were significantly more likely to have been depressed. Forty-two of the sixty agoraphobics were women, and the excess women were found in the subsample with depression. Other studies show that 40 to 90 percent of agoraphobic patients experience major depressions and confirm that these depressions often antedate agoraphobic symptoms.[19] Based on a large-scale study, Chambless claimed that depression is an integral feature of agoraphobia.[20] On the other hand, Schapira and coworkers found high rates of agoraphobia in depressed patients.[21] This and similar findings led Bowen and Kohout to argue that most agoraphobia results from affective disorder.[22]

Family and treatment studies suggest that panic and agoraphobia share etiologic factors with depressive disorders. Munjack and Moss, for example, found that first-degree relatives of agoraphobics with panic attacks had a 38 percent risk of depressive disorder, compared with a 14 percent risk for relatives of patients with simple phobias.[23] Bowen and Kohout found that 84 percent of their sample of agoraphobics with panic attacks had first-degree relatives with major affective disorder.[24] Leckman and coworkers found that the co-occurrence of anxiety and depression increased family risk for either of the disorders, suggesting that the same genes contribute to both disorders.[25] As for treatment studies, many antidepressants are effective for treating panic as well as depressive symptoms.[26] Exposure and antidepressants are effective for agoraphobics.

Just as they attribute women's risk of depression to physiological factors, some biological theorists believe that there are physiological reasons for women's risk of anxiety.[27] Anxiety disorders are sometimes associated with premenstrual syndrome, suggesting that reproductive hormones play a role in their genesis. Kenneth Kendler and his colleagues studied anxiety syndromes in the twin pairs they identified from birth registries.[28] All of the phobic disorders appeared to be modestly to moderately dependent on genes, but agoraphobia in particular appeared to be highly dependent on nonspecific environmental factors. These factors increase the risk for several types of anxiety syndromes, but their strongest effect is on agoraphobia. Once again, however, Kendler and his colleagues found little or no evidence for pathogenic effects of environmental factors shared by twins raised together. Whether this is because rearing environment has little impact on the environmental factors causing adult anxiety or because of a methodological problem in Kendler's study remains to be seen. In studying anxiety disorders, Kendler and his colleagues used much the same methods as when they studied depression. Other studies have shown that low social class, which presumably should have appeared as a shared environmental factor in Kendler's study, is associated with increased rates of anxiety (see below).

Perceived Lack of Power as a Causal Factor

Several influential psychological theories attribute depression and anxiety to subjective perceptions akin to perceived lack of power. None of these theories actually refer to "perceived lack of power," but they do use other terms that have about the same meaning. While these theories differ in several important respects, they all emphasize the patient's subjective impression of his or her social power, in the most general sense. Most modern-day clinicians subscribe to one of these theories, in the sense that they use them in their clinical practice.

First, interpersonal theorists believe that depressive disorders arise from a matrix of disturbed social relationships.[29] Patients prone to depression may lack social support, be engaged in hostile or dysfunctional relationships, or be involved with others whom they are afraid of losing. These interpersonal problems are thought to arise in large part from personality problems related to poor self-regard. Thus, recovered depressives have been found to lack self-confidence, to be excessively pessimistic about the future, and to perceive themselves as inadequate. All of these self-perceptions relate in an obvious way to perceived lack of social power. The patient does not believe he or she can provide for his or her needs, stand up to others, or freely make decisions that might displease other people. Not surprisingly, patients have trouble asserting themselves or expressing anger. Indirect expressions of hostility often contribute to their relational problems.

Similar observations have been made by attachment theorists, who believe that patients prone to depression differ from other persons in having more salient, childlike attachment needs.[30] John Bowlby, the British psychiatrist who studied children's responses to separations from their attachment figures, noted that these responses resemble adult depressions.[31] Patients prone to depression are said to be dependent on attachment figures, whom they resent but nonetheless fear displeasing. Threats to the relationship trigger depressive episodes, exactly as separations trigger responses in childhood. Bowlby initially thought that depressives had suffered early disruptions of their attachment relationships due to divorce, death, or parental desertion. Later studies, however, failed to support this hypothesis or indicated that it is only partially true.[32] For example, while some depressives have suffered loss of a parent in childhood, most report that their childhoods were more or less uneventful. Many of those who lost parents suffered other stresses that may have been even more critical. Attachment theorists now speculate that parenting styles or more subtle disruptions in attachment relationships than outright loss of the parent alter children's models of themselves and others so as to maintain intense later attachment needs.

If it is true that depressives have more intense or childlike attachment needs than others, it must be because they believe they need more assistance in life. They do not believe they can provide for their needs, stand up to others, or make successful decisions without extraordinary aid from other persons. Bowlby and others have shown that attachment-seeking behaviors wax and wane with self-confidence in particular situations.[33] Thus, children in unfamiliar or frightening situations seek their attachment figures, while children in situations that they know they can handle show less overt attachment-related behaviors. Generalized blows to their confidence increase children's attachment needs across a range of settings. The catastrophes cited by Bowlby, which cause recrudescent childlike attachment needs in adults, represent blows to self-confidence in the most general sense. They point toward a lack of control in life and create a sense of helplessness.

Learned-helplessness theorists have made an especial study of the perceived lack of power of persons prone to depression. Learned helplessness was first described in animals subjected to inescapable shocks or other noxious stimuli.[34] After a while, animals in these conditions stop trying to escape. They may become unresponsive even in other conditions, when responses would be rewarded. Seligman noted the similarities between human depressives and animals with learned helplessness and suggested that human depression may be a form of learned helplessness. He showed that, compared with normals, depressives doubt their ability to influence future events. They entertain this doubt even when not depressed. They foresee unpleasant events, but they cannot imagine ways they can forestall or prevent these. Because they lack faith in the possible efficacy of their actions, they fail to learn new behaviors or to act when needed. Later, Seligman and other learned-helplessness theorists adopted a more "attributional" theoretical framework.[35] Unlike the original learned-helplessness paradigm, which implied that learned helplessness results from earlier trauma, the attributional framework traces learned helplessness to faulty cognitive habits. Thus, people who habitually attribute untoward events to global and enduring, rather than to specific and temporary, causes or who overestimate their own role in misfortunes are thought to be more likely to doubt their own effectiveness. Treatments aimed at changing attributional styles have been said to change attitudes associated with learned helplessness in patients prone to depression.

The fact that depressives express greater feelings of helplessness should not be understood to mean they distort reality. In fact, some studies suggest that mildly depressed subjects assess their abilities and environments more realistically than subjects who are not depressed.[36] Nondepressed subjects exaggerate their past achievements and overestimate their present-day prospects. They claim credit for successes but disavow failures, and thus they overestimate their talents and capabilities. They think they are better liked and more attractive than they are. This point is important in regard to women depressives; insofar as women lack power, women's perceived lack of social power is often accurate.

In citing cognitive habits responsible for learned helplessness, Seligman and other learned-helplessness theorists have joined the larger camp of cognitive behavioral therapists. Modern-day cognitive behaviorists attribute depression to faulty cognitive habits, such as misattributions of failures and successes, which leave the depressed patient feeling powerless and incompetent.[37] Patients faced with difficulties, for instance, are sometimes said to engage in "catastrophic thinking." They assume that their difficulties will escalate to the point of catastrophe, regardless of what they do. Thus, the patient who is temporarily out of a job may well assume he will never again be employed. Obviously, patients who engage in this type of thinking have little or no feeling of social power, as I define it here. Therapy proceeds by training the patient in thoughts that are more likely to lead to constructive action.

John Price and Leon Sloman, who are among the pioneers of an evolutionary approach to mental disorders, have argued that depression is a submissive strategy for dealing with powerful others.[38] According to this view, depression-prone patients are chronically too submissive. They thus form unequal relationships with others whom they try to please. Whenever anything happens that lowers their social status, depression-prone patients become even more submissive, in the form of overt depression. Depressed patients "throw themselves" on the mercy of those around them. Through helplessness and passivity and by playing on manifest weakness, they extract concessions from others while avoiding direct confrontations. This model implies that depression is a strategem, akin to an illness role (see chapter 3), which is universal, though it has cultural variants. It might be patterned after separation responses in children precisely because such responses once gained adult assistance and blunted adult aggression.

Price and Sloman's model implicitly links depression to perceived lack of social power. In the ethological literature, dominance and submission are understood to be dependent on judgments made of relative power.[39] "Resource holding power" is frequently used to denote subjective impressions of power in nonhuman populations. Paul Gilbert, a British psychologist who has written extensively on application of ethological concepts to psychopathology, has developed this model into a coherent theory of depression dependent on perceived lack of social power.[40] He cites convincing evidence that correctly judged lack of power increases the risk of depression.

As for anxiety disorders, attachment theorists, who trace depression to the exigencies of attachment needs, liken panic anxiety and agoraphobic avoidance to separation fears.[41] Very young children separated from their attachment figures, especially in unfamiliar situations or when strangers are present, appear to be markedly anxious. In strange situations, for instance, children become inhibited unless their mothers are with them. The Ainsworth Strange Situation Test, which is now widely used to assess attachment bonds, was originally designed to measure such inhibition in the mother's absence.[42] Like children, agoraphobics experience anxiety in settings where strangers are present, unless they are accompanied by close friends or relatives. Contrary to earlier views, agoraphobic anxiety does not result from merely having experienced panic in public settings.[43] Some agoraphobics have never had panic attacks. Instead, public places in which strangers are present must be inherently stressful for susceptible patients. Attachment theorists claim that many agoraphobics have suffered childhood losses or had school phobias or intense separation anxiety in their early relationships, but studies have generally failed to confirm these claims.[44] As in the case of depression, if agoraphobics do show excessively salient childlike attachment behaviors, it must be because they lack faith in their ability to manage without assistance. That is, they must perceive themselves as lacking in social power, as I define it here.

According to Seligman, who developed learned-helplessness theory, anxiety is the first response to threatened loss or danger.[45] As the threat increases, feelings of anxiety give way to helplessness. Those who suffer anxiety in everyday situations are hence those, like depressives, who lack confidence in their capacity to manage normal events. Individuals who generally lack self-confidence might show either anxiety or depressive symptoms in response to perceived threats, depending upon the magnitude of the threats and upon transient fluctuations in their self-regard. Albert Bandura and others have shown that lack of self-confidence leads to subjective anxiety; it is not just epiphenomenal.[46] Bandura refers to "self-efficacy," by which he means a person's faith in his or her ability to manage particular situations. Self-efficacy is partly dependent on skills pertinent to specific phobic situations, but it is also determined by general beliefs about coping abilities. In most situations, self-efficacy is closely akin to perceived social power, as I define it here. Individuals who believe they can provide for their needs and security, protect their interests from others, and freely make decisions will necessarily feel self-efficacious in most or all social situations. Significantly, Bandura and others have shown that it is lack of self-efficacy, and not subjective anxiety, that leads to avoidant behavior. This might explain why agoraphobic avoidance can occur without panic attacks ever being experienced in a public setting. In numerous studies, Bandura and his coworkers have shown that increasing confidence in the efficacy of coping skills decreases both avoidance and subjective anxiety (see below). Behavioral interventions that do not increase self-efficacy cannot relieve anxiety or avoidant behavior.

Women's Social Power, Depression, and Anxiety

If perceived lack of social power increases the risk of depression and anxiety syndromes, then women's relative lack of social power might account for the excess number of women with these disorders. In chapter 5 I will argue that men pursuing their reproductive strategies realize a potential advantage over women by controlling resources needed for rearing children. Hence, in showing that women's lack of power accounts for their increased risk of anxiety and depression, I will emphasize economic inequities. Noneconomic factors also contribute to women's relative lack of power, but these can be seen as the legacies of past male resource control.

Men who controlled resources in ancient societies created certain mores and ideologies that are still with us today, at least in modified form. Feminist authors have shown how these ideologies narrow women's educational and employment opportunities and consequently serve to decrease their social power.[47] For instance, ideological obstacles to women's control over their reproduction militate against both women's education and women's careers. Early birth-control advocates, such as Margaret Sanger, clearly understood that birth control is essential for women's gainful employment, the only alternative being giving up family life in order to have careers.[48] The battle for control of women's reproduction is still being actively fought in the United States. According to Barbara Bergman, a feminist economist, the notion that men should not have to obey women's dictates is partly responsible for women's job segregation.[49] Women are not hired into positions in which they will manage men. Job segregation confines women to low-paying jobs (see below). Invidious ideologies about women's intellect have been shown to have wide-ranging, serious impacts on women's schooling.[50] Studies have shown, for instance, that young women are discouraged from developing cognitive skills and from studying subjects that would lead to career opportunities. Because of cultural norms, young women are also less likely to learn useful skills of assertiveness. Instead, they are trained to please others and to be self-sacrificing. Some feminist therapists advocate assertiveness training for most women patients, to make up for skill deficits due to cultural norms.[51] Assertiveness training is said to greatly boost women's self-confidence in conflictual situations.

Barbara Smuts, a well-known primate ethologist, has pointed out that men's violence against women may be an important source of male power.[52] In fact, early patriarchies encouraged male violence as a means of controlling women, who were treated as chattel (see chapter 5). Mores encouraging male violence against women are still a significant factor decreasing women's real and perceived social power. For example, according to some sources, almost half of American women are sexually assaulted sometime in their lives.[53] Many of these assaults are so-called date rapes, which courts only recently defined as real crimes. Wife beating is still widespread, and many wives are threatened if they try to leave their marriages. Courts and legislators only recently redefined spousal violence as a matter of public concern and passed laws, for instance, against rape in marriage. Modern American women have also been especially hard hit by the crime epidemic occurring in large cities. The severe restrictions imposed on women by street crime have been largely ignored by legislators and jurists.

A number of studies have shown that many women who are victims of violent male assaults lose trust in their surroundings, withdraw from activities, and experience anxiety and depression.[54] In particular cases, victimization may precipitate major decisions that are ultimately disadvantageous, such as withdrawing from school or leaving a well-liked city. The high incidence of anxiety and depression is consistent with the notion that victimization decreases self-perceived power. Several women authors have dealt with the psychological aftermath of male assaults in widely read popular novels.[55]

Elizabeth Ozer and Albert Bandura of Stanford University reported an intriguing study that illustrates how fear of male violence causes clinically normal women to restrict their activities.[56] They studied forty-three women who had enrolled in a self-defense program offered at three locales in the San Francisco Bay area. The subjects, who ranged in age from eighteen to fifty-five years, were mostly unmarried or divorced; more than half worked full time; 38 percent of the subjects had been physically assaulted at one time or another, and 27 percent of them had been raped by acquaintances, relatives, or boyfriends. The self-defense program consisted of five 4½–hour sessions conducted by two women. The subjects learned how to disable assailants with powerful blows to vital body areas, and they practiced these skills with each other wearing padded gear. Two male assistants acted as assailants to provide additional practice. The subjects learned how to disable assailants attacking from the front or back, and when pinned down or in the dark. They were taught to reduce the risk of assault and to manage threats of violence in an effective manner. Ozer and Bandura administered questionnaires on anxiety, avoidance, and beliefs about self-efficacy in potentially threatening situations before the program began and at six-month follow-ups.

At the time of initial testing, those of the subjects who had been raped expressed less confidence in their ability to deal with threatening situations, they felt more vulnerable to assault, and they were more avoidant than other subjects. Those who had been physically assaulted but not raped expressed more anxiety about potential assaults, but they were not as avoidant of actual situations. Not surprisingly, mastering self-defense skills produced a marked improvement in the subjects' belief that they could handle threatening situations. The subjects also showed dramatic improvement in their belief that they could manage problems arising in recreational, social, and other activities seemingly somewhat removed from the threat of immediate violence. Involvement in these activities increased significantly following self-defense training. According to the authors, after self-defense training the subjects participated in more outdoor activities, attended more evening cultural, educational, and social events, and increased their use of public transportation. Though agoraphobics generally express other fears than of violence, avoidance of public transport is an especially common symptom of agoraphobia. Increases in self-confidence were statistically associated with increased activity levels, suggesting that decreased self-confidence had played a causal role in maintaining avoidant behavior. Apparently, at least for this group of self-selected women, avoidant, restricted behaviors were caused by the fear of assault.

In sexual harassment, implicit or explicit threats of invidious treatment take the place of threats of physical harm to women. Sometimes, however, harassment takes a more forceful turn, as in the recent notorious Tailhook incident, in which case it is hardly distinguishable from assault. Sexual harassment retards women's educational and career advancement, regardless of whether any threats are carried out.[57]

According to the theory outlined in chapter 5, resource control is a key factor in gender relations. The invidious cultural factors cited in previous paragraphs all result from past male control of resources and hence of social institutions. Today, wealth is more

widely distributed than it was in previous eras, so that large numbers of persons can meet their essential needs and even enjoy a few
luxuries—but wealth and high incomes are still overwhelmingly in
the hands of men. Barbara Bergman and others provide an excellent overview of economic inequities between men and women.[58]
These inequities have proven to be resistant to efforts to narrow
them. Victor Fuchs, an economist at Stanford University, recently
summarized data on women's income in the United States between
1960 and 1986.[59] This is the period in which economic inequities
between men and women became matters of public concern, and
efforts were made to close the economic gap between men and
women in business and the professions. In spite of these efforts,
however, Fuchs found that with the exception of relatively few
young, white, unmarried, and educated women, American women
were not substantially better off in 1986 than in 1960. Although
the proportion of women holding paid jobs increased from 35
percent in 1960 to 51 percent in 1986, women were generally paid
less than their male coworkers. From 1930 to 1979, American
women's wages were 60 percent of men's, on an hourly basis. By
the mid-1980s, they were still about two-thirds. The enduring
wage differential resulted from segregation of women in low-paying jobs and from constraints on overtime women are able to
work. One index of job segregation shows that the American
workplace has twice as much sex segregation as segregation by
race. I have already noted Bergman's hypothesis that women are
excluded from jobs that might lead to their managing men. Women
cannot work overtime because they still bear the greater part of
responsibility for housekeeping and child rearing. The highest-
paying jobs require flexible hours, with occasional overtime work.
These jobs were designed to be held by men with wives who stayed
at home, feeding the children their dinner on evenings men worked
late. According to Fuchs, women, but not men, in high-paying
corporate jobs today tend not to have children, and many of them
are unmarried. Since many women are also working in part-time
jobs, they have less job security than men in their companies.

In recent years, the "feminization of poverty" has attracted much public attention. Judging by poverty rates, women's economic conditions appear to be deteriorating, rather than improving. Fuchs found that during the 1960s the percent of poor who were women increased from 57 to 61 percent for whites, and from 59 to 66 percent for blacks. The percentage rose no further for whites in the next sixteen years, but it continued to rise for blacks to 72 percent. Most impoverished women are mothers without partners. In 1986, nearly 40 percent of white mothers without partners lived in poverty, compared to just 13 percent of childless single white women. Nearly 60 percent of black mothers without partners lived in poverty, compared to 26 percent of childless single black women. Since the number of children raised by single parents has risen, and since many of these single parents are poverty-stricken women, by 1986 the poverty rate among children was nearly twice the rate found among adults: 51 percent of white children and 70 percent of black children living with single mothers were living in poverty in 1986. Fuchs calculated that child-care costs completely consume take-home pay for single mothers working in low-paying jobs.

Fuchs's data imply that women are disadvantaged in large part because of their disproportionate responsibility for taking care of children. At the very best, being responsible for children prevents women from working the long, irregular hours required by the professions and high-paying business jobs. At worst, child care completely eats up the take-home pay of single mothers working in low-paying jobs. Indeed, Fuchs concludes that in the United States "the greatest barrier to economic equality (between men and women) is children. Most women want to have children and are concerned about their well-being once they are born. . . . The 'propensity to mother' is present and strong, and puts women at a disadvantage. . . . The fairest, most efficient, most effective way to help women is through their children." [60] He advocates public policies aimed at alleviating the child-care burden on women.

Depressive symptoms and dysthymic mood are generally more

prevalent in the lower classes, and especially among those living in or threatened by poverty.[61] This suggests that the excess number of poverty-stricken women, most of whom are mothers, might account for some of the excess number of women depressives. In this respect, it is noteworthy that the major community study that failed to find differences in rates of depressive disorders between men and women was conducted among the Amish, a generally prosperous group in which there are few single mothers, and these do not live in poverty.[62] Similar remarks may apply to anxiety syndromes. For example, although there are no clear class-related differences in aggregated fears or phobias, which are for the most part simple phobias, such as of insects or heights,[63] a study by Chambless indicates that low social class is a risk factor for agoraphobia.[64] The Epidemiologic Catchment Area Study confirmed that agoraphobia is more common in less educated subjects and in subjects with low occupational status,[65] and similar findings have been reported for panic disorder[66] and for generalized anxiety disorder as well.[67] Thus, the types of anxiety most relevant to this study do seem to vary with income and social class much as depressive disorders do.

Insofar as they are economically dependent upon men, nonworking wives and mothers have even less social power than do other women in our society. Unlike men, who generally can leave their wives and maintain their own standard of living, women in our society have much lower standards of living following a divorce. As Fuchs's data indicate, mothers especially are likely to slide into poverty following marital breakups.[68] According to the theories discussed in the previous section, perceived lack of social power might place these women at special risk of mental disorders. Due in part to the high cost of child care, nearly 50 percent of American women with children less than one year old are completely outside the labor force.[69] This compares with 44 percent of women with children less than six years old and 27 percent of women with children six to seventeen years old who do not work at all. Hence, a higher rate of anxiety or depression among economically dependent wives and mothers would have a significant impact on overall rates of illness for women as a whole.

Clinicians often encounter depressed or anxious full-time housewives and mothers who report that they last felt competent when they were employed. Popular feminist authors have dealt with this issue extensively, suggesting its importance to a great number of women. For instance, the protagonist of *The Women's Room,* the well-known novel by Marilyn French, feels rather confident as an upper-middle-class housewife until events bring her face to face with her economic vulnerability.[70] Her husband makes it clear that his money belongs to him, and not to both of them, as she had believed. A point that Marilyn French and other authors make and that is often apparent in the clinical setting is that economic dependence weakens full-time housewives vis-à-vis their husbands. When marriage becomes more valued by one partner than the other, due to economic or any other needs, then the partner who values it less may become a "dominant other," to borrow a term from interpersonal therapists, and the partner who values it more may lose his or her self-confidence.[71] Economic dependency leads to inequality in the marriage relationship, regardless of good intentions or ideologic commitments.

As expected from its effect in rendering women dependent, motherhood in societies like ours does predict an increased risk of depressive disorders. Fatherhood, by contrast, predicts improved mental health. Bebbington and coworkers, for instance, identified individuals with minor depressive disorders in a community survey in the United Kingdom.[72] In the first phase of their study, they found that 30 of 393 (7.6 percent) men and 74 of 406 (18.2 percent) women were depressed. This is approximately the same finding reported by surveys summarized by Nolen-Hoeksema. But when parenthood was examined, a surprising pattern emerged. Only 17 (10.4 percent) of 163 childless men, 16 (11.3 percent) of 141 childless women, and 13 (5.6 percent) of 230 fathers were depressed. But an astounding 58 (21.8 percent) of 265 mothers had an affective disorder. In other words, nearly all the excess female depressives were found among the mothers in the study sample. In order to further clarify factors predicting depression, Bebbington and his coworkers reinterviewed 52 of the above subjects who had been found to be depressed and 223 who were mentally well. Their findings support the importance of caring for young children as a contributing cause for women's depression. Thus, 17 (18.0 percent) of 94 women without children under the age of fifteen, but 18 (35.2 percent) of 51 women with such children were in the depressive group. The effect on mothers, moreover, is highly specific. None of the 39 men with children under the age of fifteen were found to be depressed. The rate of depression for men not caring for young children (17 of 91, or 18.6 percent) was the same as the rate of depression for women in similar situations. Consistent, too, with the thesis that employment decreases depression, 31 (14.9 percent) of 208 subjects who worked outside the home but 18 (29.5 percent) of 61 subjects who did not work had a depressive disorder. The risk of depression was doubled by lack of outside employment. Depression was also more common in the working-class subjects, as compared with those of the middle class. The very high rates of depression found in these follow-up figures reflect Bebbington's choice to include a disproportionate number of ill subjects. Other studies confirm Bebbington's major findings.[73] I have already cited reasons to doubt that maternity causes depression hormonally.

Costello studied 541 women recruited for a study of cardiovascular health.[74] Her results suggest that employment reduces the risk of depression, regardless of marital status. Costello's subjects were between forty-two and fifty years of age, premenopausal, and free of known mental disorders. Women who had never married, women who had stable first marriages, and unmarried widows reported the least depression. The highest rates of depression were reported by divorcees and by other women who had had unstable relationships. Whether they worked or not, educated women had low rates of depression, while uneducated women reported high rates of depression. Lack of education reduces women's ability to earn a living wage. Uneducated women who were not currently working had three times the risk of depression as the entire sample. The rate of depression was 10.1 percent in those who were unemployed, 6.1 percent in those with blue collar jobs, 7.4 percent in clerical workers, and 3.2 percent in professional workers. The husband's occupational status did not predict the risk of depression in Costello's sample. Costello found that parity did not predict depression, but since the average subject was forty-seven years old and since most of the subjects (74 percent) worked at least part-time, Costello's sample included very few unemployed housewives caring for very young children.

Cochrane and Stopes-Roe reported data from the British Department of Health and Social Security that show that women are 40 percent more likely to be hospitalized for mental illness than are men and that a large number of the excess female admissions are due to depressive disorders.[75] Married women, especially, are likely to be admitted, in comparison with married men, while single or widowed women are at no special risk. Divorced men and women alike had very high rates of admission, but men's rates were actually somewhat higher than those for women. To follow up on these data, Cochrane and Stopes-Roe conducted a door-to-door survey of 150 men and 109 women, aged twenty to sixty years, who were living in large English towns. Subjects were administered the Symptom Rating Test, a checklist of thirty symptoms aggregated into four subscales. The depression subscale, for instance, is composed of symptoms such as guilt, failure, hopelessness, poor appetite, and fatigue, and the anxiety subscale is composed of symptoms such as nervousness, panic attacks, restlessness, and tension.

Women as a whole had significantly higher scores on the depression and anxiety subscales and also on a subscale comprised of somatic symptoms. Marital status per se was not related to symptom level, but women who were unemployed had much higher symptom scores than did working women. Thus, for women as a whole, unemployment doubled depression subscale scores and was associated with at least 50 percent increases in anxiety and somatic symptom scores. Employed women reported about the same symptom levels as did male subjects. Married women who worked had fewer symptoms than housewives, the greatest difference being on the depression subscale. Cochrane and Stopes-Roe concluded that employment outside the home is a major determinant of sex-related differences in rates of mental disorder.

Insofar as maternity predicts a higher rate of depressive disorders, men's and women's rates of depressive disorders should be similar in populations in which maternity is uncommon or is a less significant factor. I have already noted that Bebbington and his coworkers found that childless women were at no greater risk for minor depressive illness than were childless men. Likewise, women without young children (under fifteen years) were at no greater risk than men without young children, according to Bebbington's study. In summarizing Nolen-Hoeksema's review of depression rates, I noted that two studies had failed to find sex differences in college-age populations.[76] College-age women, of course, are less likely to be mothers than other women their age, and they also are more likely to enjoy economic advantages. Similar findings have been reported in teacher trainees.[77] Among the elderly the rates of depression are high for both men and women, but several studies indicate that they are the same for both sexes.[78] Men's advantage from work and women's disadvantage from child rearing both disappear with retirement and old age. Elderly widows and widowers likewise do equally poorly.[79] In one study, 19 percent of widowers and 17 percent of widows participating were found to be depressed a year after their bereavement.

Two studies in particular shed some light on this issue. Both of these studies used subjects with minimal sex-role divergence in order to determine the effect of sex per se. The first, by Rachel Jenkins, used the General Health Questionnaire and the Clinical Interview Schedule, a structured interview, to identify cases of psychiatric disorders in 321 entry-level executives in the Home Office of the United Kingdom over a one-year period.[80] All of

Jenkins's subjects had attained their positions by competing in examinations, were between the ages of twenty and thirty-five years, and worked in the vicinity of London. The 183 men and 138 women had approximately the same educational level and had been raised in families of the same social classes. Although a third of the men and women were married, only seven percent of the women had children. According to Surtees and Bancroft, of women born in 1955 in England and Wales, 37 percent were mothers by age twenty-three and 70 percent were mothers by age thirty.[81] Hence, Jenkins's women subjects were leading very different lives from those of most women about their age. Consistent with the low parity rates in her subjects, Jenkins also found no sex-related differences in domestic burdens.

Neither the questionnaire nor the structured interview showed differences in psychological morbidity between men and women during a one-year follow-up. Rates of minor morbidity for men and women were 36 percent and 34 percent, respectively. Regarding particular symptoms, women tended to report significantly more somatic symptoms, and men were rated as showing significantly more psychomotor retardation. Somewhat more women than men complained of depression, fatigue, and irritability, but these differences were not significant and in any event did not produce differences in morbidity. Jenkins concluded that her findings were consistent with studies of college students, which showed no sex differentials in psychiatric morbidity: In the absence of role divergence and without the effects of motherhood, women are no more likely to be depressed than men.

A study by Wilhelm and Parker controlled for sex-role divergence and had a much longer follow-up period.[82] Parker had earlier shown that men and women trainees in a teaching program in Sydney, Australia, showed no differences in their short-term risks of depression.[83] In 1978, Wilhelm and Parker enrolled 170 trainees from the same program in another study to determine long-term risks. Of these, 165 subjects, including 109 women and 56 men, completed the five-year project. At entry into the study, men and women subjects were closely matched in employment and social class. Average age was twenty-three for both men and women; 21 percent of the women and 16 percent of the men were married, and 8 percent of the women had at least one child. At the end of the five-year study, 53 percent of the women and 44 percent of the men were married, and 36 percent of the women had at least one child. Still, only 9 percent of the women were full-time homemakers at the end of the five-year study. Since the average subject was twenty-eight years old at the study's conclusion, the 36 percent parity rate is in fact quite low, at least in comparison with figures like Surtees's and Bancroft's (see above). Wilhelm and Parker found that, by the end of their five-year study, 28 percent of the women and 27 percent of the men had at one time or another sought psychological treatment. Using the Diagnostic Interview Schedule, a structured interview, to generate diagnoses, Wilhelm and Parker found no sex difference for lifetime major or minor depressive episodes. Incidence rates for depression were also identical for men and women subjects during the study period. Witnesses were interviewed and confirmed diagnostic conclusions in all but three cases of major and more than 80 percent of cases of minor depression. Wilhelm and Parker conclude that "as social variables effectively remained controlled throughout the study, in that age, marital status, parenthood, and employment (apart from home duties) did not differentiate the sexes, a sex difference was prevented from emerging." The 9 percent of women who were full-time homemakers did not comprise a large enough group to raise the risk of depression for women subjects in general. Wilhelm and Parker did not separately report depressive risks in the third of the women subjects who had become mothers.

Wilhelm and Parker also administered self-esteem scales to subjects at entry and follow-up and occupational attitude scales to subjects at follow-up. Men and women had equal self-esteem at baseline and follow-up, and self-esteem improved significantly for both sexes during the five-year study. At the study's conclusion, women considered their work important and satisfying. Men, on the other hand, reported more dissatisfaction and considered their work less important.

The relation between marriage and motherhood and the risk of depression is probably not universal; even in our society, it probably varies from one subculture to the next. Marriage and motherhood testify to at least a minimal level of social functioning, they confer prestige on women, and they are sources of pleasure. In those societies in which women lack other options, marriage and motherhood insure women's survival. Wherever the benefits of marriage and motherhood outweigh their disadvantages, either because wives and mothers enjoy more social power than in our society generally or because women lack other options in life, marriage and motherhood should reduce the risk of depression. Romans, Walton, and colleagues studied women living in Otago province, New Zealand.[84] Questionnaires concerning demographic, social, and mental health variables were mailed to 2,044 women. Interviews were conducted with 314 women who returned these questionnaires, of whom 65 could be considered psychiatric "cases," and thirty months later, 272 of the 314 women were reinterviewed. Most of the ill subjects suffered from depression. In contrast to findings reported in other settings, marital status failed to predict illness or recovery. Number of children correlated with psychological symptom scores only among rural women, whereas lack of outside employment predicted illness only among urban women. Lack of employment training, however, predicted illness in both urban and rural settings. The authors explain the absence of a generalized effect of maternity by noting that childbearing and child rearing are more valued and supported in New Zealand than in other countries. Also, most of the women in this sample were employed: 60 percent of women living in urban areas and 52 percent of women living in rural areas had at least part-time employment outside the home, and many of the nominally unemployed rural women actually worked in partnerships that sold wool or livestock. Consistent with the importance of social power, moreover, financial problems predicted illness and poor recovery.

Subjects who were initially ill had lower socioeconomic status than those who were well. Of those who became ill during the thirty-month follow-up, 72 percent reported financial crises, in comparison with 49 percent of those who remained well. Women who described their financial status as "poor" were more than twice as likely to become psychiatrically ill as those who reported "sound" financial conditions; 72 percent of those initially ill subjects who reported no financial crisis recovered by the follow-up interview, in comparison with only 44 percent of those who had had financial crises. Of those who improved, 69 percent reported having "sound" finances, in comparison with only 36 percent of those who failed to improve. Twenty-nine percent of women who were separated, divorced, or widowed at the time of the initial interview developed a psychiatric illness by the time of the follow-up interview. By comparison, only 10 percent of never-married women and 7 percent of initially married women developed an illness during the follow-up period. Whatever benefits women in this area get from marriage, they apparently pay a high price should their marriage not last. There are also apparently problems due to the natural history of the mothering role. The authors noted the problems faced by mature women whose child-rearing role has come to an end but who have few opportunities for valued employment outside the home.

Aderibigbe and colleagues administered questionnaires to 277 women seeking prenatal care at the University College Hospital in Ibadan, Nigeria.[85] Four and nine-tenths percent of the women met screening criteria for depression, 5 percent met criteria for generalized anxiety disorder, and 4.5 percent met criteria for phobic disorders, which most often were agoraphobia. One hundred sixty-two of these women, including 49 who had been found to be psychologically disturbed, were reassessed six to eight weeks after delivery. Of the 49 who were initially ill, all but 8 (16 percent) were recovered six to eight weeks after childbirth. At the time of the follow-up interview, only 23 of the 162 subjects met screening criteria for illness. In this particular sample, birth of a child reduced anxiety and depression.

Aderibigbe and colleagues note that in Nigeria, a woman's ability to bear children is seen as a "true test of womanhood," and the "sole reason for marriage." In light of this cultural milieu, the authors observe, "It is likely that pregnant women . . . feel under considerable pressure to prove themselves. . . . A safe delivery would represent a tremendous triumph and lead to the disappearance of the fear."[86] According to these authors, "fear" was the most common morbid emotion prenatally, and anxiety symptoms were more common in women who were pregnant for the first time. What is unclear from this report is whether prenatal anxiety was related to pregnancy per se or to childbirth, or how Nigerian mothers compare with nonpregnant women on psychological measures. In any event, this report shows that becoming a mother can lead to improved mental health, at least under some conditions.

Insofar as agoraphobia and panic anxiety are related to depression, one would expect that, in societies like ours, unemployment and motherhood would predict higher incidences of these disorders, too. In fact, the typical agoraphobic is said to be a housewife.[87] Women who go to work are exposed to public places, and exposure is a good treatment for agoraphobic avoidance. The story is more complex, though, concerning motherhood. Chambless found that agoraphobic women with more young children living at home experienced fewer panic attacks, had less chronic anxiety, and were less depressed than agoraphobic women caring for fewer children.[88] Costello's study showed no relationship between number of children living at home and phobias in women in Calgary, Canada.[89] Buglass and coworkers compared thirty married agoraphobic women to an equal number of married, age-matched controls.[90] The agoraphobic women had fewer children than the controls, but the authors did not report the children's age distributions. Since the agoraphobics and controls were matched for age, however, it seems unlikely that the children of the two groups could have differed too greatly on the same dimension. Phobic women were less involved in group activities than were normal controls, suggesting that they may have been more completely immersed in housekeeping roles. Agoraphobic women have been shown to lack masculine features on sex-role inventories in comparison with norms for women as a whole.[91] They adopt more exclusively nurturant, self-sacrificing roles consistent with traditional expectations of mothers. Chambless notes that many agoraphobic women first complain of their symptoms after their children have grown.[92] Some agoraphobics can function well as mothers, but as their children mature, they have less to do within their homes and their avoidant behavior becomes more confining. Children keep mothers company, so that women afraid to be alone may take comfort from them.

Unlike the case with depression, there seems to be little data comparing the risk of panic or agoraphobia in single and married women. Also, though attachment theorists claim that some agoraphobics fear losing their spouses and others they relate to as attachment figures,[93] agoraphobic marriages do not appear to be grossly unstable or conflictual.[94] Insofar as both depression and agoraphobia reflect perceived lack of power, the present viewpoint predicts that agoraphobics, too, might have relational problems like those of depressed patients (see above).

In chapter 5 I will argue that men can realize their potential power advantage over women by monopolizing resources needed for rearing children. Resource monopolization, both between men and between men and women, varies greatly from one culture to another, and hence the relative social power wielded by men and women differs greatly too. In our own society, we see an especially complex picture. Traditional housewives and mothers, being dependent on men, control fewer resources—in comparison with their own and their children's potential needs—and have higher rates of illness. Working women, at least those not living in poverty, have better control of resources and appear to be mentally healthier. Working women living in poverty with their children have not been sufficiently well studied to characterize, but there is every reason to think that their mental health suffers.[95] We may be reaching a point at which women's excess risk of certain mental disorders reflects the number of women who are still in traditional roles or living with children in poverty, rather than conditions of women generally. In a later chapter, I note that women prone to anxiety or depression might be well counseled to pursue a career and to limit their parity as that career requires, rather than to take on traditional women's roles.

The points raised in this and in the following chapter pertain to powerless people in general, and not just to women in male-dominated societies. In fact, in our society, lower-class men are also more likely to be depressed, and possibly anxious too, than men from higher classes.[96] In chapter 4 I will mention certain possession illnesses afflicting lower-class men in stratified societies, which resemble possession illnesses that are elsewhere confined to women. Yet there are differences between the conditions faced by disadvantaged men, even in stratified societies, and those faced by women in male-dominated societies, and these should be considered before generalizing the points made in this and the following chapters.

The differences between women and lower-class men include, but are not limited to, the following: Although lower-class men may be unable to provide for themselves and their families, they are nonetheless not reliant upon a powerful other who can do better than they can. They do not reexperience in their daily lives the type of enforced dependency children, for example, have on their parents. Lower-class men are usually respected in their class. Whereas women in male-dominated societies may feel devalued by their close acquaintances and even by their families, lower-class men are likely to feel devalued only by persons from the upper classes. In male-dominated societies, lower-class men have dominion over lower-class women, and that makes them feel like masters in their own small realm. It also makes them satisfied with the social order. In Judeo-Christian and Islamic societies, lower-class men are also dignified by their religion in ways that women are not. Although ill-timed assertion may be dangerous, lower-class men can assert themselves without stepping out of their gender role. But part of the female gender role in many societies is to be passive and docile. Finally, if they obey laws serving the upper classes, lower-class men can limit their exposure to violence. Women, on the other hand, are subject to violence regardless of their precautions. Compared to men of their social class, women in many societies are subject to much greater danger in public places.

3

•••••••••

Women's Mental Disorders as Illness Roles

Individuals who lack social power, as I have defined it, cannot provide for their needs and security or the needs and security of loved ones, or make life decisions based on their own desires. Individuals who believe they lack social power must find ways of getting by in life. Insofar as they believe that direct efforts will fail, they may have to fall back on stratagems that serve their needs indirectly. Indirect stratagems may work by enlisting support of more powerful others and/or by disguising their ultimate goals. In the following pages, I argue that some women's mental disorders are really illness roles that patients adopt because, among other reasons, they believe they are powerless to meet their needs more directly. Possibly, women have had these disorders more frequently than men because women in fact have lacked needed social power. These illness roles enlist support from physicians and other helpers, whose own needs are served by offering treatment for them, and the functions served by these roles are often disguised. In discussing these illness roles separately from anxiety and depression, I run the risk of introducing an artificial distinction, which serves a heuristic purpose but is more hard and fast than in real life. In real life, women with disorders mentioned in this chapter are often depressed and anxious as well.[1] Depression, too, can be seen as an illness role, as many experienced clinicians are no doubt aware. I have already mentioned the theory that relates depression to submissiveness, which implies that depression is a specialized strategem akin to an illness role. Real patients manifest complex admixtures of processes we might like to distinguish for theoretical reasons.

In this chapter, I will define and discuss the concept of illness roles and apply this concept to so-called grand hysteria, to the lesser hysterias, and to Briquet's hysteria, which is today called somatization disorder. These forms of hysteria encompassed most of the cases of hysterical illness of nineteenth-century women. Neurasthenia, which also is mentioned below, occurred in both men and women. In the following chapter, I will discuss two disorders, multiple personality and anorexia nervosa, which also have their roots in the nineteenth century but which have increased in incidence just in recent years. Concepts of social roles developed in this chapter turn out to be applicable to these disorders, too.

Roles and Illness Roles

In referring to illness roles, I will be using concepts from sociology and social psychology.[2] A series of well-known experiments conducted by social psychologists has shown that human behavior is controlled much more by immediate social situations, and controlled less by enduring personal attributes, than had previously been realized. Social psychologists, in fact, now refer to the tendency to assume that behavior reflects enduring personal attributes as the "fundamental attribution error." Many of them now call themselves "situationists," by which they mean they emphasize control by social settings.

Some sociologists and social psychologists describe social control in terms of roles or schemata. Roles are behavioral patterns dictated by social settings, while schemata are the internalized conceptions, including beliefs and emotional valuations, that underlie these roles. In a social setting, individuals learn to take on rewarded roles, which sooner or later become genuinely felt, or real, for them in that setting. Since roles are often conveyed by subtle cues, and since individuals adopt these roles and their corresponding schemata unself-consciously, the whole process by which individuals adopt advantageous roles in a particular social setting most often goes unnoticed. Also, most people stay in the same social settings for very long periods of time, imparting an apparent stability to their behavior, which belies their potential for change in response to new demands.

Rapid role adoption is most obvious in the social psychology laboratory. Here, subjects can be exposed to radically new, contrived social settings, which call for adoption of roles discordant with "normal" behavior. The ease with which subjects adopt new roles and unwittingly come to accept the schemata appropriate to them is invariably surprising to those not familiar with studies of this kind. Perhaps the most famous, or in any event the most notorious, of studies of role adoption was conducted by Phillip Zimbardo, of Stanford University.[3] Zimbardo wanted to know whether undesirable behavior patterns shown by prison guards and by prisoners reflect the enduring personalities of those who choose to be prison guards and those who choose to be criminals, or whether they are created by role demand characteristics of the prison situation itself. To study this question, Zimbardo recruited a group of normal college-age men to participate in a paid experiment. Half of these men were randomly assigned to act as uniformed guards in a makeshift prison constructed in the basement of the psychology building. The guards were instructed to enforce certain prison rules and to prevent their prisoners from escaping. The remaining subjects were clothed in makeshift prison garb and locked in barren cells.

After just a day or two or in this situation, both prisoners and guards began to lose perspective. The guards became physically and emotionally abusive and the prisoners became apathetic, sullen, or servile. The guards expressed their contempt for the prisoners by inventing degrading routines, which the prisoners were forced to follow. Some of the prisoners broke down; one had to be removed from the experiment and another refused to eat. Others plotted revenge. After five or six days, feelings were running so high on both sides that Zimbardo stopped the experiment. The guards and prisoners seemed to be emotionally harming each other, and the potential for violence seemed to be present too. Films made of the experiment and interviews with participants made it clear that the study had altered not only behavior, but thinking and feeling as well. Values and self-identities had changed during the study, as guards and prisoners absorbed the roles they played.

Another, more naturalistic, setting in which rapid changes in role are evident is in religious cults or similar groups. There is a general consensus among those who study cults that many cult members join cults to gain a sense of belonging. For example, Marc Galanter, from New York University, surveyed 119 recent converts to the Divine Light Mission, an eastern religious group that once gained notoriety for having a thirteen-year-old guru, known as Maharaj Ji.[4] Converts reported that membership in the mission had relieved symptoms of psychological distress from which they had previously suffered. The degree of symptom relief correlated closely with the extent to which converts saw the Divine Light Mission as a cohesive social group and with the convert's stated distrust of outsiders. Galanter hypothesized that his respondents had been alienated from larger-than-family groups and that they had gained this kind of camaraderie in joining the Divine Light Mission. Since alienation is psychologically distressing, those who felt more of the camaraderie they were seeking experienced greater relief from mental distress. Sociologist Robert Bellah and his coworkers have shown the extent to which modern American life encourages alienation, which might be a cause of distress.[5]

According to Bellah and coworkers, the individualistic ethic first described by Alexis de Tocqueville has flourished in the United States at the expense of community, which is now disturbingly out of reach for many Americans.

Other studies echo Galanter's observations. In a famous study of conversion to a cult, the sociologists John Lofland and Rodney Stark found that converts were, in fact, globally disaffected from noncult social contacts.[6] Saul Levine, a psychiatrist, interviewed members of numerous cults and reported the same phenomenon.[7] Alienation from noncult groups appeared to be important in leading to conversion. Galanter later studied participants in cult workshops intended to recruit members.[8] Consistent with his earlier observations, the major predictor that participants in these workshops would later convert to the the cult was lack of outside social ties.

Observers of cults also agree that conversion depends upon social ties, not upon ideology.[9] Thus, potential recruits to the more successful cults may be invited to a dinner or social meeting at which they are fed and emotionally coddled. Members of the cult will go out of their way to make their guests feel special. The potential recruits become the targets of "love bombing," as the process has been called. Potential recruits who show interest in further contact with the cult are invited to lengthy "retreats" in isolated locations. During these retreats, intensive efforts continue to make potential recruits feel at home among friends. Practical help may be offered them. Religious dogma is mentioned only after recruits have become sufficiently attached to the group that they express an interest in joining it. In Lofland and Stark's phrase, adopting the dogma at that point is merely "to accept the opinions of one's friends," in this case friends who place a high premium on agreement.

One way of increasing feelings of camaraderie is for new recruits to spend as much time as possible with other cult members. Lofland and Stark considered communal living arrangements essential to consolidation of new members' loyalties. Recruits cannot be counted on until they have lived with the cult for an extended period. Cult members Galanter studied spent 94 percent of their nights in communal quarters.[10] Typical cults discourage maintenance of family ties or of noncult social relationships that might prevent complete immersion in the cult milieu.[11] Physical separation from the cult milieu leads to a loss of commitment and religious faith.[12] To ensure that members are exposed only to other believers, some cults establish settlements in isolated locales. Rajneeshpuram, in Oregon, was a typical example of what cults seek to accomplish.[13] There, the followers of the late Bhagwan Shree Rajneesh spent their days entirely surrounded by their comrades.

Seeking acceptance, recruits to religious cults quickly learn the role, and adopt the corresponding schemata, appropriate to cult members. They profess belief in their cult's doctrine, and they report cosmic and out-of-body experiences, visions, voices, ecstasies, and possession states consistent with that doctrine. They act on their cult's doctrine in ways that leave no room for doubt as to the genuineness of their beliefs. In Rajneeshpuram, for example, followers of the Bhagwan labored from sunup to sundown on communal projects. Inspired religious cult members have mutilated or killed themselves because they believed cult doctrines required these sacrifices. These roles and schemata, moreover, are often at odds with the previous lifestyles and values of cult members. Many of the Rajneeshees held advanced degrees and were religious skeptics before becoming Rajneeshees. Many other cult members were raised in liberal families with values antithetical to those they now espouse. Apparently, transient group processes can effectively sweep aside enculturated roles and deeply ingrained schemata.

Observers impressed by the malleability of beliefs and behavior shown by religious cult members have likened cult conversion to a state of hypnosis.[14] This metaphor may be apt. As discussed below, hypnosis is related to social role malleability in the most general sense. Military units, political parties, and other institutions have been known to produce equally rapid changes in adults' beliefs and behaviors, showing that cult phenomena are not sui generis.

The sociologists Henry Sigerist and Talcott Parsons were the first to observe the social-role aspect of bodily illness.[15] Sigerist noted that sickness brings characteristic changes in social relationships. The sick person is released from obligations that are incumbent upon well members of his or her society and also receives attention from friends and family members. According to Parsons, who elaborated on Sigerist's observations, to be defined as ill one must appear disabled. The disability, which prevents the patient from meeting his or her obligations, must be such that others do not believe it can be overcome through an act of will, and it must be validated by an authority figure, such as a doctor or shaman. The individual must appear to dislike his or her disability, and he or she must show good-faith efforts to be cured.

People, of course, can try to take on an illness role when they are not really ill. In this case they have to persuade others that they are disabled and that they have made every effort to be cured. They must find authority figures, physicians in our society, to validate their claim to the illness role. Actually, finding such physicians may not be terribly difficult. As I show below, medical institutions can teach and reward false illness roles in much the same way cults impress roles on their members. Doctors sometimes need patients with a particular illness as badly as cult leaders need their devotees.

The psychiatrist Thomas Szasz attributed mental disorders to falsely claimed illness roles.[16] Szasz took as his models the very same mental disorders I will discuss in similar terms in the following pages. Szasz's analysis, though, differs from the one presented in this chapter. The most significant difference is that Szasz did not employ concepts of roles and schemata as these are understood by social psychologists. Instead, his frame of reference was psychoanalytic. The social-role viewpoint implies that those who take illness roles lack better alternatives. Hence, it draws attention to social conditions that block access to functional roles. By contrast, psychoanalysis draws attention away from social conditions, especially of women patients.[17] The social-role framework distinguishes between false illness roles adopted unself-consciously and malingering. By contrast, psychoanalysis blurs this important distinction. The social-role framework implies that doctors and patients create illness roles together. Szasz's framework ignores doctors' social psychology and the sociology of medical institutions.

An illness-role approach is deconstructionistic in the sense that it treats some mental disorders as social fictions. However, it differs from that deconstructionism advocated by feminists. As I noted in chapter 1, some feminists claim that psycho-diagnoses are tools for oppressing women and that women with these disorders are martyrs rather than patients. Even Jane Ussher, who was cited in chapter 1, came to the conclusion that feminist deconstructionists understate the problems of women with these disorders, which she attributed to many of the same etiological factors emphasized in this and the previous chapter.[18] By treating illness roles as joint enterprises between physicians and patients, rather than as labels imposed on unwilling patients, the approach taken here keeps sight of patients' life problems, which lead them to adopt unpleasant and difficult roles. Patients' willingness to take on unpleasant and difficult roles reflects the social forces to which they have been subjected, as well as more personal factors peculiar to each patient.

Social-role concepts are familiar to feminists, since at least some feminist theorists have used them to argue against the reality of sex differences. Sandra Bem, for instance, argues that those differences that are evident now, such as boys' and men's preference for rough-and-tumble team sports or girls' and women's greater interest in babies, result from differential rewards for gender roles.[19] Girls are rewarded for behavior consistent with the "feminine" role, and boys are rewarded for behavior consistent with the "masculine" role. These roles are arbitrary, but they serve to maintain men's and women's place in a sexist society. In contrast to so-called difference feminists, who believe that there are real differences between men and women, Bem claims that men's and women's attitudes, values, and preferences would be identical if men and women were exposed to identical situational forces. Some of the implications of this claim are discussed in chapter 6. Within certain limits, the debate between difference feminists and gender-role theorists like Bem turns out not to be critical to the argument here.[20]

Grand Hysteria

To turn to women's illness roles: In the 1870s and 1880s, the neurologist Jean-Martin Charcot and his students described the syndrome of what they called grand hysteria among female patients in the Salpêtrière Hospital in Paris.[21] Charcot, an imposing figure sometimes referred to as the "Caesar" of the Salpêtrière, was famous for his lectures and clinical demonstrations. One well-known painting shows Charcot standing in his lecture hall, which is filled with male physicians. Beside Charcot, supported by attendants, an attractive, partially undressed female patient is shown falling into a swoon. Charcot became a consultant to the nobility and to the rich of Paris. His salon was attended by artists and intellectuals, and his students included the founders of modern neurology, as well as Pierre Janet, a pioneer in psychology. Early in his career, when he was still a neurologist, Freud traveled to Paris to study at Charcot's side.

The manifestations of grand hysteria observed in the Salpêtrière consisted of seizure symptoms and so-called stigmata, which were present between the seizures. The stigmata included anesthesias, tremors, paralyses, gait disturbances, tunnel vision, and other disabilities. These could not be explained on physiological grounds. The sensory losses and paralyses, for instance, failed to correspond with nerve distributions. The gait disturbances differed from gait disturbances seen with known neurological lesions. Visual problems came and went without objective findings. Charcot divided the seizures into four phases. During the first, or "epileptoid" phase, the patient dropped to the floor and showed flailing and jerking movements. These movements resembled true epileptic convulsions. During the second phase, that of "grand movements," the patient assumed bizarre or unusual postures. Some patients, for instance, arched their backs sufficiently to bear their weight entirely on their heads and heels for long periods of time. During the third phase, that of "passionate attitudes," the patient seemed to hallucinate. She babbled or spoke incoherently and showed rapid changes in mood. She assumed and maintained prayerful postures, spread her arms as if crucified, or mimed sexual intercourse. During the last, or "delirious" phase, the patient became incoherent, laughed or wept uncontrollably, and eventually became stuporous. In grand hysteria, seizure episodes could be started or terminated by pressure on parts of the body, which Charcot referred to as "hysterogenic points." Hysterogenic points were thought to affect seizures by means of reflex activity. Consistent with this explanation, patients reported that pressure on hysterogenic points, which were often over the breasts or lower abdomen, set off a local tingling that spread to the throat and head before the seizure started. Charcot and his students built corsets and other devices to apply constant pressure to hysterogenic points, in order to block the seizures in some of their patients. Spiteful hysterics were observed pressing each other's sensitive points in order to set off seizures.

In the 1870s, under the influence of his colleague, Charles Richet, Charcot began experimenting with hypnosis. He found that grand hysterics were readily hypnotized. After staring at bright lights and listening to suggestions, hysterical patients lost consciousness. In this state, their limbs could be moved into different postures, which they would maintain, or they could be made to mime a suggested emotion. If the lights were then dimmed, or the patient's eyes were closed, the hypnotized grand hysteric became limp. In this state, muscles could be made to contract with apparently superhuman force merely by touching them. One hypnotized patient held herself rigid between two chairs, her head on one and her feet on the other, after her muscles were touched. Similar demonstrations are a staple of modern stage hypnotists, but they were thought more extraordinary in Charcot's day. If instead of the lights being dimmed, the patient's head was scratched, the hypnotized hysteric would enter a so-called twilight state, during which she talked and behaved as if sleepwalking. Charcot was especially surprised to find that long-standing stigmata of grand hysteria, including blindness and paralysis, resolved temporarily in response to hypnotic suggestions.

Charcot, who was first and last a neurologist, reasoned that hypnotizability and hysteria were signs of the same brain disease. Hence, hypnotizable subjects, even if clinically well, were prone to hysterical illness given the right conditions. This theory set the stage for the so-called battle of the schools, waged between Charcot and his students at the Salpêtrière and Hippolyte Bernheim and others at the medical school at Nancy. Bernheim, a professor of internal medicine, had been inspired to experiment with hypnosis by Auguste Liebeault, a small-town general practitioner who used hypnotic instructions to treat medical problems in mentally healthy patients. His 1866 book on hypnotic therapy sold only one copy, but his consulting room, a whitewashed shack in his garden, attracted numerous colleagues who came to observe his methods. Bernheim was one of his visitors. Based on his own experience, Bernheim concluded that responsiveness to hypnosis is perfectly normal and depends on suggestibility rather than brain disease. He argued that both the hypnotic and nonhypnotic signs of grand hysteria were caused by Charcot's expectations, which Charcot unwittingly conveyed to highly suggestible patients. Their suggestibility showed itself in the ease with which they were hypnotized.

Bernheim's critique of Charcot became a cause célèbre of nineteenth-century science. By 1887, Charcot, Bernheim, and their followers had published more than eight hundred medical papers supporting one side or the other, and newspapers and magazines had brought the dispute to the public. In spite of Charcot's fame and the fame of the Salpêtrière, Bernheim and his followers gained the upper hand. They reported data on thousands of hypnotized subjects, rather than on just a few. They conducted controlled experiments to show the effect of suggestion on mentally healthy persons. Most importantly, they showed that the full syndrome of grand hysteria described by Charcot and his students was rare if not nonexistent outside the walls of the Salpêtrière. Apparently, to respond to Charcot's expectations, patients had to be in the master's presence. By the time Charcot died in 1893, Bernheim and his followers had already carried the day. After Charcot's death, his syndrome of grand hysteria essentially disappeared.

Pierre Janet, a founder of depth psychology and one of Charcot's students, later argued that the real link between hysteria and hypnotic responsiveness was not suggestibility, but dissociation. According to Janet, hypnotizable subjects and hysterical patients differ from other persons by virtue of their greater ability to dissociate, or to segregate mental contents. Dissociation is shown by the hypnotized person's ability to follow instructions he or she cannot recall hearing, and by the grand hysteric's somnambulistic states. Rejected by psychoanalysts, dissociation theory nearly disappeared until it was used by the Stanford University psychologist Ernest Hilgard in the 1970s to account for results of hypnotic experiments.[22] As a result of Hilgard's work, dissociation theory is once again widely cited in clinical work. The American Psychiatric Association's *Diagnostic and Statistical Manual* now calls certain illnesses "dissociative disorders."[23] Today's dissociationists essentially follow Janet in believing that certain illnesses and hypnotic responsiveness manifest an ability to segregate mental contents, thereby dividing the seeming stream of consciousness.

In spite of the recrudescence of dissociation theory, modern-day social psychologists have continued to study hypnosis in terms akin to Bernheim's. Experimental psychologists following in the footsteps of T. R. Sarbin and T. X. Barber have shown that many, and possibly all, of the phenomena of hypnosis—including apparent memory feats, analgesia, and so-called hypnotic regression, in which subjects appear to relive an earlier time—are readily understood in terms of social roles.[24] According to these social cognitive theorists, as they call themselves, both hypnotist and subject play culturally defined roles. The hypnotist is expected to do something to "induce" hypnosis and to issue certain commands, and the subject is expected to follow the hypnotist's guidance. If the hypnotist tells the subject his arm is getting lighter, the subject is supposed to raise his arm in the air while disavowing any active intention to do so. If the hypnotist tells the subject he cannot remember his name, the subject is supposed to refrain from speaking his name while making an apparent effort to recall it. Highly responsive subjects are those who can wholeheartedly lose themselves in their role. Barber and others believe that highly responsive subjects are responsive to social cues and have vivid imaginations, such that they can convince themselves that something special is happening.

Actually, even dissociationists agree that hypnotizable subjects are highly responsive to subtle social cues. Thus, Herbert and David Spiegel, who claim that their widely used test of hypnotizability measures physiological talent for dissociation, note that highly hypnotizable subjects are anxious to please and extremely sensitive to interpersonal cues and social expectations.[25] According to these authors, clinicians treating such patients have to be careful to avoid suggesting roles, which these patients would then adopt. In effect, these patients become what they are thought to be, if these thoughts are conveyed to them even by subtle cues. They enter whatever state they are believed to be in. Unhypnotizable patients, according to Spiegel and Spiegel, respond to cues only reluctantly and resist adopting roles suggested to them by others.

The hypnotizable patient described by social cognitive theorists and by authors like Spiegel and Spiegel resembles the patient with a "hysterical style" described by David Shapiro, the "high self-monitoring" individual described by Mark Snyder, and the "other-directed" personality type described by David Riesman.[26] According to Shapiro, a psychoanalyst, hysterical personalities are highly responsive to social cues and little concerned with logical inconsistencies, either in their own behavior or in their beliefs. Snyder, a social psychologist, notes that high self-monitoring individuals define themselves by the social roles they happen to be playing. They are highly attuned to role cues, and they avoid situations lacking clear role expectations. Riesman's well-known other-directed personality type is likewise highly sensitive to role expectations. Steered by social "radar," the other-directed person contrasts with the inner-directed, who steers by an internal "gyroscope."

In the same vein, patients with so-called hysterical psychoses, some of which resemble grand hysteria, have been said to have "antennae" to pick up social cues and to be habitual role players.[27] According to Spiegel and Fink, patients with these disorders are readily hypnotized.[28] Cross-cultural studies show that societies in which forms of hysterical psychosis are common emphasize conventionality, conformity with social roles, and the importance of sensitivity to social-role demands.[29] Children in these societies are raised to conform to subtly expressed expectations.

It is worthwhile to review the stories of Charcot's patients, to show how their situations and their concomitant lack of power impelled them to take on illness roles suggested to them by physicians.[30] Louise, one of the most famous of Charcot's patients, entered the Salpêtrière in 1875, at the age of fifteen years. She was the oldest of five children of Parisian domestics, but three of her four siblings died in early childhood. Between the ages of six and thirteen Louise lived in a boarding school run by Catholic nuns. There she was taught to read and write, but she was frequently beaten for violating the rules. She tried to establish relationships with her surviving brother and with her parents, but these efforts were unsuccessful, and at age thirteen she went to live with a family her parents had introduced her to, as an apprentice seamstress. The head of this family raped Louise; his wife then threw her out. She was sent as a maidservant to live with a spinster in Paris, but her parents brought her home after learning she had become sexually involved with two adolescent boys. At home, she started having screaming fits, which led to her admission to the Salpêtrière, where she stayed for the next five years.

Another grand hysteric, Genevieve, was an orphan from Loudon without any education. As a child she had fits of violent anger. At age twelve she intentionally cut her hand. Today, Genevieve might have been diagnosed as a borderline personality.[31] At age fifteen, Genevieve became engaged to a young man, Camille, but he died shortly afterward of a mysterious illness, leaving her grief-stricken. She entered a hospital in Poitiers, where she stayed for about a year. She then was employed as a chambermaid, but her master seduced her. She returned to the hospital with a hysterical pregnancy. Shortly thereafter, she attempted to kill herself with pills and with scissors. At age seventeen, she escaped from the hospital with her lover, a medical student, but this relationship did not last, and Genevieve went to Paris to work as a chambermaid. After a series of fits and suicide attempts, she first entered the Salpêtrière in 1865. She twice escaped from the Salpêtrière, and both times became pregnant. A daughter was left in the country and a son died of exposure. In 1875, Charcot became impatient with Genevieve's misbehavior. He threw her out of the hospital, but he shortly thereafter relented and allowed her to return.

The Salpêtrière, built on the site of an ancient saltpeter depot from which it took its name, was a wretched public institution filled with lower-class women with every conceivable untreated neurological and psychiatric disorder. Charcot's reputation today rests on his having delineated important and still incurable neurologic diseases among the inmates of the Salpêtrière. The only thing the inmates of the Salpêtrière had in common was that they all had nowhere else to go, in an age in which the poor in general, but especially poor women, were dying on the streets from exposure and malnutrition. Tens of thousands of women in late-nineteenth-century Paris were forced into prostitution in order to stay alive. The Salpêtrière was run by ambitious middle-class doctors, who hoped to further their careers by solving the problem of hysterical illness. Having the most dramatic form of hysterical illness, grand hysterics stayed in the hospital when they otherwise might have been discharged, and they also were accorded extra attention and privileges. By developing grand hysteria, poverty-stricken women like Louise and Genevieve could assure their place in the Salpêtrière and in the status hierarchy of the Salpêtrière, in roughly the same way modern religious converts assure their place in the cult by ideologic conversion and by religious experiences. Today's cult members, of course, join due to alienation, whereas women like Louise and Genevieve had to maintain their positions in the Salpêtrière just to be provided for in a hostile world.

Actually, Charcot himself drew a parallel between hysteria and epidemic religious ecstasies, but he tried to assimilate the latter to the former by proclaiming that ecstasies, such as occurred during the seventeenth century at Loudon, were symptoms of hysteria. In this way he set in motion a long-standing opposition between psychiatric and religious thinkers. Yet from a social-role viewpoint, hysteria and religious ecstasies are more plausibly viewed as secular and religious versions of one phenomenon, rather than one being subsumable to the other. Consistent with this notion, studies of subjects who report intense religious experiences show hysterical features on psychological testing.[32] They are not mentally ill, nor are they hysterics in the nineteenth-century sense, but their personality types are such as to promote adherence to role expectations. As I note below, some patients are "cured" of illness roles by becoming religious seers.

It also seems improbable that grand hysteria was a product of conscious simulation, any more than the religious experiences claimed by today's cult members are merely simulated. Many features of grand hysteria seem to preclude simple malingering or play-acting. Blanche Wittman, one of the most famous of Charcot's hysterics, was asked in the 1920s if she had simulated symptoms of grand hysteria. After Charcot's death, Wittman had remained in the Salpêtrière, where she was treated for a time by Jules Janet, Pierre Janet's brother. Jules Janet thought Wittman had two distinct personalities, one of whom was accessible during hypnotic trances. Eventually, Wittman's symptoms abated and she went on to work in the hospital as an assistant with the newly invented X-ray machines. At the time she was interviewed, she was dying from cancer contracted due to exposure to the X-ray beam. She vehemently denied ever faking symptoms. She said that some had tried, but that Charcot could see right through them.

The Lesser Hysterias

Although grand hysteria was limited to the Salpêtrière, less dramatic forms of hysteria were extremely widespread among nineteenth-century women. Women afflicted by these disorders lacked the seizures of Charcot's grand hysterics, but they nonetheless showed a panoply of physical symptoms that, not being intelligible in physiological terms, must have been produced in conformity with illness roles. Several factors explain the high incidence of these disorders. For one thing, nineteenth-century doctors lacked objective markers for physical illnesses, so patients with subjective complaints could seldom be proven well. Patients were therefore freer than they are today in adopting illness roles of many different kinds. John Bowlby's study of Darwin's psychosomatic complaints illustrates quite clearly the extent to which bodily-illness roles served to express emotions in some nineteenth-century families.[33] Darwin and others in his extended family routinely took to bed when something upsetting happened. Also, women in particular were expected to be ill at least part of the time. Excessively robust health, as shown by physical stamina, resistance to disease and stress, vigorous movements and loud speech, or a pink complexion, was considered a sign of poor breeding, at least in the upper classes.[34] A healthy appetite for food, especially for red meat, was thought to be a sign of unladylike carnal desire. Nineteenth-century men honored and worshiped women whose hold on this world seemed tenuous. As Thorstein Veblen noted, men who could afford it were more than willing to pay for the additional status a frail wife conferred.[35] Frail wives had to be sent to spas and treated with kid gloves. In some cases, wives' disabilities prevented sexual intercourse, but many upper-class men had mistresses they could turn to. Finally, the poor eating habits, lack of fresh air and exercise, and severely restricted activities of nineteenth-century middle-class women rendered many of them really frail and sickly. Insofar as middle-class women saw themselves as sickly on realistic grounds, it would have been all the easier for them to become more disabled by adopting illness roles. These roles would have been consistent with their previous self-perceptions.

Case histories clarify the types of personal factors that led nineteenth-century women to adopt illness roles. In each case these factors relate to frustration of women's preferences in societies in which they lacked social power. "Anna O.," for example, was a patient seen by the Viennese physician Josef Breuer during the early 1880s and described by Breuer and Sigmund Freud in their *Studies on Hysteria,* which they published in 1895.[36] Anna O.'s real name was Bertha Pappenheim; she was the only daughter of a wealthy Jewish family. Pappenheim became ill while nursing her father each night during his terminal illness, a tuberculous lung abcess. Her symptoms at first included loss of appetite, cough, and headaches. Soon, however, she suffered intermittent visual disturbances, paralyses, and anesthesias. As her father's death approached, she began to have somnolent episodes and to hallucinate snakes, skulls, and skeletons. At times she spoke as a child; at other times she could speak only French, English, or Italian rather than her native German. She developed two personalities, one of whom was aggressive and poorly behaved, the other of whom was docile. She refused to take any fluids. She complained of abdominal pains, and she disconcerted the proper Victorian Breuer by claiming to bear his child. In spite of the fact that Breuer found that talking with Pappenheim alleviated her symptoms—a process that Pappenheim dubbed her "talking cure"—she was sufficiently ill at the end of Breuer's treatment to require continued therapy in a Swiss sanatorium.

The Pappenheims were an Orthodox Jewish family with very traditional views of women's rights and abilities. Breuer described Bertha Pappenheim as "markedly intelligent, with an astonishingly quick grasp of things and penetrating intuition . . . [possessing] a powerful intellect . . . which stood in need of [application]."[37] Yet she had stopped school at age sixteen, five years before her illness, and had since then lived a sheltered and extremely monotonous life awaiting eventual marriage. She told Breuer she spent her days in her "private theater" filled with adventurous daydreams that helped her tolerate the tedium in her home. Shortly before her illness, Bertha's less-talented brother, her father's favorite child, entered the study of law.

Breuer thought Pappenheim fell ill because she was upset by her father's terminal illness. Yet Bertha Pappenheim's later writings suggest that she was not as devoted to her father as Breuer thought. She complained that her father had scoffed at her youthful ambitions and that he had made no effort to hide his preference for her younger brother. She observed that he was unwilling to provide for her education. She condemned treatment of women in Orthodox Jewish families like hers. As for her father's plans to marry her off, Bertha Pappenheim later wrote that in Orthodox Jewish families like hers, the wife was expected to live as a "beast of burden," serving the needs of men. Her intellect was undeveloped and her spirit dulled. "Her lovesong," according to Pappenheim, "was sung . . . serving Gefilte fish!"[38] In hindsight, we can see that Pappenheim's mysterious illness expressed more ambivalence than devoted love. This energetic and ambitious young woman, held prisoner in her home for five years at the time Breuer met her, waiting for a married life she did not look forward to and having to watch her less competent brother pursue the education she wanted for herself, was forced by her mother to care for the bodily needs of the man who had scoffed at her dreams, the very man responsible for her current plight. Her care, moreover, was really intended to show her devotion; the family could easily have afforded professional nurses. By becoming ill, Pappenheim excused herself from taking care of her father and even competed with him for her mother's attention, a theme we see repeated in other similar histories (see below).

After her father's death, Bertha Pappenheim and her mother moved from Vienna to Frankfurt, her mother's native city. There Bertha Pappenheim became a leading figure in the German social-work movement. Her concern for women's rights and her feelings about men in general were manifest in her activities and in her subsequent writing. She began programs, for instance, for women who had been seduced and abandoned by men, for women whose husbands had left their families to emigrate, and for Jewish women in brothels in Turkey and Palestine. Poor Jewish parents in Poland, who did not value daughters, would sell them to merchants who raised them and later resold them as prostitutes in the Ottoman Empire. Pappenheim condemned Jewish leaders and merchants in Poland and Istanbul for failing to take steps against the white slave traffic. As for her writing, Pappenheim wrote the first German-language translation of Mary Wollstonecraft's classic book, *A Vindication of the Rights of Women,* which advocates women's education, and she wrote a play called *Women's Rights,* which dealt with exploitation. The men in this play are either rapists or heartless seducers who give no thought to the harm they inflict on women.

Consistent with a social-role view of her earlier illness, Bertha Pappenheim never evinced the slightest hysterical symptoms once she had found ways, through her work and writing, to satisfy her needs outside the stifling confines of her traditional family. Her career gave her opportunities to express her ambition and talents and to protest men's domination of women, which she had experienced in her family home. She apparently never had much use for psychoanalysis, though she was aware of Breuer and Freud's case study.

"Dora," whose real name was Ida Bauer, did not fare as well as Bertha Pappenheim.[39] Freud published her case in 1905, five years after treating her for a three-month period. The only daughter of a wealthy Bohemian Jewish family, Ida was only eighteen when her father brought her to Freud. Her symptoms included headaches, a persistent cough, whispering speech, a mysterious limp, and what was thought to be irrational hostility. She was intermittently depressed and had expressed suicidal thoughts. Ida complained to Freud that her father had a lover, a Frau K., whose husband had made sexual advances toward her. The K.'s were friends of the family, and Ida believed that her father countenanced Herr K.'s behavior to secure Herr K.'s complicity in his own affair with Frau K. Ida's mother was said to suffer from "housewife's psychosis," which apparently meant she spent her time obsessively cleaning the house. She was, as a result, quite unavailable to protect her teenage daughter. Few cases in the psychoanalytic literature show such a complete failure of rapport between analyst and patient as is evident in Ida's case. Freud found nothing remarkable about Herr K.'s attentions. His theory of sexuality led him to assume that if Ida found these disgusting, as she claimed, then it must be because her sexual drives had been subject to repression. Freud had met Herr K. and considered him pleasant and handsome, and not the least bit disgusting. Nor did Freud consider what it meant to Ida to be traded for her father's satisfaction or what it meant to her to have Freud, whose fees her father paid, tell her there was nothing wrong with Herr K.'s propositions. Not surprisingly, Ida left treatment abruptly without having been helped. Leaving, she told Freud that since men were detestable, she would never marry.

Ida in fact did marry, but her marriage ended in tragedy. Her husband, a composer, suffered a serious head injury during World War I, which left him chronically ill and mentally impaired until his death in 1932. After her husband's death, Ida and her son fled to France and then to the United States. Her only sibling, Otto Bauer, a principal leader of the Austrian Socialist Party, also fled to France, where he died in 1938. In 1922, Ida was seen in New York by Felix Deutsch, who found that she had many of the same somatic symptoms as when she had seen Freud, nearly twenty-five years before.[40] According to Deutsch, Ida's psychosomatic and mental symptoms made her a burden to others right up to her death in the 1950s.

Ida may have inherited illness from her mother. Relatives of patients with obsessive-compulsive disorder, which is what "housewife's psychosis" signified, have an increased risk of emotional illness.[41] However, only a social-role view can explain Ida's actual symptoms. Except for an occasional patient with somatization (see below), modern-day patients seldom manifest mental problems by coughing, whispering, or limping. That Ida's mental problems led to these various symptoms suggests that her milieu, in contrast to that experienced by most modern-day patients, promoted these physical symptoms, just as it promoted them for Bertha Pappenheim. I have already cited some reasons that illness roles came readily to nineteenth-century patients, and to women in particular. Actually, before adopting an illness role, Ida had unsuccessfully tried to solve her problems directly. She complained to her father and mother about Herr K.'s advances and asked them to take steps to shield her from Herr K. But Herr K. and her father charged her with living an overwrought fantasy life. They claimed that she had read too much on the theme of love. It was only then that Ida resorted to physical symptoms suggested by her milieu. Where words had not sufficed, physical symptoms effectively stymied Herr K.'s advances. They blocked her father's plan to trade her for Frau K., which Ida must have experienced as a profound betrayal. Because of her mother's illness, Ida had grown up unusually close to her father and dependent on him. Frau and Herr K. later admitted to Ida that the situation had been as she described it.

Alice James, the sister of Henry and William James, presented an especially tragic case of hysteria.[42] Her history shows how destructive the invalid role could be for nineteenth-century women. Born in 1848, Alice was the youngest of five children and the only daughter in the James household. Her father, Henry James, Sr., had inherited enough money that he could devote himself to writing obscure books on his religious theories. A kind and indulgent parent, who took more interest in his children than most men of his era, he nonetheless had typical Victorian notions of womanhood, with which he hobbled his brilliant only daughter. To begin with, he saw women more as household idols than as real people.

He admired what he saw as their spiritual superiority, manifested in motherhood, and he even wrote paeans to it, but he thought that women lacked men's mental abilities. Bram Dijkstra, an art historian and a professor of comparative literature at the University of California, San Diego, has shown that the notion of woman as household saint was ubiquitous in late Victorian art and literature.[43] Jean Strouse, Alice James's biographer, noted ambivalence even in Henry senior's praise of feminine spirituality.[44] Insofar as women were spiritual by nature, and not by moral effort, their spirituality was ultimately of less account than men's in James's moral universe. He also thought women belonged in the home. In an 1853 article, he claimed that the feminist movement would lead to muscular women and effeminate men. Finally, he believed that women should be selfless. Being innately saint-like, they should think first of others, and not of their own needs. Jean Strouse quotes from a letter Henry senior wrote on a New York shopping spree, which shows how he taught Alice the art of selflessness.

He had picked up (he wrote) a "half-hundred" foreign photographs for William, "But they are too dear to permit me to buy any fancy ones for you . . . I shall go into Stewart's this morning to enquire for that style of ribbon for you. If I had only brought a little more money with me! I went into Arnold's for a scarf for you, but the clerks were so rapid with me, I couldn't buy & bought two pairs of gloves for myself, one of which turns out too small for me but will suit Harry. . . . Goodbye, darling daughter, and be sure that never was daughter so beloved. . . . Keep my letters and believe me ever your lovingest Daddy." [45]

Alice's problems began when she was eighteen, after the James family had moved to Cambridge in order to be near William, who had just entered Harvard. This, of course, was the time in Alice's life when she came face to face with the narrowness of her options, which contrasted so sharply with her older brothers'. Previously bright and cheerful, she developed severe fatigue and "nervous excitability." Local doctors thought that she had hysteria. She was sent to New York City, where Charles Fayett Taylor diagnosed nervous exhaustion. Taylor believed that the female brain was especially vulnerable to exhaustion from overuse, and thus he was frequently cited in arguments against women's education. Taylor's cure for exhaustion consisted of massages and enforced mental inactivity, a sick role, in other words, to which Alice took all too readily. She spent the next ten years living with family members. Relapses and nervous fits were followed by long convalescences. She was bedridden much of the time.

In 1884, after her parents' deaths, Alice moved to England with a friend, Katharine Peabody Loring, whom she had met through the Society to Encourage Studies at Home, a correspondence school for women students. Alice had a better relationship with Henry James, Jr., than with her other brothers, and Henry had lived in England for many years. But, even with Katharine and Henry, life in England failed to help Alice's health. English doctors divined "suppressed gout," a nonexistent disease much in vogue at the time. Cared for by Katharine, Alice spent much of her time frequenting various spas. Hypnosis helped relieve some of Alice's symptoms, especially if Katharine was the one who induced the trance, but Katharine had to be absent on occasion to care for her sister, who was ill with tuberculosis. Alice tended to backslide when she was away. Alice died of cancer in 1892, three years after she started to keep a diary. In her diary, she wrote of her "relief" on learning that she finally had a terminal illness after a lifetime of suffering and debility. Katharine preserved her diary, which her family might have destroyed, and this was eventually published in 1964. The diary reveals a powerful intellect stymied and frustrated for lack of a proper outlet. Handicapped by her upbringing and by the era in which she lived, and no doubt saddled with problems that are hidden from us, Alice had never been able to find a "healthy" role that satisfied her needs. In lieu of such a role, she had lived her life as an invalid.

Though they are much less common today than they were in the nineteenth century, disorders resembling the lesser hysterias have not yet disappeared. For example, 1 to 2 percent of modern American women have somatization disorder, which was once called Briquet's hysteria, after the man who described it around the turn of the century.[46] Somatization disorder is rarely found in men. The patients described by Briquet complained of diverse traveling pains, most commonly in the abdomen and chest, along with conversion symptoms. According to the American Psychiatric Association's *Diagnostic and Statistical Manual,* third edition, revised (DSM-IIIR), the diagnosis of somatization disorder requires that patients have had at least thirteen symptoms from the following impressive list:

Vomiting, abdominal pain, nausea, bloating, diarrhea, multiple food intolerances, arm pain, leg pain, back pain, joint pain, painful urination, shortness of breath, palpitations, chest pain, dizziness, amnesia, difficulty swallowing, loss of voice, deafness, double vision, blurred vision, blindness, fainting, seizures, trouble walking, paralysis, weakness, urinary retention, rectal or genital burning pain, lack of sexual interest, dyspareunia, impotence, painful, irregular, or excessive menstrual periods, or vomiting throughout pregnancy.[47]

According to the DSM-IIIR, each of the thirteen or more symptoms must have been severe enough to have caused an alteration in the patient's lifestyle or to have caused the patient to seek medical care, and none of them may be accounted for by known organic illnesses. This last condition ensures, of course, that somatization disorder must be an illness role, as a matter of definition. The patients state their complaints in dramatic and vivid terms and often have undergone multiple operations, including emergency exploratory procedures. Most have had unneeded diagnostic procedures performed by several physicians. Clinicians treating patients with somatization disorder agree that these patients are dependent and manipulative. If their wishes are refused, they respond with increased symptoms or with angry outbursts. Many are very depressed, and suicide gestures are commonly used to influence doctors and members of their families. Patients with somatization disorder spend much of their adult lives debilitated and bedridden or seeking medical care.

Women with somatization disorder often have male relatives with antisocial personalities. Antisocial persons are highly manipulative, lack a sense of guilt, and engage in exploitative or criminal activities. They do not generally complain of physical symptoms. Some researchers interpret these findings to mean that somatization disorder and antisocial personality are genetic disorders, caused by genes that express themselves differently in the two sexes.[48] However, both somatization disorder and antisocial personality are more common in lower-class, highly stressed families, in which both boys and girls are more likely to be abused (see below). In the following section, I will discuss evidence that parental abuse predisposes to illness roles of many different kinds. Hence, in many families, somatization disorder and antisocial personality may co-occur for reasons related to family environment, not just because of genes.

Patricia Draper and Henry Harpending, two leaders in the effort to apply evolutionary concepts to human behavior, argue that somatization disorder and antisocial personality are similar, in that both involve cheating in reproductive relationships.[49] According to this view, women with somatization disorder feign distress in order to increase material and other assistance specifically from men, while antisocial men mainly exploit women. However, the apparent specificity of somatization disorder may be adventitious. If somatization disorder occurs mostly where women lack power, then somatizing women will have to seek help from men because men alone have the power to give the aid they need. Care-seeking behaviors must be addressed to whatever powerful figures the social environment offers.

A patient described by Phillip Slavney shows how similar the histories of some patients with somatization are to the histories of patients with grand hysteria seen in the Salpêtrière some one hundred years before.[50] These histories are remarkable for prolonged deprivation of love and caring attention and for overwhelming vicissitudes of life, especially those to which women today are most vulnerable, such as being a single parent, lack of education, marginal jobs, economic distress, and abusive partners. At the time of her presentation with somatization disorder, the patient, dubbed Mrs. V., had suffered from numerous symptoms, including nausea, abdominal pain, chest pain, palpitations, headaches, amnesia, back pain, leg numbness and weakness, disturbance in walking, and allergies. She took many medications and had undergone operations for some of her complaints. Like many other patients with somatization disorder, Mrs. V. was also severely depressed and had tried to take her life on more than one occasion. According to Slavney's case history, Mrs. V. had lacked support and care from others for much of her earlier life. Her mother abandoned her at a neighbor's home when she was nine months old. The neighbors raised her, but her "foster mother," as Mrs. V. called her, resented having to care for her. She recalled asking her foster mother why she was not allowed to play with other children. Her foster mother told her she did not belong with other children since she had no mother. As a child she had depression, eczema, asthma, and frequent colds, but her foster mother refused to take her to doctors or dentists. Medical services may have signified caring attention for this deprived young girl. At the time of her presentation, Mrs. V. had not seen her foster mother for eight years, though they lived in the same city. She was raped at age twelve by a neighborhood boy and punished when she reported it. In the eleventh grade, she became pregnant and had to withdraw from school. Although she married the father, he left her soon after the child was born, so she had to support both herself and her infant son. She soon was involved with a man who became her common-law husband. An alcoholic, he gambled to excess and beat her, until she eventually told him to leave the house. He fathered her second son, who had grown into a notably antisocial adolescent by the time Mrs. V. presented herself to Slavney. Mrs. V.'s jobs were all manual labor and culminated in work as a school cafeteria aide. She claimed that her back pain resulted from an injury on the job at school, and after surgery for a ruptured disk, she had managed to get herself a substantial monthly allowance as long she stayed disabled. At the time of her presentation, Mrs. V. was stressed by her younger son's behavior, which was blatantly out of control, and by her third husband's failure to give her the emotional support she felt she needed. Treatment consisted largely of helping Mrs. V. deal with her present environmental stresses in ways more adaptive than assuming an illness role.

Some patients today also present themselves with disorders that resemble the more colorful forms of hysteria, in which bizarre mental alterations appeared alongside the physical symptoms. Like Bertha Pappenheim, patients with these disorders may become mute or incoherent, see visions, have screaming or crying fits, or become aggressive and difficult to manage. These more dramatic syndromes are rare among Western women, who generally have sophisticated concepts of disease, but they still occur with some frequency in women from other cultures. For example, Malcolm Weller, a British psychiatrist, described four women with dramatic hysterical syndromes among Cypriot immigrants living in North London.[51] According to Weller, Cypriot immigrant families, being extremely patriarchal, resemble Viennese families at the turn of the century. One patient Weller described, a twenty-eight-year-old unmarried woman, had fits and muteness and painted her face with shoe polish. She threw food, struck her mother with a metal rod, smeared jam in her hair, and set off fire alarms. In the hospital, she neglected her personal hygiene and had sexual intercourse with several male patients. In spite of her odd behavior, she was able to clearly voice complaints about her family. In order to prevent her from losing her virginity, her parents had severely restricted her freedom of movement and even her telephone calls. They had tried to force her to accede to an arranged marriage. Another patient, the daughter of a domineering Greek Orthodox priest, had been singing and screaming at night and complained of visual hallucinations. She was sexually provocative and even got into bed with a demented patient in the ward in which she was hospitalized. She later developed senseless sighing, crying, and giggling and episodes of aggression. Two of Weller's patients presented themselves with what might be called hysterical psychoses, characterized by seemingly psychotic thoughts and behavior, emotional volatility, and disordered thinking. I noted earlier that patients subject to hysterical psychoses, most of whom are women, are said to have acute "antennae" to pick up social cues and to be habitual role players. These characteristics sound like those of the highly hypnotizable subjects described by the social cognitive theorists and others cited earlier, and in fact, as I mentioned, a very high capacity for hypnotic phenomena may be used to diagnose hysterical psychoses mimicking other disorders.

Finally, Susan Abbey and Paul Garfinkel, from the University of Toronto, argue that the so-called chronic fatigue syndrome is the modern-day equivalent of neurasthenia, an illness described by George Beard in 1869.[52] Both disorders are characterized by disabling fatigue or exhaustion, decreased activity levels, muscle and joint pain, headaches, and various "neuropsychological" symptoms, such as memory problems or lack of concentration. Both lack the more dramatic symptoms once seen in hysteria. Beard thought that neurasthenia resulted from depletion of electrical energy in the nervous system, due to overactivity or mental stress. Late-nineteenth-century doctors believed the nervous system was simply unprepared for steam travel, telegraphy, and what they considered the hectic pace of nineteenth-century commerce. As might be expected in light of Beard's causal theory, neurasthenia often occurred in successful men. Beard himself had suffered from neurasthenic symptoms, and he claimed to have learned much about the disease from highly accomplished men who had depleted their energy through excessive work. Most of the patients nonetheless appear to have been women. Most patients with chronic fatigue syndrome are also women, but I have not included it among women's mental disorders because there is still debate as to its etiology. Although most physicians believe it is psychogenic, some think it is caused by viruses or by immune dysfunction.

Given the etiologic significance attached to commerce, nineteenth-century doctors might have been hard pressed to account for the fact that most neurasthenics were women. But Beard ascribed the illness as it occurred in women to the recent emphasis on women's education. Having less nervous energy than men, ambitious women especially were likely to be depleted by prolonged mental application. However, in her 1910 autobiography, Margaret Cleaves, herself a neurasthenic, argued that ambitious women became neurasthenics because their ambitions were frustrated by society, not because they were overworked. Charlotte Perkins Gilman, who also had neurasthenia, believed her symptoms were caused by dissatisfaction with her life as a wife and mother. Silas Weir Mitchell, who was perhaps the most famous American physician of his time, ridiculed Gilman's theory and advised her to give up writing if she wished to recover her health. Gilman not only failed to follow Mitchell's advice, but she later ridiculed Mitchell in one of her short stories. Jane Addams, the founder of Hull House, also thought her symptoms of neurasthenia resulted from dissatisfaction. As he had with Gilman, Mitchell insisted to Addams that her problems were physiological.

According to Abbey and Garfinkel, not only were Cleaves, Gilman, and Addams correct in their theories about their own illnesses, and Beard and Mitchell mistaken, but chronic fatigue syndrome is now caused by similar factors. Thus, according to Abbey and Garfinkel,

among chronic fatigue syndrome sufferers are a number of women and men who feel conflicted about their working lives, and the difficulty in balancing their careers with their family obligations and personal wishes. The diagnosis of chronic fatigue syndrome provides a legitimate "medical" reason for their fatigue, emotional distress, and associated psychophysiological symptoms and allows them to withdraw from situations they find intolerable. . . . This dynamic has been observed for patients in a number of differing situations, including high achievers who are motivated by pleasing others . . . and women who are ambivalent about leaving paid employment to stay home with young children.[53]

Thus, if it is true that chronic fatigue has no organic basis, we may be witnessing the emergence of yet another medical illness role, occurring mainly in women, which differs in its symptoms from somatization disorder. Consistent with this hypothesis, some patients who once presented themselves with somatization disorder have presented themselves recently with symptoms of chronic fatigue. Insofar as chronic fatigue serves some of the same functions as somatization disorder, it is likely that it too will appeal to persons who believe, often rightly, that they lack social power to meet their needs more directly.[54]

4

Two Modern-Day Epidemics

In the previous chapter, I applied social-role concepts to certain disorders of women that were common in nineteenth-century Europe and America. Analysis of these disorders as illness roles explains why they might have been more common in those who lacked social power. In fact, case histories of women who suffered from these disorders, or who suffer from still extant variants of these disorders, point toward lack of power, usually in combination with overwhelming exigencies of life, as an etiological factor.

In this chapter, I will discuss two disorders with nineteenth-century roots that have gone on to become more common than ever before. The first of these, multiple personality disorder, can be analyzed in the same terms as the various forms of hysteria. That is, most or all cases probably result from illness-role behavior, and those who adopt the role are handicapped or disadvantaged. Studies of patients with multiple personality disorder also point to exposure to childhood abuse as a factor shared with other similar illnesses. Eating disorders, first anorexia and more recently bulimia, or a combination of the two, are not illness roles per se, since patients with these disorders often deny being ill, but they too can be understood using social-role concepts presented in chapter 3. Bodily form and appetites are part and parcel of complex social roles, and as such they have been used to make social statements of several different kinds, in our culture and in others. They are especially likely to be used this way by those who lack social power to meet their needs more directly. Both multiple personality disorder and eating disorders are much more common in women.

Multiple Personality Disorder as an Illness Role

In the last decade, many women previously thought to have other mental disorders have been "discovered" to have multiple personalities.[1] Men with this diagnosis are exceedingly rare. I use quotation marks because it is still uncertain, as I hope to show, exactly what is discovered in making this diagnosis, at least in most cases. Although some authorities on multiple personality disorder assert that only ignorance can account for doubts about it, other scholars continue to observe that the only clinicians to discover multiple personalities are those who first believe in them. Like the concentration of grand hysterics in the Salpêtrière, this type of case distribution implies to social-role theorists that multiple personality disorder is an illness role. If so, like many other illness roles—in fact, like grand hysteria—multiple personality disorder must depend on collaboration between patients and doctors for its full expression. Enthusiasts counter this argument by claiming that most clinicians overlook the disorder. The alter personalities are said to be so shy, and the host personality so resistant to the diagnosis, that only a clinician skilled in treating multiple personality disorder will show the perseverance needed to demonstrate that the disorder exists.

In one influential text, Frank Putnam, a psychologist and a leading authority on multiple personality disorder, recommends aggressive probing for evidence of the disorder.[2] Over long periods of time, under hypnosis and in the "nontrance" state, patients are prodded to acknowledge lapses in their memories and to speak and act as if they had separate parts. Putnam claims that this type of probing can do no harm if the patient is not a multiple personality, and that with repetition it may lead to information about alter selves if the patient has the disorder. According to Putnam, the median length of time it takes to diagnose multiple personality disorder in this way is six months, with some cases taking several years. The diagnosis is made when the patient speaks to the therapist in an alter voice. Putnam's method of inquiry seems an ideal procedure for shaping patients' behavior to conform to expectations. Like grand hysterics, patients with multiple personalities are said to be exceedingly easy to hypnotize. If they are like the highly hypnotizable subjects described in the previous chapter, they are acutely sensitive to social-role expectations conveyed by repeated questions like those described by Putnam.

Actually, patients can now learn how to behave like multiples before they ever meet a therapist who believes in the disorder.[3] In 1957, *The Three Faces of Eve* informed the lay public about the case of Eve White, a subdued and shy young woman from Augusta, Georgia, who turned out to have two alter personalities. The first, whom the authors dubbed Eve Black, was carefree and flirtatious, and the second, whom they called Jane, was calmer and more mature. *The Three Faces of Eve* became a popular movie, and Eve herself, whose real name is Christine Sizemore, wrote an autobiography. Sizemore apparently had an additional nineteen personalities emerge before her ultimate cure. In 1973, a lay science writer informed the public about a similar patient, whom he dubbed Sybil Dorsett. Sybil had thirteen personalities, including an aggressive alter called Peggy Lou, a child alter called Vicky, two carpenters called Mike and Sid, and a pianist named Vanessa. Kenneth Bianchi, the notorious "Hillside Strangler" arrested in 1979, made the front pages of major American newspapers by claiming that he suffered from multiple personality disorder. An alter named Steve confessed to the many murders of which Kenneth was accused but denied that Kenneth knew anything about them. *The Minds of Billy Milligan,* a popular book published in 1981, described a case of multiple rape committed by an alter outside the host's awareness. Most recently, paperback readers can buy a book authored by some of the alters of a woman called Trudi Chase, who is said to be host to more than ninety personalities. One of these, called Rabbit, does not speak but howls. A psychologist who treated this patient, to whom the book is dedicated, outlined the modern theory of multiple personality in the introduction. A television dramatization of Trudi Chase's story appeared on a national network.

Proponents of multiple personality disorder sometimes cite the original cases of this disorder as proof that it is not just a social construction. The earliest patients, presumably, developed the disorder without benefit of guidance from clinicians or the popular press. In chapter 3, I mentioned that Jules Janet believed that Blanche Wittman, one of Charcot's grand hysterics, had an alternate personality that appeared under hypnosis. Another well-known early patient was Christine Beauchamp, described by Morton Prince in 1900 and again in 1905.[4] While hypnotized, Beauchamp referred to her waking self in the third person. When challenged by Prince she eventually laid claim to other names. H. Merskey, a psychiatrist from the University of Western Ontario, reviewed these and others of the earliest cases of multiple personality.[5] According to Merskey, suggestion and training were crucial from the very beginning. He notes, for instance, that by asking Beauchamp for names for her hypnotic states, Prince may have encouraged her to demonstrate full-blown alters. Not surprisingly, the earliest patients said to have multiple personality were facing social problems very much like those faced by hysterical patients.

Actually, shortly before the first cases, the concept of multiple selves caught the imagination of the reading public. Robert Louis Stevenson's *Dr. Jekyll and Mr. Hyde,* which became an instant success in 1886, actually embodies many of the themes—such as multiplicity, lack of control over switching, and division of alters according to moral development—evident in the first cases and in cases today.[6] Having taken a potion that once released his baser self, the hapless Dr. Jekyll finds himself reverting at unpredictable moments to the character of Mr. Hyde. Mr. Hyde's activities, from running over a child in the street to murder, repulse the civilized Dr. Jekyll, who wages a failing struggle to maintain control of himself. In a posthumous note to his friends, Dr. Jekyll foreshadows another clinical theme: steady growth in the number of alter selves (see below).

> I thus drew steadily nearer to that truth . . . that man is not truly one, but truly two. I say two, because the state of my own knowledge does not pass beyond that point. Others will follow, others will outstrip me on the same lines; and I hazard the guess that man will be ultimately known for a mere polity of multifarious, incongruous and independent denizens.[7]

The gulf between Jekyll and Hyde embodies the split between human and animal selves in a post-Darwinian world. Like some of the alters described by early clinicians, Hyde is more vital than Jekyll. Being closer to nature and unencumbered by civilized mores, Hyde has sharper senses and instincts than civilized men.

Certain features of multiple personality disorder have changed as the condition has spread. Authorities on the disorder argue that these changes reflect scientific progress; that is, armed with modern knowledge about multiple personality, today's clinicians supposedly have become more accurate in their history taking.[8] Features of the illness that were never revealed in the earliest cases are now uncovered routinely. But change is also typical of illness roles, as clinicians refine and enhance their expectations. Details of grand hysteria changed in a similar way as Charcot and his colleagues gained more experience with it. The features of multiple personality disorder that have changed the most since the first descriptions near the turn of the century are the numbers of personalities, their types and classifications, and the role and nature of early child abuse. Many of the earliest cases had only two personalities, and few had more than four. But as Dr. Jekyll suggested, multiplicity has a certain momentum, and in recent years patients have averaged ten to fifteen alters, and many have been reported with over fifty alters. Modern clinicians recognize types of alter personalities that were not always evident in the early cases. Thus, modern patients typically manifest alters who are children or animals, self-destructive or artistic, or who are persecutor, protector, or helper personalities. Before the late 1970s, the majority of case reports of multiple personality made no mention of childhood trauma. However, modern authorities on multiple personality agree that childhood trauma, especially severe physical and sexual abuse, plays a causal role. The fact that early reports failed to mention abuse is ascribed to inadequate probing of patients' defenses by clinicians who did not understand the importance of past abuse. Today, treatment cannot be considered complete until the supposedly resistant and amnesic patient has reconstructed in detail the history of abuse to which she was subjected.

Of course, reporting abuse may be part of the illness role. Just as they repeatedly question patients about experiences consistent with their having alter personalities, many therapists who treat multiple personalities repeatedly urge their patients to "get in touch" with heinous events they cannot recall experiencing. In this way, they pressure patients to spin victimization fantasies, if the real events in their lives have not been sufficiently dreadful. So-called hypnotic regression is used to recover memories of especially traumatic abuse. Patients are hypnotized, told they are children again, and asked to describe events unfolding before their eyes. Studies conducted by those who believe that hypnosis is a social role show that accounts of events obtained in this fashion are really fantasies about what might have happened, rather than memories in any real sense, but these studies have not deterred overzealous clinicians.[9] In effect, the hypnotic stage setting implicitly gives permission to patients to fantasize stories that will please and shock the hypnotherapist.

All of these efforts to recover memories are based on the belief that traumatic memories are very likely to be repressed out of conscious awareness. Some memory researchers, though, deny that this is true, thereby questioning the scientific basis for what has become a large industry.[10] If traumas are not repressed, then what the patient remembers spontaneously is as likely, or perhaps even more likely, to be true than what is remembered with assistance.

Features of illness roles have a way of inflating with time, and memories of abuse have thus become more improbable. Thus, many patients with multiple personality disorder today are said to have been childhood victims of "cult abuse," meaning that they were subjected to sexual satanic rituals by their parents and other adults. Not surprisingly, since the interests of therapists provide an impetus for illness roles in general, clinicians who diagnose cult abuse often see many patients who claim to have had this experience. On the basis of stories told to them by hypnotically "regressed" patients, some therapists claim that tens of thousands of children are murdered and cannibalized each year by an organized conspiracy of devil worshippers. The sociologist Jeffrey Victor and other researchers have shown that these claims are simply impossible.[11] Nor have the claims of particular patients ever been verified on the basis of objective evidence, which should be obtainable.[12]

James Gordon, a psychiatrist who wrote an intriguing account of the Rajneeshees, the religious cult founded by the Bhagwan Shree Rajneesh, reported on the eleventh annual Rocky Mountain Conference on UFO Investigation, held in Laramie, Wyoming, in 1991.[13] Gordon's account puts lurid "memories" of ritual abuse into perspective, and it shows just how little faith can be placed in hypnotic regression. The Rocky Mountain Conference was started in 1980 by a man named Leo Sprinkle, who was then a professor in the counseling-psychology department at the University of Wyoming. Sprinkle, who believed that he himself had traveled aboard a UFO when he was only ten, had been counseling individuals who believed they had been abducted by UFOs. He thought that an annual conference might provide a supportive setting in which these people could tell their stories without fear of ridicule. UFO abductees ostensibly suffered anxiety, were bothered by amnesic periods corresponding to their abductions, and experienced flashbacks and nightmares. They had headaches and muscle tension and felt detached from others. They had to fight powerful impulses to leave their jobs or families, or to move from town to town. Some of their lives had been wrecked by the psychological aftermaths of their abduction experiences. Although only twenty people came to Sprinkle's first conference, attendance grew tenfold over the next decade. Sprinkle's story had been told in a popular 1985 book called *Aliens among Us* and in 1987 in the *National Enquirer*. Some of the nearly two hundred people in attendance at the conference described by Gordon had long-standing interests in UFOs but did not claim to have met aliens themselves. The remainder, though, came because they had had experiences that frightened or alarmed them, which they interpreted in extraterrestrial terms. For example, one individual, Donald, recounted an experience that had occurred the year before. At 11:30 P.M., while on a camping trip, he was walking toward his car when he was approached by a strange-looking group of people. He thought of running away, but he felt himself to be paralyzed. The next thing he knew, it was morning, and he was inexplicably driving out of Reno, Nevada. Troubled afterward by recurrent nosebleeds and a sense that he was being "visited" at night, Donald went to a therapist who used hypnosis to help him "recover" memories of alien abductions dating back to his childhood.

Hypnotism is the method of choice for uncovering memories that UFO abductees cannot otherwise recall. Sprinkle himself first learned of his own UFO travels by being hypnotized by a professional colleague. Thus, the role played by hypnotism at the conference described by Gordon parallels its role in diagnosis and treatment of multiple personality disorder, in which it is used to uncover alter personalities and memories of abuse. Some of the memories obtained in this way from ostensible abductees sound remarkably like memories of abuse proffered by those who claim to be victims of satanic cults. For example, under so-called hypnotic regression, a woman in attendance at the conference described by Gordon recounted lying helpless and naked while alien beings inserted objects into her vagina. Helplessness, nakedness, and rape with foreign objects are all common themes in stories of cult abuse offered by mental patients.

On the basis of stories told to them by their hypnotically regressed patients, some therapists now claim that abduction by aliens is a major mental health problem in the United States.[14] Oddly, some of these therapists are in academic centers.

If there is still any doubt as to the reliability of hypnotically obtained memories or of subjects' abilities to spin intriguing tales that they claim are true, hypnotic regression is also widely used as a means for remembering past lives! Some clinicians even practice past-life therapy. The emotional aftereffects of traumatic events in past lives are said to cause psychological problems that can be resolved only by recovering memories. Studies of past-life reports obtained with hypnotic regression show that they are merely historical fantasies.[15] A few therapists even offer hypnotic "progression" therapy, allowing patients to glimpse "memories" of future events.

However, even though the abuse may be more prosaic in most cases than patients and therapists claim, and the value of hypnotic regression nil, many if not most patients said to have multiple personalities probably have been abused to some degree or another. Thus, specialists in multiple personality disorder claim to have verified numerous instances of abuse claimed by patients.[16] The numbers of ostensibly verified claims are sufficiently large that, even if most others are false, there is still an association between multiple personality disorder and trauma that cannot be explained by chance. In an article on dissociation, Putnam described a study of children with multiple personality disorder whose traumatic experiences could be objectively documented.[17] Significantly, abuse and neglect have also been well documented in histories of patients with borderline personality.[18] Many and possibly most of the patients now said to have multiple personality disorder meet diagnostic criteria for borderline personality as well.[19]

Victims of childhood violence and sexual abuse lose confidence in their ability to exercise social power. Many of them, for this reason, grow up to be chronically depressed and anxious.[20] Feeling powerless and afraid, they are also exquisitely sensitive to others' role expectations. They might be especially likely to seize on illness roles as means for meeting their needs. The reader should recall that Charcot's grand hysterics had also suffered childhood abuse, neglect, and violence, as had Mrs. V., Slavney's patient with somatization disorder. Patients with somatization disorder, with inexplicable chronic pain syndromes, and with conversion disorders all report surprisingly high levels of childhood neglect or violence.[21] Freud originally thought that childhood sexual traumas were at the root of cases of hysteria too, but he later retracted this theory in favor of another, which claimed that patients simply imagined being abused. With the exception of Sandor Ferenczi, who broke ranks on this issue, psychoanalysts, even revisionists, have assumed that Freud was correct in making his volte-face. As late as 1981, Jeffrey Masson was fired as director of the Freud Archives for suggesting that Freud had really suffered a loss of nerve in retracting his earlier theory.[22] As noted in chapter 3, hypnotic susceptibility, which closely correlates with all of these disorders, reflects role malleability in a general sense. Significantly, highly hypnotizable but mentally well adults report having experienced more severe childhood physical punishments than less hypnotizable subjects.[23]

Incest especially tends to occur in families characterized by violence or the threat of force, applied over very long periods of time. Rosalyn Schultz has noted that female incest victims grow up to be so attentive to social-role cues that they see themselves as pawns of the people around them.[24] Her description of their behavior in the treatment setting sounds remarkably like descriptions of highly hypnotizable subjects. Thus, according to Schultz,

When such patients enter treatment, they frequently experience a heightened pathological need to comply with what they believe that the therapist's expectations will be of them. Unable to initiate interaction, they may wait for the therapist's direction and respond with attempts to conform to what they assume to be expected. If the therapist colludes with this "false self" . . . the "true self" remains hidden away.[25]

Not surprisingly, their compliance increases the chance that victims of childhood incest will be revictimized as adults. Richard Kluft described what he called the "Sitting Duck Syndrome" in survivors of childhood incest.[26] According to Kluft, these patients are even at risk from therapists, who take advantage of their excessive compliance in order to have sexual relations with them. Kluft described some advice he received from a Roman pimp, who was making a living off what we would call heightened role compliance. He explained to Kluft what he looked for in recruiting his prostitutes:

Beauty, yes. Sexual expertise, somewhat. That can be taught easier than you think. What is important above all is obedience. And how do you get obedience? You get obedience if you get women who have had sex with their fathers, their uncles, their brothers—you know, someone they love and fear to lose so that they do not dare to defy. . . . They will do anything to keep you happy.[27]

Carmen, Rieker, and Summit, among many others who have studied incest victims, have drawn conclusions similar to those of Schultz and Kluft.[28]

Recently, psychological tests and physiological measures have been used to try to prove that the alters enacted by patients with multiple personality disorder are not mere simulations. However, as the psychologist Ray Aldridge-Morris has shown, studies employing these measures have thus far suffered from serious methodological defects.[29] There are also conceptual problems, resulting from confusion between mere fakery and adoption of social roles. A patient adopting a social role, as opposed to merely faking, adopts the cognitive and emotional correlates of that role. The multiple personality role requires the individual to shift back and forth between emotionally distinct states. Emotions affect physiological measures. Hence, it is not surprising that patients adopting this role also shift back and forth between physiologically distinct states. I am discounting the wilder claims made by authorities on multiple personality disorder: that alter personalities have different allergic, and hence, immunologic, responses and suffer from different illnesses of bodily organs. Some authors even claim that tumors come and go with changes in personalities.

Other students of multiple personality disorder have thought to search for possible genetic contributing factors. Discovery of such factors would bolster the claim that dissociation, if not specifically multiple personality disorder, manifests nervous activity different from that responsible for everyday behavior. Along these lines, Bennett Braun studied families of eighteen patients with multiple personality disorder, and he showed that dissociation and multiple personality occurred "transgenerationally" in affected families.[30] Braun thought that his data might support genetic models, but actually, detailed review of his cases supports an illness-role viewpoint at the expense of genetic hypotheses. Thus, while many of the patients whose families were studied by Braun had parents, children, uncles, or cousins with multiple personality disorder, many others also had nominal kin with this illness. Braun's case number three, for instance, had parents and a daughter with multiple personality disorder, but her husband also had dissociative episodes and probable multiple personality disorder. Cases four, seven, twelve, and seventeen also had husbands with similar diagnoses. Cases nine and eleven had ex-husbands with probable multiple personality disorder, and case ten had two ex-husbands who Braun thought had the disorder. Case eleven had a stepdaughter with dissociative episodes and probable multiple personality disorder, and in case number five, the live-in babysitter and the babysitter's daughter had apparently caught the illness! Case number sixteen had two adoptive parents who appeared to be multiple personalities, as well as two adopted siblings with dissociation or multiple personality disorder. Certainly, no genetic disorder should affect probands' spouses, stepchildren, stepparents, or foster kin, much less the live-in help. Instead, the very high incidence of dissociation and apparent multiple personality disorder in these genetically unrelated individuals testifies to the appeal the illness role has to those who see it, so to speak, in the flesh. Because they are less set in particular roles than adults and are correspondingly more responsive to suggestions, children in particular are likely to be susceptible to strong parental models. What child, seeing a parent blame his or her misbehavior on alter personalities, would not perceive an advantage in assuming this illness role? It appears from Braun's data that most if not all children with multiple personality disorder have witnessed family members in similar illness roles. The extreme rapidity with which children with multiple personality disorder improve in treatment testifies to the ease with which children can switch social roles.[31]

Studies of mass hysteria are pertinent to the evidence Braun and others offer. For example, in April 1989, 247 members of junior-high-school and high-school choirs performing at a recital in Santa Monica, California, suddenly fell ill with headaches, dizziness, weakness, abdominal pain, and nausea.[32] Sixteen of them fainted. Fire trucks and paramedics were dispatched to the scene, and an emergency triage center was established on the auditorium lawn. Nineteen students were taken to hospitals by ambulance. At a rehearsal earlier in the day, some students thought they had smelled fresh paint, but city officials could not detect any toxic fumes that may have caused the outbreak, nor was there evidence for an infectious or food-borne toxic process. Hearing about what appeared to be an episode of mass hysteria, Gary Small and others from the University of California, Los Angeles, School of Medicine distributed questionnaires to the student performers. The responses they obtained from 519 students shed light on susceptibility to powerful illness roles. According to Small and his coworkers, 51 percent of the girls and 41 percent of the boys fell ill, a difference that, though small, is statistically significant. Girls, moreover, were likely to have had more severe symptoms. Those who fainted came exclusively from the ranks of the soprano girls. Given that girls and boys stood in separate sections, differences between them may have resulted from differences in models they were exposed to (see below), or they may have resulted from differences in what boys and girls view as acceptable for their respective genders. Boys, for instance, might see fainting as entailing a loss of face, whereas girls may perceive it as a sign of feminine delicacy. Consistent with the notion that younger children are more malleable and suggestible, the younger children were more likely to fall ill. Thus, nearly 60 percent of sixth-graders fell ill, compared with less than 40 percent of twelfth-grade students. Consistent with the notion that illness roles are more readily adopted if they are familiar, children who fell ill were much more likely to have suffered previous chronic illnesses than students who were unaffected. They were also somewhat more likely to have lost a friend or relative. Presumably, most of these losses followed on serious illnesses that the children witnessed. Finally, and perhaps most relevant to Braun's study above, students who fell ill were much more likely than others to have witnessed a friend fall ill, as opposed to witnessing illness in those who were not friends. Apparently, children are most susceptible to illness roles shown by others to whom they are linked affectively. If the same is true of adults, it would account for the large number of spouses Braun found to be affected with multiple personality or other dissociative symptoms.

Almost all of the patients who adopt the multiple personality role are first depressed and anxious.[33] Either by chance or intentionally they come in contact with a therapist who believes in the disorder, and then they develop it. The obvious question is, What do such patients get out of playing this illness role? Multiple personality is not an easy role. Keeping several stories straight—as many patients manage to do—requires attention and effort, and some creativity too. From a social-role viewpoint, there must be a payoff to justify the effort the illness role requires. Even casual scrutiny reveals several such payoffs.

First, many of the patients thought to have multiple personality disorder have been depressed and anxious for many years, not just for a short time. Many of them have so-called borderline personalities, meaning that they have trouble with impulse control as well.[34] Therapists, being human, tend to lose interest in treating patients who are depressed too long, who fail to get better in response to their ministrations, or whose behavior causes them too much worry and concern.[35] Yet the patients, having been treated for a number of years and having no social lives, are more dependent than ever on their therapists, or on the attention of mental health professionals in general, who are their only friends. In this situation, multiple personality disorder serves as a gambit to recapture attention lost over a period of years. Insofar as a new therapist, or an old one who has just returned from an educational conference, is interested in multiple personality disorder and communicates that to the patient, the patient makes herself more interesting by adopting the role. Also, in adopting the role, the patient tells the therapist that she is not hopeless, she was merely misdiagnosed by her previous, less astute, therapists, or by the present therapist himself before he got educated. Many of these patients are treated in public clinics or by large institutions. Where before they were treated coolly, everyone suddenly knows their name and wants to be part of their treatment team. Thus, multiple personality disorder serves for some patients today somewhat the same function grand hysteria served for young women in Paris—that is, it engages attention and concern by medical staff—and somewhat the same function religious beliefs and experiences do for people in cults—that is, it prevents their extrusion by a group they have come to depend upon.

Second, multiple personality disorder allows some patients to disavow hostile or other behaviors that might anger others. Many of those said to have multiple personalities were previously docile, hard-working, and compliant. Many of them were in relationships with which they were dissatisfied but which they were afraid to leave and felt they could not change. The alter personalities express their dissatisfaction and act on their secret impulses without the "host" personality having to take the blame. Previously suppressed blameworthy behavior can now be indulged in and attributed to their condition. The case of Mrs. P., described in chapter 6, shows this dynamic at work.

Finally, the patient who is thought to have a multiple personality, as that role is understood now, is certified as a victim. As noted above, multiple personality disorder is thought to be caused by horrendous childhood trauma. The disorder is conceived of as the cost of psychic survival in untenable circumstances. Specialists in this disorder even refer to patients, especially those who claim to have survived satanism, as heroines of sorts. Having survived despicable attempts to degrade or destroy them, these patients are seen as equals of survivors of Nazi death camps or of the Russian gulag. Thus, though they may have previously felt despised, patients who take on this illness role are accorded an awed respect just for being alive. Assuming that every ghastly detail must be true, clinicians retell their stories in hushed, reverential tones.

Aldridge-Morris likened multiple personality disorder to culture-bound illnesses found in other societies.[36] In fact there is a large group of culture-bound possession illnesses that affect mainly women and that closely resemble multiple personality disorder, both in form and function. In each case, the victims are thought to be displaced by foreign agents who control the body and whose behavior leaves something to be desired. In each case the victim cannot be held responsible for actions taken by these interlopers. In each case the victim is seen as a casualty of some sort of mistreatment, and in each case therapy aims to restore control over the body to the host personality.

I. M. Lewis, a cultural anthropologist, found that possession illnesses were common in societies in which women lacked social power.[37] In these societies, especially unhappy or dissatisfied women are thought to be susceptible to possession by malign or foreign spirits, such as the ancestor spirits of a hostile tribe. The possession illness is treated by offering the victim concessions, in the form of material goods, reduced workload, or attention, to combat the unhappiness or dissatisfaction that lowered the victim's resistance to the possessing spirit. Among Somali pastoralists, for example, women become ill due to *sar* possession, *sars* being evil spirits who are said to hate men. Somali women are hard pressed to feed themselves and their children. Their polygamous husbands neglect them, and they have little security. Men, but not women, can easily obtain divorces. Women afflicted by *sar* spirits develop physical symptoms. Speaking through their victims, the spirits demand new clothes, perfumes, and other luxuries the victims themselves could not request. If the demands are excessive, Somali husbands may beat their wives or threaten them with divorce, which sometimes is effective in ending states of possession, but husbands will meet more modest demands in order to appease the spirits and make them go away. Tanzanian women with "devil's disease" also develop baffling physical symptoms. The spirits causing these demand not only gifts, but expensive curative rituals, as a condition of leaving. The ritual healer lives with the victim and her family and teaches family members to modify their behavior so as to be more considerate of the victim's needs. Luo women in Kenya develop possession illnesses that can be treated only by respite from everyday labors. Once restored to health, victims are thought to be liable to relapse unless they are treated with more respect and kindness than they received before falling ill. Among the East African Taita, women develop illnesses that can be cured only by allowing them some prerogatives of the opposite sex. Black Carib women from the British Honduras are plagued by an evil spirit known as the "devourer." Victims possessed by this spirit dance uncontrollably until the devourer is appeased with gifts pleasing to the victims. Twenty percent of Havik Brahmin women from the state of Mysore fall victim to possession at some point in their lives. In conformity with the pattern established by other cases, the spirits afflicting these women can be appeased only by granting the victims certain desired concessions. Lewis cites many other examples.

Women in these societies, in which they are generally powerless, are aided by these syndromes regardless of whether they themselves fall ill. Somali men, for example, know that if they mistreat their wives, their wives may become possessed by man-hating *sar* spirits that will voice their wives' complaints. Cures are expensive and require lasting concessions, so the wise husband avoids treating his wife too badly. Wanting to maintain the ideology of spirit possession, women organize cults that specialize in the management of spirits plaguing female victims. These cults provide women who are otherwise shut out of communal social life membership in supportive social groups. In some cases membership is open only to women who have been cured of affliction. In these cases we see once again how assuming a social role, now corresponding to possession by evil spirits, confers the right to membership in a group.

Consistent with the hypothesis that lack of social power makes illness roles more attractive, Lewis noted that lower-class men in highly stratified societies are also subject to possession illnesses. Stratified societies disempower lower-class men in the same way that patriarchy disempowers women. In Ethiopia, for example, ex-slaves and Sudanese Muslims form marginal social classes lacking in wealth or power. Men belonging to these groups are susceptible to possession by the same *sar* spirits afflicting upper-class women. Since the 1930s, the membership in Ethiopian *sar* cults has included more and more lower-class men and fewer upper-class, Amhara Christian, women. Handicapped Amhara men have also made an appearance in *sar* cults once reserved for women. To cite another example, Mafia island, off the coast of Tanzania, is a stratified society dominated by persons of ethnic Arabian background. Both men and women of the Pokomo people, who are indigenous to the area and despised by other islanders, are susceptible to possession by *shaitani* spirits, who cause physical and mental illnesses. Both men and women join the possession cult charged with controlling these illnesses. Within this cult, both men and women can rise to positions of power as diviners and shamans. Significantly, higher-class women on Mafia island, who must contend with patriarchy, are susceptible to afflictions caused by other spirits, in this case from Arabia, which speak through their victims in Arabic and require expensive treatments. The cult charged with treating illnesses caused by these upper-class spirits is open only to women.

There are also possession states that are not defined as illnesses, and these in fact are reserved for the powerful, not the weak. Lewis, for instance, described what he called "central" possession cults. These frequently coexist alongside female or lower-class cults like those described above. Shamans in central possession cults, who are typically male, are important and powerful persons in their communities. In order to heal, to arbitrate, to judge, or to advise they allow themselves to be possessed by ancestral spirits or deities. The spirits or deities speak through the entranced shaman, who stakes his claim to a leadership role through the idiom of possession. For example, male shamans among the Korekore Shona of the Zambezi Valley embody ancestor spirits who are thought to control rainfall and fertility of the soil. Speaking through these shamans, the spirits condemn moral flaws that lead to drought and famine, settle disputes, and decide succession of chieftancies. In Zambia, male Tongan shamans are possessed by the souls of "big men," or long-dead powerful leaders. While possessed, Tongan shamans resolve disputes, divine the future, and lead rain-making rituals. They are arbiters of morality and of sound social judgment. Male Kaffa shamans in Ethiopia serve as mediums for their patrilineal ancestors. Shamans lend their authority to political leaders whose interests coincide with their own.

In one especially fascinating study, 72 Apaches living on the Mescalero Indian Reservation in New Mexico were given Rorschach tests.[38] The results support the hypothesis that central shamans, who in the Apache tribe can be either men or women, are remarkable for being skilled at adopting social roles. Fifty-two of the Rorschach tests were given to a control group of individuals who never claimed to be shamans, twelve were administered to recognized shamans, and seven were given to persons who claimed to be shamans but were not accorded this status by their fellow Apaches, who were unconvinced of their powers. Tests were read by raters who were unaware of the status of the person tested. Rorschach tests from both the recognized and unrecognized shamans differed from the control tests, but in opposite ways. In comparison with the control group, the recognized shamans appeared to have a high potential for phenomena that, in our society, would be called hysterical. The social-role viewpoint developed in the previous chapter suggests that this potential indicates responsiveness to social-role demands. The authors of this study concluded that shamans were skilled at what they called "regression in the service of the ego." This is a psychoanalytic term for the ability to suspend rational judgment and to become wholly immersed in forms of art and showmanship, including role performances. Unrecognized shamans, on the other hand, lacked social-role flexibility. They seemed to be incapable of creative regression as the researchers defined it.

Finally, the sex distribution of any particular illness role is a historical process, with its own inertia. This is especially evident with multiple personality disorder, which began as an illness role that might have appealed to the powerless of both sexes. However, since late-nineteenth- and early-twentieth-century women who could afford to see physicians lacked social power in comparison with men of their class, the earliest cases were disproportionately female. Clinicians who came to believe that women were more at risk pressed the diagnosis mostly with women patients. Also, a causal theory developed that attributed women's risk to their liability to sexual abuse. This causal theory further encouraged clinicians to look for the disorder mostly in women patients. Thus, multiple personality disorder is a women's disorder today partly because it was believed to be a women's disorder many decades ago. It would no doubt continue as a women's disorder for some years to come, even if the power relations between men and women were radically changed today in women's favor. The disorder would then fade away or the sex distribution equalize. In the latter case, researchers would probably argue that the male cases had been overlooked all along!

Bodily Form as a Social Role

Self-starvation, too, mostly occurs in women. Joan Brumberg, a social historian, has shown that self-starvation has had different meanings in different historical epochs.[39] Until the end of the last century, self-starvation generally had a religious significance. It was not so much part of an illness role as of a spiritual one. Control of the body and appetite was the major arena for women's religious achievement. At the end of the nineteenth century, cases began to appear resembling modern-day anorexic patients. For these patients, self-starvation is also more than an illness role. While weight loss serves to control the family and social environments, in the same way that illness roles might, it also reflects an attempt to excel at a feminine role that has gripped modern popular culture. Like women's religious roles from hundreds of years ago, this role makes control of the body the major determinant of women's self-esteem. Insofar as this role reflects misogynistic attitudes expressed in the popular culture, anorexia too, results from women's relative lack of social power.

According to Brumberg, female religious ascetics in the late Middle Ages practiced food refusal as part of a social role showing spirituality and scorn for bodily needs. When eating was seen as carnality, food refusal served to demonstrate one's existence on a higher plane. Mary of Oignes and Beatrice of Nazareth, two thirteenth-century ascetics, vomited from the smell of meat and could not swallow other foods. Catherine of Siena, who lived in the fourteenth century, voluntarily ate only small amounts of herbs. If she was forced to eat something larger, she induced herself to vomit by shoving twigs down her throat. Columba of Rieti, a fifteenth-century figure, died of starvation due to food refusal. As late as the seventeenth century, Saint Veronica ate nothing at all on most days. On Fridays she chewed five orange seeds representing the wounds inflicted on Jesus Christ.

Brumberg points out that "anorexia mirabilis," as seventeenth- and eighteenth-century physicians called religiously inspired food refusal, was only one part of a social role demonstrating disregard for bodily drives and needs. For example, like other medieval ascetics, Catherine of Siena also demonstrated her disregard for the body by scalding and beating herself, by self-flagellation, and by sleeping on beds of thorn. Angela of Foligno demonstrated her disregard for her bodily needs by drinking pus from sores and eating scabs and lice. Religious food refusal cannot be understood except as part of the larger culturally sanctioned social role of which it was a part. In particular, it should not be likened to modern food refusal, which reflects a secular, idealized feminine role. Brumberg also notes that there were few male medieval ascetics known for extended fasting or for food refusal. This is in spite of the fact that mortification of the flesh was an established means for men to demonstrate sanctity. It may be that women are better at self-starvation than men for physiological reasons and therefore more readily use it as a social-role element. Or denial of appetite, as opposed to self-inflicted pain, may not have meant the same thing in men's religious social roles as it did in women's. For example, even holy men were understood to experience sexual temptations. Their triumph over temptation contributed to their holiness. Chaste women, on the other hand, were expected not to experience sexual needs at all. As late as Victorian times, food and sexual appetites were closely linked in the popular imagination, so that by denying the former women denied the latter. It is also true that ambitious holy men in the Middle Ages could achieve renown and status by means other than denying their bodily needs. They could rise to positions of power, both secular and religious, that were completely closed to women.[40]

Eighteenth- and nineteenth-century women preserved the fasting traditions of the female saints. Since appetite for food continued to be linked in the public mind with other carnal appetites, food refusal remained a sign of spirituality. Ann Moore, the "Fasting Woman of Tutbury," came to public attention in 1807. The daughter of a laborer, Moore married briefly at the age of twenty-seven, but she and her husband separated shortly thereafter and Moore went to work as a housemaid. She had two illegitimate children by her employer, and in order to support them, she went to work "beating cotton." This probably meant she worked in one of the new cotton mills or in a cottage sewing shop. In either event, her living conditions must have been wretched. By 1807, she was poverty-stricken and dependent on an allowance given her by the parish. Ann Moore's anorexia was said to originate in her work as a domestic. Among her other duties, she washed the foul-smelling bedclothes of a man with open sores. Food came to smell to Moore like the sheets she cleaned. She said she could not swallow, and she suffered convulsions if she ate anything more than a few black currants. Moore explained her fasting on religious grounds. She renounced her earlier sexual sins and espoused Christian doctrines. Previously a pariah, she became a local celebrity.

In 1808, the Royal College of Physicians studied Ann Moore's anorexia. More than one hundred persons observed her every move for days on end. They never saw her take nourishment. Having passed this test, her fame grew more widespread. Pilgrims came from distant towns to witness the scientifically established miracle. They contributed hundreds of pounds to Moore, a small fortune to someone in her social class. In 1813, Moore agreed to a second, more careful, study, conducted by Leigh Richmond, a prominent scholar and cleric. Carefully monitored to prevent surreptitious eating, Moore became gravely ill in a matter of days. She was expected to die, but instead she was caught drinking medicines and sucking on dampened handkerchiefs. In May 1814, Tutbury town authorities forced Moore to admit she had "occasionally taken sustenance" for the past six years. Brumberg observes that once she was known not to have been totally abstinent, the public and physicians evinced no particular interest in how or why Ann Moore had managed to eat so little. From the present point of view, it seems very likely that she believed in her social role—that of the once fallen woman who has now risen so high as to leave behind carnal needs. Her pretense consisted in claiming to have risen somewhat higher than she really had. In fact, she still had one foot in the material world.

Sarah Jacob, the "Welsh Fasting Girl" of the 1870s, was one of seven children of Welsh crofters who farmed 120 acres of rented land. She began to fast at age twelve, in 1867, and her father claimed that she never passed stool or urine after December of that year. In 1869, the local Anglican vicar attested that she had not eaten in sixteen months. His letter to a magazine brought her to public attention. A two-week watch by local men validated the vicar's claim and made Sarah a celebrity. Village men and boys made a regular industry out of escorting visitors from the railway station to the Jacobs' house, where Sarah, dressed in fanciful costumes made by her mother, could be seen lying in a bed strewn with ribbons and flowers and religious books. Robert Fowler, a member of the Royal College of Surgeons, examined Sarah Jacob and concluded she was a hysteric. He shrewdly observed that the attention Sarah was receiving was inimical to her recovery, and he urged that she be removed to a hospital, where those who believed in her "miracle" could no longer encourage her. Her parents refused to heed Fowler's recommendation. In November 1869, at the behest of concerned local citizens and with the approval of Sarah and her family, four nurses came from Guy's Hospital in London to verify Sarah's fast for a two-week period. The house was searched for hidden food and Sarah was isolated from anyone who might try to feed her. By the sixth day of observation Sarah had clearly weakened. The concerned nurses were ready to give up their watch, in the hope that Sarah would then take some nourishment, however she managed to get it, but the Jacobs all refused. By the ninth day Sarah was clearly in extremis, and she died ten days after the watch began. Her parents were later tried for encouraging Sarah's fasting, and her father was convicted on a charge of criminal negligence. The *Lancet,* then as now a prestigious medical journal, offered the following comment on Sarah Jacob's death: "A girl in a weakly state of health, with a highly impressionable, emotional nervous organization, that has been unduly stimulated as well as disordered by religious reading and the sympathy of visitors, and having her vanity gratified by fuss, flowers, and ribands, will simulate anything almost well enough to deceive herself into believing it."[41]

Although the *Lancet*'s comment echoed contemporary opinion about the nervous systems of hysteric women, it nonetheless acknowledged that Sarah Jacob's food refusal was part of a social role and that Sarah herself must have believed that she could live without sustenance. Robert Fowler wrote that Sarah suffered at the end from a form of insanity. Autopsy evidence suggested that Sarah habitually ate food on the sly; for example, an indentation under her arm was thought to be due to her hiding a half-pint bottle there. Yet, by the time of her death, according to Fowler's analysis, Sarah was deceived by her own deception: "she had got herself into that state of mind in which she believed she could last out the fortnight without food."[42]

Finally, Mollie Fancher, who was known in her time as "America's most famous invalid," stopped eating at age sixteen, in 1864. Two years later, the *Brooklyn Daily Eagle* reported that Fancher had eaten nothing at all for seven weeks. At a later date, she was said to have eaten four teaspoons of milk punch, two teaspoons of wine, one banana, and a piece of cracker in a six-month period. The *Daily Eagle* attributed Fancher's problem to nervous exhaustion resulting from education. Like Alice James, and in contrast to Ann Moore and Sarah Jacob, Mollie Fancher hailed from an upper-class family capable of providing her with an education. She had been an avid reader before losing her appetite. After a streetcar accident, Fancher had also developed baffling physical symptoms, including loss of all her senses, which could only be explained as the result of hysteria. Consistent with the notion that not needing worldly sustenance indicated existence on a higher plane, Mollie Fancher later claimed clairvoyant powers. The reader should recall that spiritualist notions were popular in the late nineteenth century. Fancher was said to foresee events, to read unopened letters, and to hear conversations thousands of miles away. P. T. Barnum solicited her for his circus, which she refused to join, but she did lend her name to a line of prosthetic products, and she sold wax-work flowers that she made in bed. She enjoyed a stream of visitors who came for her advice. Eclectic physicians, who rejected the materialism of nineteenth-century mainstream medicine, supported Fancher's claim that she could live without food, and one of them went so far as to try to emulate Fancher by fasting for forty days. However, well-known neurologists ridiculed Fancher's claim and asserted that she was hysterical.

These and other cases of food refusal from the nineteenth century illustrate again how women in societies dominated by men adopt difficult and unusual social roles in order to seek goals that cannot be sought directly. Ann Moore in particular reminds us of Louise or Genevieve, two of Charcot's patients, who were also impoverished and in desperate straits before they became grand hysterics. A normal daughter of crofters could never aspire to a status like that Sarah Jacob earned by her prolonged fasting. Like any tourist attraction, she became a regular industry for the local citizens. Mollie Fancher's food refusal made her a celebrity. Showing her independence of the material world, it gave her an authority she could never have otherwise claimed. In many respects, the nineteenth-century fasting women described by Brumberg resemble the many lay women who claim to have seen the Virgin in the last hundred years. A review of modern Marian apparitions by Sandra Zimdars-Swartz shows that most seers who claim to have seen the Virgin since about 1850, when these sightings became more common, have been impoverished peasant girls much like Sarah Jacob.[43] As the result of their visions, these young girls received attention, prestige, and material aid completely out of the reach of women in their social class. Their followers believed in their spirituality and their moral authority. Some older women seers have been cured of mysterious illnesses suspiciously resembling somatization disorder. Rosa Quattrini, for instance, who claimed to see the Virgin in San Damiano, Italy, starting in 1964, had become bedridden with chronic abdominal pain before the Virgin appeared to her. Mary Ann Van Hoof, a farm wife from Wisconsin who claimed to see the Virgin starting in 1950, was incapacitated by mysterious heart and kidney pains before the Virgin's appearance. Like the women described by Brumberg, Mary Ann Van Hoof also claimed that she could live on liquids alone. In an eerie repetition of nineteenth-century vigils, Van Hoof was observed at Marquette University Medical School. She failed to maintain her weight or mineral balance while taking only liquids, nor did stigmata appear when her hands were bandaged.

According to Brumberg, patients resembling modern-day women with anorexia nervosa first began to appear at the end of the nineteenth century. In 1873, Sir William Gull, a renowned London physician, first used the term anorexia nervosa to refer to food refusal among young girls without medical illness. A Parisian neurologist, Charles Lesegue, had recently coined the term hysterical anorexia to refer to the same syndrome. The modern-day anorexic differs from fasting saints and from women like Ann Moore, Sarah Jacob, and Mollie Fancher in her preoccupation with thinness. The modern-day anorexic believes she is overweight, even when she is starving. Unlike her predecessors, she does not claim to be in touch with God nor that she is sustained by her spirituality. She fasts in order to lose weight, not for the sake of fasting.

From the late nineteenth century until about 1960, anorexia nervosa was still considered rare. Since 1960, however, a sharp rise has occurred in the incidence of this disorder in Europe, Japan, and the United States, that is, in all countries influenced by Western values and media.[44] Recent estimates are that between 1/2 and 1 percent of young girls in England and the United States have anorexia nervosa, a prevalence that compares with that of other serious mental disorders, such as schizophrenia or manic-depressive disease. In underdeveloped countries, by contrast, anorexia remains extremely rare.

Its increased prevalence and the concentration of cases only in certain countries suggest that anorexia reflects recently changing aspects of Western culture. Consistent with this hypothesis, modern-day anorexia first emerged when thinness became a status symbol for women in Europe and North America. Brumberg notes that genteel Victorian women were supposed not to respond to lower senses like taste and smell, but only to higher senses, such as sight and hearing. Women asserted their gentility by becoming excessively thin. Fat women, by contrast, could not be considered genteel or refined, and they might be considered vulgar. Lord Byron, whose Romantic followers equated excessive thinness with delicacy of the soul, ostensibly pronounced that women should not be seen eating! George Beard, whom we have already encountered, wrote that "young ladies live all their growing girlhood in semi-starvation" for fear of "incurring the horror of disciples of Lord Byron."[45] Hester Pendleton, an American writer, had already lamented the adverse effects of dieting on young girls' development. Around the turn of the century, another physician, Clifford Albutt, noted a "panic fear of obesity" that led young women to starve themselves and to take unhealthy potions. Thorstein Veblen, observing that the dread of overweight was confined to upper-class women, who were also those falling victim to the new form of anorexia, argued that pursuit of thinness was a class phenomenon.[46] According to Veblen, excessively thin women, being excessively frail, signified nonproductivity and hence a life of leisure. Men valued very thin women as a demonstration of affluence, thinness in this respect serving the very same function as bound feet served in China. A sturdy frame became a sign of low-class origins.

Women today no longer aspire to the kind of gentility they sought in Victorian times. Yet, as Brumberg documents, thinness is still a means of demonstrating social and moral worth, and women seek to be even thinner than before. Annette Kellerman, who epitomized female beauty in 1918, was 5 feet 3¾ inches tall and weighed 137 pounds. If she were living today, Kellerman would be "overweight." Marilyn Monroe, the beauty ideal of the 1950s, was pudgy by modern standards. Weight is now a ubiquitous feminine preoccupation. At any one time, half of American women, and a higher proportion of girls, consider themselves on a diet. Eighty percent of fourth-grade girls in the city of San Francisco were recently found to be dieting. Studies of girls in private schools in Washington, DC, revealed a similar pattern. A 1984 survey by *Glamour* magazine of thirty-three thousand women eighteen to thirty-five years of age found that three out of four of them thought they were overweight, often without regard for actuarial data. As in the nineteenth century, upper-class women especially strive for extremes of thinness. Americans currently spend thirty-three billion dollars yearly on goods and services intended to help lose weight.[47] Women spend most of this money. Today's woman has also taken up exercise. More women are walking, jogging, and swimming than ever before in history. Unfortunately, for many women who exercise, fitness is incidental to the primary goal of weight loss.

In general, women in our society are expected to show their worth as much through their bodily form as with diction and language, jewelry, clothing, and other goods. They no more want to be overweight than to speak ungrammatically, wear tawdry jewelry, or dress in shabby clothes. Their tastes in bodily form, as much as their tastes in jewelry and clothes, are determined by social norms and tend toward idealization of excessive thinness.

Societal expectations regarding bodily form play a critical role in initiating anorexia.[48] The force of long exposure to societal expectations can hardly be overstated, especially for insecure youngsters. By the time they are teenagers, girls in our society have been exposed for years to media and cultural messages valuing excessive thinness. They are thoroughly indoctrinated. Many anorexics report that, before the start of their illness, they were repeatedly criticized by parents, friends, or schoolmates who thought they should lose weight.[49] The diets these young girls started in response to such criticism often led directly to medically dangerous weight loss. A number of authors have argued that self-starvation carried to an extreme degree becomes an addictive process and that this accounts for the problems in treating anorexics once they have embarked on their dangerous course.[50] Others have cited psychological reasons that girls will not give up dieting, once they have begun.[51] In effect, psychological theorists claim that entrenched eating patterns serve adventitious communicative and defensive functions, which must be addressed in treatment before patients can improve.

Certainly, societal expectations that lead women to starve themselves are in some sense invidious to women and hence reflective of women's lack of social power. The nineteenth-century prejudice against women's sensuality reflected strong misogynistic cultural trends. Feminist authors have argued that modern-day standards of beauty that demand excessive thinness or other alterations of the female body reflect intense hostility to women's aspirations.[52] Such standards serve to depreciate women's intellectual and character assets and to reinforce the notion that women's worth is determined by their physical attractiveness to the opposite sex. For instance, the girl who is thoughtlessly criticized for being overweight is essentially being told that intelligence, humor, loyalty, and other personal traits will not suffice to gain approval of other persons if she is not thin. She is being encouraged to concentrate on her appearance to others, and especially on her appearance to men, and hence to pursue traditional women's roles. From this point of view, more and more difficult standards for acceptable female form reflect an ongoing backlash against women's ambitions in the last one hundred years. Girls are shown few compelling examples of powerful women whose power is not derived from bodily form or appearance.

In the last ten years, so-called bulimia nervosa has become increasingly common among young American women.[53] Bulimics, most of whom are of normal weight, go on eating binges and then purge with laxatives or by inducing vomiting. Twenty years ago, binging and purging patients were relatively rare. Now, however, there may be as many as five bulimic patients for each one with anorexia. Like anorexics, bulimics are obsessed with weight, rather than with food. When they are not binging or purging, bulimics are often starving themselves. In many cases, the binges occur in the setting of chronic caloric restriction.

Society also dictates standards of male attractiveness, but these call for muscularity rather than extreme thinness. Viewed in these terms, the male counterpart of anorexia nervosa is abuse of anabolic steroids. Just as anorexic women starve themselves to be thin, so some men abuse steroids to be muscular. Anabolic steroids are derivatives of testosterone, which, in conjunction with strenuous exercise, rapidly build muscular strength and change bodily form, at the same time leading to heart, liver, and other serious medical and psychiatric problems. Illegal use of steroids came to public attention in 1988 when Ben Johnson, the Canadian track and field star, was disqualified from the Olympics after a positive urine test. This led to allegations that steroid hormone use was common in professional sports in the United States. Regardless of whether these particular allegations were true, steroids are apparently widely abused today, mostly by young men of high-school and college age. High-school and college women, of course, are more likely to be anorexic. Athletes and body builders often use extremely high doses of steroids and employ hormone combinations to maximize their impact. This also has the effect of maximizing their side effects. A recent nationwide survey estimated that more than 6 percent of twelfth-grade boys use or have used anabolic steroids.[54]

Case reports suggest that anabolic steroid use is a type of addiction. For example, one recent study reported that steroid users experience depression, fatigue, decreased sex drive, insomnia, anorexia, dissatisfaction with their body images, and a desire to resume steroid use after stopping it.[55] The authors of this study interpreted these complaints as signs of withdrawal from steroids, akin to withdrawal symptoms following cessation of other addictive drugs. These symptoms are not too dissimilar from those reported by patients with anorexia nervosa following modest weight gains, except that instead of wishing to take steroid hormones the anorexics wish to resume their self-starvation. Part of the problem in treating steroid abusers is that, like anorexics, they never seem to believe that they have achieved what they wanted in the way of bodily form, even when others think they have already gone too far.

5

An Evolutionary, Cross-Cultural View of Women's Social Power

In the previous chapters, I argued that mental disorders that are more common in women are caused in part by lack of social power. Hence, women's relative lack of social power may be responsible for their greater risks. Consistent with this hypothesis, the women most at risk appear to be those most handicapped, often economically but also for other reasons, or those who have less security, such as mothers of young children.

Insofar as this argument is correct, clinicians who treat women should be familiar with contemporary, culture-specific social factors—such as job segregation or divorce and child-support laws—affecting women's lives. Such factors determine women's perceived and real power. They should also know something about cross-cultural factors affecting women's power. Such knowledge speaks directly to questions of choice and preference that are necessarily central to the clinical situation. Do women somehow choose to lack social power? Was Freud right in thinking that the healthiest women want to play second fiddle? Or do women lack social power for reasons outside their control? Was Horney right in thinking that women envy male power and prerogatives? In this chapter I present an evolutionary and cross-cultural overview of women's social power that will serve to answer these questions. This overview points toward a power struggle, waged between men and women, which has gone one way or the other at various times and places. Given the long history of this battle between the sexes and its roots in human biology, women's excess risk for certain mental disorders can be understood only in the context of human nature and cultural history.

Other authors have offered varied accounts of the power relations between men and women. As I will discuss, a few of these are similar to that presented here. In drawing on modern-day theories of behavioral evolution, together with anthropological studies informed by these theories, I hope to portray the issues in the most fundamental terms.

Behavioral Evolution

Although evolutionists have long believed that species-typical behavior in general and human behavior in particular evolved in the same way as bodily form and function, coherent theories of behavioral evolution have emerged only in the last few decades. These theories do not rely on group selection, the long-discredited doctrine, mentioned in chapter 1, that social behaviors evolved for the good of the group. Instead, they assume that advantages from social behaviors accrue to individuals or their genetic kin. Readers interested in detailed accounts of these theories are referred to works cited in the Notes.[1]

In the last few decades, it has become apparent that certain social strategies, or patterns of social responses, confer reproductive and other fitness advantages. Because these strategies are highly advantageous, mental dispositions have evolved that have the effect of promoting adherence to them, at least in social environments resembling those of our ancestors. Modern-day individuals may fail to adhere to these strategies because they are living in unusual social environments, very different from the conditions in which human behavior evolved, because they are mentally ill, or because they have been trained to suppress dispositions integral to a strategy. The first possibility is illustrated below. I have discussed the second and third possibilities elsewhere.[2] However, most individuals do adhere to these strategies, even in modern times.

These strategies are contingent—that is, they depend on environmental, or contingent, cues—and they are highly flexible at the tactical level. Behaviors subserving these strategies, far from being stereotyped, differ according to environmental conditions. Tactical flexibility is shown by most higher primates—especially ingenious chimpanzees, for instance, have enhanced their displays of dominance by banging together garbage cans found at research stations, something they could not do in a more natural setting—but it is still more salient for human beings. Means for achieving the same goals vary tremendously between individuals and between different cultures.

Some readers may be misled by the everyday usage of the word 'strategy.' In everyday usage, to say that someone has a strategy implies that they are adhering to an intentional plan. Thus, "Admiral Raeder's strategy was to cut Britain's supply line" implies that Admiral Raeder planned to cut Britain's supply line. To evolutionists, though, 'strategy' does not imply an intentional plan. Thus, a commonplace male strategy to maximize fitness, discussed below, is to father children by as many women as possible. However, what evolved to promote this strategy was not a desire for children but for varied and frequent coitus. In an environment like that in which humans evolved, men who had strong desires for varied and frequent coitus may have had more children than men with weaker desires. Some primitive peoples described by anthropologists, and presumably our ancestors too, did not even know that sexual intercourse leads to pregnancy. Now that we do understand the relation of coitus and pregnancy, some men and women take steps to separate what they do want, sexual intercourse, from what they may not want, babies. Moderns can break the linkage between motivation and consequence precisely because they no longer live in an environment like that in which humans evolved. In this new environment, motivational factors like the desire for coitus may not produce adherence to strategies, like those described below, as reliably as they once did. However, these strategies retain much heuristic value.

Nonreproductive Strategies

Most evolved strategies are not directly related to reproduction and hence differ relatively little between the two sexes.[3] Kin and reciprocal altruism are the best known of these strategies. Kin altruism is the strategy of rendering assistance, at least under some conditions, to genetic kin. The conditions and types of assistance dictated by kin altruism are readily expressed in mathematical terms.[4] Cross-cultural studies confirm that people everywhere adhere to kin altruism in providing aid to their relatives.[5] The biological basis of kin altruism may consist of emotional processes that cause us to feel friendly toward those with whom we have had the longest associations. At least in societies like those in which humans evolved, long association was a reliable clue to genetic kinship.

One particular type of kin-altruistic behavior, which is especially familiar to mental health clinicians, is parenting behavior. Children carry half of each of their parents' genes, and they need adult assistance to reach reproductive maturity. As predicted by kin-altruism theory, parents in all societies provide their young children with food, shelter, and clothing. They clean them, protect them from dangers, and educate them in the ways of their social group. Recent research inspired by the British psychiatrist John Bowlby, who studied children separated from their parents during World War II, has shown how parents become "attachment figures" for children.[6] That is, they allow themselves to become the object of the child's own proximity- and aid-seeking behaviors, and they respond to these behaviors in a supportive fashion. Numerous studies have aimed to elucidate the processes that lead parents to be altruistic to children. It now seems clear that some of these are innate.[7]

Reciprocal altruism is the strategy of providing cost-effective aid to associates who are likely, as judged by their past behavior, to reciprocate in the future. As in the case of kin altruism, the conditions and types of assistance consistent with reciprocal altruism are also readily expressed in mathematical formulas.[8] Cross-cultural studies confirm that people everywhere behave like reciprocal altruists,[9] and emotional processes dependent on brain biology are likewise implicated in producing this type of behavior. For example, reciprocal altruists must have the minimal affiliative dispositions to ensure their prolonged contact with other persons. Robert Trivers, a biologist who stated the theory of reciprocal altruism, argues convincingly that cognitive demands due to this social strategy contributed to enlargement of the human brain during the Pleistocene epoch.[10]

"Mutualism" is a social strategy conceptually related to reciprocal altruism.[11] Individuals practicing mutualism cooperate with each other in flexible ways to reach mutually advantageous goals. They deny the benefits of these goals to those who did not help reach them. The fitness advantages of mutualism are considerable, above and beyond the advantages conferred by gregarious living. Groups of mutualistic individuals can mount organized defenses against predators, hunt for large game, define and protect territory, and invent and perfect technologies. The activities of mutualistic groups, such as exploiting food supplies, tend to harm unaffiliated outsiders. Consequently, once mutualistic groups are formed, the advantages to the individual of participating in such a group become even greater. Like reciprocal altruism, mutualism is evident in all human societies. Also, numerous human perceptual, cognitive, and emotional dispositions increase the chance of adherence to mutualism, and many of these are innate or dependent on innate processes. Tendencies to adopt rewarded social roles, described in chapter 3, probably also promote adherence to mutualism. Groups reward roles to induce individuals to help them meet their goals.

There are also several so-called agonistic strategies, which dictate possible options in agonistic encounters. Readers interested in such strategies are referred to works cited in the Notes.[12]

Reproductive Strategies

The strategies mentioned thus far relate to reproduction only indirectly. That is, kin and reciprocal altruism, mutualism, and agonistic strategies affect mating opportunities and determine the fate of offspring, but they do not directly specify efforts to find or interact with potential mates. Strategies directly related to reproduction play a greater role in shaping gender relationships, and hence they are more pertinent to the point of this study.

Charles Darwin laid the basis for modern thinking about reproductive strategies in his 1871 book *The Descent of Man, and Selection in Relation to Sex*.[13] Since Darwin's time, ethological studies have confirmed the validity of his approach in numerous species. Here I will summarize modern thinking about reproductive strategies for Homo sapiens, which differs from other species in having extremely precocious young, who consequently require prolonged postnatal care.[14]

First, human males must have evolved to compete with each other for exclusive sexual access to women. Since a healthy man can father many more children than any woman can bear, ancestral men could realize their own reproductive potential only by mating with more than their "share" of women. Given the equal number of men and women, a man who mated with more than one woman and prevented other men from mating with them effectively deprived at least one other man of women altogether. Insofar as the behavioral dispositions or abilities that caused ancestral men to mate with more than their share of women were hereditary, these dispositions and abilities must have been passed on to later generations. In effect, we are all the descendants of men who outcompeted other men for exclusive sexual access to available women.

Second, women must have evolved to compete with each other for mates with the best genes, that is, those genes that confer the greatest advantage on their children, and if need be, for mates who are able and willing to help them raise their children. Since ancestral women would not have lacked sufficient sexual opportunities to bear their maximal number of offspring, women would not have evolved to compete for sex per se. By choosing to mate with men who are vigorous, healthy, and smart, women may be choosing mates with better genes. Certainly, men whose genes are ill suited for their environment are unlikely to be robust or especially healthy. The importance of choosing mates who are able and willing to provide needed assistance follows from human children's prolonged dependency. In ancestral societies, men apparently provided women and children with needed high-protein foods.[15] In other societies, men provide their children with social position and rank or with education and other like advantages. The extent to which women choose mates for paternal assistance will vary with availability of resources needed for rearing children in their society. Women in societies in which such resources are readily available to them, or at least widely distributed among men, will be able to choose their mates without much consideration for resource availability. Women in societies in which such resources are concentrated in the hands of very few men will have to choose mates on the basis of such resources, if they are to adhere to their reproductive strategy.

Women's concern with resources needed for rearing children is part and parcel of their concern for children's well-being. Each of her children represents a large reproductive investment for a woman. She has carried the child to term and, in an ancestral environment, breast-fed it for several years. A woman who loses a child of whatever age has lost a large proportion of her possible reproduction. Thus, women must have evolved so as to provide care for children. Men, by contrast, may have little investment in children. A single child represents a much smaller proportion of a man's than of a woman's possible reproduction. Hence, men may have evolved to have more variable, and often minimal, concern with children's welfare, depending upon their particular reproductive situation.

Although the form and extent of male competition and the extent to which women depend upon male parental assistance for basic resources needed for rearing children vary enormously from society to society, both men and women adhere to these basic reproductive strategies in all societies in which issues of mate choice and sexual behavior have been studied.[16] For example, David Buss, a psychologist at the University of Michigan, performed a cross-cultural survey of differences in men's and women's mating preferences. In every case differences were consistent with predictions following from these strategies. Men in all the societies Buss surveyed are less sexually choosy, more desirous of mating with maximally fecund partners, and less concerned with commitment than women from their societies. Not that men intentionally pursue the most fecund females; their choices in female attributes, though, coincide with fecundity. Likewise, women in most cultures choose sexual partners based in large part on availability of resources needed for rearing children.

As the models also predict, women in all societies assume most of the burden of child care. In many societies, men are wholly free from the exigencies of child care, although they may materially support mothers and children. Anthropologists Lionel Tiger and Joseph Shepher provided intriguing data from Israeli kibbutzim that show how women's concern for the well-being of children helps to create this discrepancy in the provision of child care quite independently of cultural injunctions.[17] Some Israeli kibbutzim were specifically established with the aim of freeing women from their child-care burdens. From the earliest age, children were to be raised in communal nurseries, spending only one or two hours each day with their parents. Mothers were encouraged to work in kibbutz jobs unrelated to child care, in order to avoid overinvolvement with children. Tiger and Shepher found that, although men were willing to accept care of their children in nurseries, with only occasional parent-child contact, women lobbied against the nurseries and, in many kibbutzim, succeeded in having children live at home with their parents. Although men were happy with jobs in farming or factories, women sought and took over positions caring for children. Tiger and Shepher conclude that women in kibbutzim have chosen preferred activities in seeking involvement with children and that these preferences reflect their innate dispositions.

As expected from their reproductive strategy, in all societies men are more likely than women to kill or injure each other in fights for sexual access.[18] Young men, especially, fight each other for women. Humans are also dimorphic with respect to bodily size. The average man is 10 percent taller and heavier than the average woman and has more muscle and a lower proportion of body fat. Greater bodily size in males of other species is seen as an adaptation for success in intrasex combat.[19]

Finally, men who control resources useful for rearing children can attract the greatest number of maximally fecund mates. According to Bobbi Low, an evolutionary ecologist at the University of Michigan, men in most societies seek to control such resources by forming coalitions with some, but not all, of their fellows.[20] These coalitions are fluid and often end in hostility, but they nonetheless accomplish their purposes while they last.

Numerous innate dispositions increase the chance that men and women will adhere to their respective reproductive strategies. For example, sexual object choice, which is a prerequisite for adherence to both male and female strategies, is now thought to be determined prenatally or shortly after birth by fetal sex hormones acting on brain structures.[21] Fetal sex hormone levels normally are determined by the presence or absence of genes carried on the Y, or male, chromosome. Sex-related differences in arousal patterns may be determined in a similar fashion. Male sexual arousal, which is rapid, visual, and conditionable to culturally specific signs of female sexual availability, promotes adherence to the male strategy, which is to take advantage of sexual access to women.[22] Female sexual arousal, which is slower and more determined by emotional cues than by visual stimuli, promotes adherence to the female strategy, which is to mate selectively. Numerous studies suggest that men's greater aggressiveness and women's concern for children are also partly determined by hormonal or other biological factors.[23]

The Male Power Advantage

Insofar as men and women adhere to the reproductive strategies described above, men are likely to have more power than women under most conditions. Men are advantaged for several related reasons. First, male reproductive strategies are such that, in societies that permit resource monopolization, men in positions of power use their resources in order to monopolize as many women as possible. They seek to have multiple wives, concubines, or other dependent women, to whom they alone are permitted sexual access. In order to maintain their exclusive sexual access, powerful men in such societies extend their control over women in general. They restrict women's rights and activities and cloister them in the home. They may treat women as chattel, as the historian Gerda Lerner described in her study of ancient society.[24] Commodification of women, as Lerner called the process, manifests male attempts to monopolize sexual partners. No one seeks to own that which they do not monopolize in one respect or another. Restrictions of women's activities and their reduction to property are justified ideologically, with long-lasting effects on later gender relations.

Second, insofar as men tend to band together to pursue reproductive goals, women will be still further disadvantaged. Women's relative power in social groups depends upon the extent to which resources needed for rearing children are widely distributed, either among women or among men in general. Coalitions that concentrate resources needed by children in the hands of rather few men allow those men greater control over women adhering to their own reproductive strategy. The power of such coalitions is especially great in large-scale societies, in which transient political groups based on a few common interests, rather than coalitions based on personal bonds, wield the greatest power. As I will describe, there is evidence that women's status deteriorated with the development of the first organized states and that men's coalitions aimed at controlling resources were a principal tool in women's subjugation.

Finally, women are disadvantaged due to their often greater concern for their children's welfare. Men who control resources needed for rearing their children can sometimes control their spouses by threatening to withhold resources. This is a credible threat precisely because the father's concern for his children's well-being may be less than the mother's. In the United States today, millions of women are forced to provide as best they can for children whose fathers refuse to help support them.[25] Lack of paternal assistance is the principal factor plunging millions of American children into poverty (see chapter 2). Many American women must be more or less afraid to displease their husbands in part because their children depend on his goodwill.

These various disadvantages are all interrelated. Whenever resources are scarce, fluid, politicized male coalitions can monopolize resources, thereby making themselves attractive prospective mates. Men in the most successful coalitions will seek to monopolize multiple sexual partners, an effort that in extreme instances may reduce women to chattel. Individual men, moreover, may be able to keep their children's mothers in line by the threat of withdrawing needed paternal assistance. As long as they themselves lack resources for rearing children, and if such resources are highly concentrated, women's reproductive strategies ensure that they will cooperate with the regnant system. They will have to accept as mates men who control resources, and for the good of their children, they will have to please their partners. Women can escape male domination only by controlling sufficient useful resources that they can provide for their children without a male, if need be, or if such resources are widely distributed among men in general.

It is worth contrasting this evolutionary model of male dominance with two well-known "classical" models, both of which identify resource monopolization as a vital factor in male domination but which hypothesize different motives and chains of events. The first of these, outlined by Frederick Engels, attributes male domination to the invention of private property.[26] According to Engels, prehistoric groups were communist societies. There was no private property, there were no exclusive sexual relationships, and children belonged to everyone. Once they had invented private property, however, ancient men wanted to pass it on to heirs, but these could not be identified in the offspring of group marriages. By instituting monogamy, and by restricting female sexuality, these men secured legitimate heirs and thus their property interests. It follows from Engels's argument that female rights can be realized through demise of the propertied class. That is, working-class men, having no capital to pass on to their heirs, should have no particular motive to deny women equality.

Engels's work was a mixed blessing for women. On the one hand, by treating patriarchy as a historical issue, Engels encouraged others to work for women's rights. In socialist countries, however, Engels's hypothesis was used to block discussion of women's political issues.[27] For example, in 1908 Alexandra Kollontai, the leading Russian woman Marxist before the revolution, organized a congress of feminist groups in St. Petersburg. The Social Democrats, who were the forerunners and later enemies of the Communist Party, condemned Kollontai's congress, which they thought would draw attention away from the class revolution that would solve women's problems. They considered feminism a bourgeois diversion from the real struggle. After the revolution, Kollontai asked Lenin to found a women's department to address feminist issues. Lenin at first refused, citing the very same argument used before in St. Petersburg. When he relented, he prevented the new department from raising feminist issues. Until Stalin closed it, the Women's Department functioned as a specialized propaganda arm touting the party's line among working women. When Stalin restricted divorce and access to abortions, moves opposed by Russian feminists, he was able to cite Engels's thesis, that the interests of women would be served by socialism more or less automatically. Stalin's moves were motivated, among other factors, by his fears about the long-term geopolitical consequences of falling birthrates in the Soviet Union. The revolution, it seemed, needed women's bodies.

In fact, the revolution failed to live up to its claims for women's liberation, just as it apparently failed to live up to its other claims.[28] Like their counterparts in the industrial West, women in recently socialist countries are less highly educated and work in lower-paid and less-prestigious jobs than men. Apparent exceptions to this rule turn out to be misleading. Thus, most women professionals in formerly socialist countries, such as the large number of women doctors practicing in Russia, work at the lower levels of their professions, whereas the more prestigious posts are occupied by men. Like many Western women, women in these countries work outside the home but still assume most of the burden of housework and child-care duties.

From the viewpoint developed here, Engels's model seems to place the cart before the horse. Rather than dominate women to protect private property; men seek control of property—or of useful resources—in order to attract women. (Recall that evolved social strategies do not imply definite plans [see above]. Men seeking resources are not necessarily thinking about the opposite sex.) When resources can be monopolized, male coalitions can vitiate female choice and subordinate women, who are dependent on them for resources needed for rearing children. Resource control is a strategy for gaining control over women, not vice versa as Engels's model has it.

The second model was proposed by Thorstein Veblen.[29] Veblen believed that the motive for male domination was invidious self-display, or "emulation," during what Veblen called the "predatory" phase of cultural life. Veblen believed that the wish for invidious self-display was a prime mover of human social behavior. In the predatory cultural phase, powerful men did not produce wealth but attained it by plunder or fraud, and thus they valued attributes attesting to force and fierceness. Because women could be taken from other men by force, they came to be valued as trophies of prowess in war, and in this way they served the same function as enemy scalps or ears in more recent times. According to Veblen,

The practice of seizing women from the enemy as trophies, gave rise to a form of ownership-marriage. . . . This was followed by an extension of slavery to other captives and inferiors, besides women, and by an extension of ownership-marriage to other women than those seized from the enemy. The outcome of emulation under the circumstances of a predatory life, therefore, has been . . . a form of marriage resting on coercion.[30]

In contrast to Engels, who thought that women were subjugated in order to secure property rights, Veblen thought women comprised the original properties from whom the whole concept of property rights evolved. "From the ownership of women," Veblen wrote, "the concept of ownership extends itself to include the products of their industry, and so there arises the ownership of things as well as persons."[31] In this regard, Veblen seems to concur with Claude Lévi-Strauss, the cultural anthropologist who argued that exchange of women by primitive men constitutes the primal form of property trade.[32]

Although Veblen seems to recognize the male sexual motives described in this chapter—otherwise why would victorious men take women in the first place?—he would have men monopolize women for honorific reasons. Whatever sexual motives men have for "owning" women, in the various senses that women are owned in patriarchal societies, Veblen passes over in favor of self-display, this being the cornerstone of his social theory. From the point of view of theories of evolution, it makes no sense to divert attention from reproduction—which affects fitness directly—in favor of matters like self-display that affect fitness indirectly. Gerda Lerner agrees with Veblen that ownership of women served as the model for slavery,[33] but the models of behavioral evolution described above suggest that the concept of ownership in a general sense must rest on much more ancient attempts to control resources than those considered by Veblen.

Finally, cultural anthropologist Marvin Harris recently formulated another well-known theory of male domination.[34] Harris's theory, too, is instructive in the present context. According to Harris, men's advantage resides in their greater physical strength, particularly their upper-body strength, which affords them superiority in the use of primitive weapons and some agricultural implements. This advantage is realized mostly in warlike societies, in which men are highly trained in the use of weapons, or in societies dependent on those implements men can more readily use. Regarding the latter, for instance, Harris notes that women in West Africa, where the main agricultural implement was the hoe, wielded much more power than women in northern India, where soil and weather conditions required that plows be used. Women could use the hoe almost as well as men; but men were greatly advantaged in using the oxen-drawn plow. As Harris himself observed, his theory in this instance is compatible with the notion that resource control determines women's relative power. Because they could grow their own food, women in West Africa were more independent of men.

Harris notes that women in warlike societies have less power than women in more peaceful but otherwise comparable societies. Thus, men are more dominant in warlike Australian Aboriginal tribes than in comparable, but peaceful, tribes of !Kung Bushmen. Warfare and male dominance seem to go hand in hand in settled, village societies that often fight with their neighbors. In these societies, women work the land while men, being stronger, spend their time preparing for war. For example, men of the Yanomämo, who are described below, spend much of their time preparing for raids on neighboring villages. Yanomämo women are little more than chattel, in spite of the fact that they produce most foods. Harris argues that men in warlike societies are able to dominate women because of their training in use of dangerous weapons. Men in such societies not infrequently turn their weapons on women. Even here, however, resources may be important in establishing male control. Men in warlike societies fight neighboring tribes or villages to secure territory and to capture women. Both hunter-gatherer peoples and agriculturalists must have adequate land to meet their material needs. The latter, especially, need long-term control over land, which may account for the greater ferocity of warfare in settled village societies. By securing land, warriors gain control over most resources needed by women and children. In the absence of male protection, women could not work the land without being killed or abducted by men from enemy villages. Hence, women's livelihoods are as wholly dependent on men as in societies in which only men can farm. By driving off neighboring peoples, who might compete for game, men might also improve their hunting prospects, enhancing their control over the protein supply.[35]

A Cross-Cultural and Historical View of Women's Relative Power

In the previous section, I noted that differences between men's and women's reproductive strategies confer a power advantage on men under most conditions. This power advantage varies with the extent to which women are dependent upon men for material resources needed for rearing children, and it is greatest in those societies in which relatively few men monopolize those resources, thereby undermining women's freedom of choice.

Bobbi Low studied men's and women's relative social power by reviewing data on the 93 odd-numbered societies listed in Murdock and White's Standard Cross-Cultural Sample.[36] The Standard Cross-Cultural Sample is a compilation of ethnographic data on 186 societies, chosen for their linguistic and geographic diversity.

Low's studies confirm the pattern of male advantage predicted by the evolutionary model, together with the hypothesized importance of resource control.

First, consistent with men's adherence to their reproductive strategy, men in positions of power in most societies monopolize two or more sexual partners. Eighty-three (89 percent) of the societies studied by Low allowed for polygynous marriages. Obviously, not every man in such societies can have more than one partner, so multiple wives, in fact, are reserved for more powerful men. Actually, even societies that permit only monogamy allow wealthy men additional sexual partners, which are not permitted to women. Monogamy is often serial so that wealthy or powerful men can take younger, more fecund, wives as their first wives age.[37] Polyandrous societies, which allow women multiple husbands, rather than vice versa, are extremely rare;[38] Low found none in her particular sample. The eighty-three societies that sanctioned polygynous marriage differed from each other in the proportion of women in multiple marriages and in the maximal number of wives permitted by custom. In studying these parameters of polygynous marriage, Low found that greater degrees of polygyny were associated with male control of inherited wealth and with lesser degrees of women's control of their husband's resources. Societies that allowed men the greatest number of wives were most often highly stratified; that is, they showed the greatest difference in wealth distribution by class. Apparently, as the evolutionary models described above predict, wealthy or powerful men obtain more sexual partners by controlling resources needed by women and children. Very large harems indicate large inequities in resource distribution not only between men and women but between men as well.

Low showed that women living in stratified societies or in societies in which women control few resources are trained to be obedient and sexually restrained. Chastity and obedience are the prized harem virtues. When women control resources, daughters are taught neither obedience nor submission and are correspondingly freer to control their own sexuality. Low's findings in this regard are consistent with Schlegel and Barry's.[39] On the basis of similar data, Schlegel and Barry concluded that men who control resources women need for subsistence also control women's sexual lives. The Yanomämo, a warlike horticultural and hunting people who live in jungle villages in Brazil and Venezuela, illustrate one extreme form of male competition and sexual domination.[40] Yanomämo villages are wholly controlled by men, who frequently kill each other in fights over sexual partners. As many as 25 percent of men are murdered or killed in raids on neighboring villages. These raids themselves are mounted to kidnap neighbors' women. Men who can manipulate kin and other allies are able to take as wives the excess numbers of women resulting from male deaths and hence to father a disproportionate share of the next generation. For example, one leader, "Shinbone," was known to have 43 children. Shinbone's father, also a successful polygamist, had nearly 150 grandchildren. Yanomämo women may prefer polygynous marriages, because only powerful men can make their wives secure. But women are also treated as commodities and traded by powerful men according to certain rules that define exogamous matings.

Yanomämo men are obsessed by the fear that their women will cuckold them, thus giving away what they consider theirs. However, having failed to invent chastity belts or to discover infibulation (sewing closed the vagina to mechanically prevent intercourse), and being frequently away from their villages on hunting or raiding expeditions, they have to rely on terror to keep their wives in line. Thus, Yanomämo men who suspect they have been cuckolded beat their wives severely. Wives who have been captured from neighboring villages have no male kin to protect them, so they will be treated especially harshly if their fidelity is suspected. In one such case described by Napolean Chagnon, an anthropologist who has spent much of his life studying the Yanomämo, a suspicious husband shot his wife in the abdomen with an arrow.[41] An aggrieved Yanomämo man might also defend his sexual prerogatives with his women by challenging suspected lovers to fight with clubs. Such fights involve allies and kin on both sides and frequently end in death or serious injury.

Another extreme of male sexual domination is illustrated by the Arab and North African tribes described by Sir Richard Francis Burton, the great British explorer.[42] Wealthy men in these tribes maintained polygynous marriages. Like Yanomämo men, they too were obsessed with the fear that their women would cuckold them. They protected themselves by subjecting girls to clitoridectomy. Burton's account made clear that the purpose of clitoridectomy was in fact to eliminate pleasure in sexual intercourse. Women who had not undergone this procedure were considered unfit for marriage. Actually, clitoral cauterization and clitoridectomy were used to prevent masturbation and to treat mental illness in nineteenth-century Europe, so Burton did not really have to travel so far to observe it (see chapter 6). The Somalis also practiced labial infibulation, using horse-hair sutures. This was first done at age fifteen and repeated by traveling husbands who suspected their wife's fidelity. In medieval Europe, of course, metal chastity belts were used by the upper classes in place of horse-hair sutures.

Low found that women lacked political power, too. Sixty-five of the ninety-three societies Low reviewed had only male chiefs or political leaders. Seven of the remaining twenty-eight societies had leaders of both sexes, though male leaders were more powerful, two allowed both sexes equal leadership roles, and there was no information on the remaining nineteen. Low notes that these latter groups were probably led by men; ethnographers would have noted unusual leadership patterns. Actually, study of the ethnographies in the Cross-Cultural Sample suggests that even these figures overstate women's political roles. For example, the Nama, of the central and northern Kalahari, are coded in the sample as affording women political positions, but in fact most Nama groups had no political offices. Instead they were led by hereditary male chieftains. On only one occasion, a woman reigned as a regent for her younger brother until he came of age. Another tribe, the Mbundu in south central Africa, was said to allow women to hold political posts, but it too had had only one woman ruler, according to tribal historians. Low's analysis showed that matrilineal kinship was the only factor increasing the probability that women could be leaders. Women in societies with matrilineal kinship may assume group leadership roles as means of promoting the interests of their kin.

None of the societies Low studied were matriarchal; that is, in no society did women exercise power similar to men's in patriarchal society. Nor is there real evidence of past matriarchal societies, in spite of a well-known theory invented by J. J. Bachofen, a nineteenth-century thinker influenced by Darwin.[43] True matriarchal societies would pose a difficult and perhaps insurmountable challenge to the hypotheses outlined in this chapter. Many observers agree, though, that hunter-gatherer tribes, which are thought to resemble the groups in which human ancestors lived, give greater power to women than do more settled societies, albeit with some exceptions.[44] The exceptions tend to be highly warlike tribes like those cited by Harris. Thus, Bachofen may have been wrong in claiming that prehistoric societies were matriarchal, but he may have been generally right in thinking the "primitive" state conferred greater power on women. Once again, resources provide an explanation for women's relative power. In hunter-gatherer tribes, women supply the bulk of caloric requirements by gathering vegetation. Men supply protein-rich game. Hunting is often cooperative; the game is shared among those who take part in the hunt. Men depend on each other for long-term assistance, and they cannot risk excluding those whose future aid may be crucial to their own survival. Cooperation, to make the point succinctly, retains a privileged position in hunter-gatherer tribes. Also, resources in such societies cannot be "owned" nor inherited. Thus hunter-gatherer women directly control a significant proportion of resources needed for rearing children, and what resources they don't control are spread among men in general, rather than being monopolized by just a few powerful men. Women retain a strong bargaining position vis-à-vis their current and potential mates.

A question closely related to the issue of matriarchy is whether powerful women might behave like powerful men in their relationships with the opposite sex. Certain historical queens, who are said to have had voracious sexual appetites, are sometimes cited as evidence that powerful men and women are cut from the same cloth.[45] But here, too, the historical evidence indicates otherwise. For example, the legendary Semiramis, the Babylonian widow of a ninth-century B.C. Assyrian king, was said to use her soldiers for her sexual gratification and then to slay them, to keep them from telling tales. Her son supposedly killed her after she tried to seduce him. But in fact little is known about Semiramis, except that she briefly served as regent for her son. According to the Russian poet Lermontov, Tamara, a twelfth-century Georgian Queen and military leader, hurled her numerous lovers over the edge of a precipice. Tamara, in fact, was canonized for her devotional piety by the Georgian Church. Caterina Sforza, the cruel fifteenth-century ruler of Forlà and Imola, and Catherine the Great, whom Voltaire called the "Semiramis of the North," did take numerous lovers to satisfy their passions, but other allegations against them apparently were invented by their political enemies. The nineteenth-century Rani of Jhansi, who died fighting the British in the Indian Rebellion, became known as the "Jezebel of India" for her alleged licentiousness, but the charges against the Rani, too, were entirely propaganda. The real Jezebel, whom the Rani was said to resemble, was a ninth-century B.C. queen of Israel whose death is described in the Bible. She may have been killed for attempting to revive the Tyrean goddess cult.

According to Antonia Fraser, a well-known women's historian, historical women rulers on the whole have been sexually puritanical, and even the most licentious of them were seldom as bad as their male peers.[46] At worst, rulers like Caterina Sforza and Catherine the Great were sexually overactive. They did not keep men in harems nor claim to own their lovers. They cannot be said to have mirrored powerful male rulers.

Conditions affecting resources periodically change, so women's relative power should also change with time. Gerda Lerner described women's loss of power in the early years of the city-states of ancient Mesopotamia.[47] Studies of neolithic settlements suggest that women enjoyed relatively high status at the dawn of the historical epoch. Some women in these settlements were buried in ways that suggest that they were important persons, and the worship of goddess figures apparently was widespread. Consistent with the relation hypothesized above between women's relative power and resource availability, neolithic settlements in Anatolia show little evidence of social stratification. For example, all of the dwellings in these settlements are the same size.

History began with the invention of writing about three thousand B.C. in the city of Sumer. Tens of thousands of documents have been found that attest to the customs and laws of Mesopotamia from three thousand B.C. to the biblical era. Lerner contends that early Mesopotamian documents show that women initially enjoyed higher status than they did later on. According to Lerner, women in Mesopotamia were gradually "commodified," becoming little more than chattels. Eventually, not only were women bought and sold, or captured as prizes in warfare, but crimes against women became property crimes against the men who owned them. Being property themselves, women could not sign contracts or make business decisions. Their movements were restricted to keep them from giving away sexual favors that belonged by rights to their owners. Extreme commodification of women in Mesopotamia provided a model for slavery in a more general sense, according to Lerner's argument. Consistent with the notion that resource distribution affects women's relative power, women's loss of power in ancient Mesopotamia followed on advances in agriculture, warfare, communication, and government that allowed rather few men to control wealth and resources to an extent unprecedented in earlier societies. Lerner cites evidence showing vast concentrations of wealth in the hands of Mesopotamian aristocrats and priests.

There is little need to review the increase in women's power in the last one hundred years.[48] Although women today are still handicapped in comparison with men (see chapter 2), they do exercise more power than their mothers and grandmothers did. Consistent with the importance ascribed here to resource control, recent improvements in women's relative social power have coincided with greatly increased average standards of living. For the first time, common men and women have had reliable access to resources needed by children. Not only can most men earn a "family wage," but according to Barbara Bergman, a well-known student of women's economic conditions, extraordinary rises in workplace productivity have brought women into the job market, hence giving them greater direct control of the nation's wealth.[49]

Women's Response to Their Relative Lack of Power

Thus far in this chapter, I have shown that models of behavioral evolution suggest that men will have certain advantages over women, such that women will often lack needed social power. The cross-cultural and historical studies described in the previous section show that this male advantage is most often realized, to some extent or another. The most powerful men in the majority of societies control resources sufficiently to circumscribe women's choices, sometimes going so far as to make women a species of property. In addition, women seldom wield real political power. Although some societies are rather egalitarian in their gender relations, there are no societies known in which the tables are turned and women dominate men.

These findings and analyses raise the question of women's responses. How do women feel about their lack of power? Are they happy to be without power and to play limited social roles? Or do they covet power and secretly hope to obtain male social prerogatives? The answer to this question is highly politically charged. Social conservatives have often portrayed women as happy playing second fiddle to men, while feminists of all stripes have insisted that women want more. Contrary to the viewpoint expressed by Cynthia Fuchs Epstein,[50] which I cited in chapter 1, an adaptive, or fitness, analysis favors the feminist claim, rather than meliorism. As noted in chapter 1, Epstein's contrary opinion rests upon confusion regarding group selection, the now-outmoded doctrine that social behavior evolved for the good of the group. Increased social power, or freedom from control by others whose interests conflict with one's own, can only increase fitness if fitness is studied in individual terms. Relative social power has probably been a major selective factor for humans, so neither men nor women could possibly have evolved to give up their power to others, if they have a choice. Given the opportunity, both men and women should seek to increase their social power.

In fact, women do seek greater social power, even in societies wholly controlled by men. Some of the illness roles described in the previous chapters represent women's attempts to achieve some control over others, in spite of adverse conditions in their daily lives. I. M. Lewis has shown how women's possession cults serve to enhance women's power in especially patriarchal tribal societies.[51] As Low observed in ethnographies in the Standard Cross-Cultural Sample, women have to be taught to be submissive to men.[52] Societies in which women control few resources, and hence are dependent on men's sexual patronage, teach girls to be obedient and to accept their places. This kind of indoctrination would not be necessary if submissiveness and obedience came naturally to women.

Insofar as male and female reproductive strategies, which are conditioned by the extraordinarily slow maturation of human offspring, give men advantages over women in some situations, and insofar as women have evolved to resist men's control, Homo sapiens is a deeply divided species. The battle between the sexes is bound to flare up whenever ecological factors allow coalitions of men control over useful resources needed for caring for children. When rather few men control resources needed by children, women are forced to mate with them on disadvantageous terms. Cease-fires will occur whenever useful resources are widely distributed, either between men or between men and women. In either case women retain rather free choice of mates and hence great influence over men's behavior.

In the previous chapters, I tried to show that certain well-known mental disorders that are more common in women represent efforts to meet needs, which take the forms they do because the women who make them lack social power. Other disorders are side effects of interpersonal stratagems shaped by lack of power, or they manifest subjective responses to lack of power. In any event, women's excess risk of these mental disorders results from their relative powerlessness in comparison with men. Women with these disorders—or at least those who represent the excess number of female cases—are the walking wounded in the battle between the sexes as it has expressed itself in their particular time.

It may seem odd to some that behavioral evolution could lead to mental illness, however indirectly, as the argument here suggests. Why did evolution create a power struggle, if the result of that struggle is that so many fall ill? Isn't evolution supposed to enhance well-being?

To begin with, the most "natural" societies, in the sense of being most like those in which human beings evolved, may be least likely to foster women's disorders. I have already noted that several ecological factors in hunter-gatherer life militate against dramatic power imbalances between men and women. Insofar as relative powerlessness causes mental disorders, the hunter-gatherer lifestyle may have been better for women's relative mental health than later-developing lifestyles that are familiar to us. Second, behaviors that look pathological in the clinical setting may nonetheless be adaptive in the real world. Cross-cultural data cited in chapter 4 suggest that certain culture-specific disorders of women are highly functional in their cultural settings. Women with these disorders can increase their relative power vis-à-vis men in their lives without incurring risks of direct confrontation. Even in our society, some women with mental disorders may thereby meet their needs. Clinicians who reify illness roles may thereby ignore these roles' adaptive functions or dismiss them as so-called secondary gains. This oversight is corrected only when illness roles—and resultant mental disorders—are viewed in their social context, with attention to relative power (see chapter 6). Finally, natural selection places no value on happiness, only on reproduction. Natural selection can act to improve mental health only if poor mental health adversely affects reproduction. There is in fact no reason to think that women's unhappiness, or women's mental disorders, have historically had much effect on women's reproduction. Anorexia nervosa is an exception, of course, since it reduces fertility, but this is a new disorder, at least in its modern-day form (see chapter 4). Depressed women are less likely to kill themselves than are depressed men, and those who do are generally past reproductive age.[53] Data cited in chapter 2 suggest that in our society, women become depressed after—not before—having children, since motherhood exposes them to the most severe disadvantages of the female role. Insofar as unhappiness has motivated some women to increase their social power, and consequently their fitness, natural selection might even have favored distress.

6

• • • • • • • • • •

Conclusion

In chapters 2 through 4, I presented evidence that lack of social power is a contributing factor in depression, in some anxiety disorders, and in a variety of illnesses that can be understood in terms of social roles. Social power was defined as the ability to provide for one's needs and security and the needs and security of loved ones and to make life decisions based on one's own interests. Insofar as lack of social power increases the risk for these disorders, women's relative powerlessness might account for their increased risk of falling ill. In chapter 5, I discussed women's lack of power in an evolutionary and cross-cultural framework. Women's lack of power results from differences in men's and women's evolved reproductive strategies in environments in which rather few men can monopolize resources needed for rearing children. If resources are widely distributed, either between men or between men and women, women are better able to defend their interests. Like men, women must have evolved to seek power, not to give it up. Hence, it is not surprising that lack of power increases women's chance of illness.

The various points made in previous chapters have important implications for the future of relationships between men and women and the future of women's mental health, for psychiatric researchers and mental health clinicians, and for our understanding of sexual equality. Here I will address each of these in turn.

Future Relationships between Men and Women

As I noted in chapter 5, the argument in this book resembles Engels's argument, in that it links disparities in wealth to patriarchal, or male-dominant, social forms. But whereas Engels thought that patriarchy was designed to provide legitimate heirs, so that wealth could be sequestered within definite families, the argument here implies that concentration of wealth makes patriarchy possible.[1] Only men with strangleholds on resources needed by families are in a position to monopolize women, or to reify their monopoly by treating women as property. Societies in which resources are more evenly distributed afford women greater power, all other things being equal. Wide availability of resources needed by children undermines the basis for men's control of women.

In the last two hundred years, progressive societies have provided more and more of their citizens sufficient resources to care for themselves and their children. For the first time in history, large numbers of common men and women are able to lead decent lives, free from the threat of starvation, disease, and grinding poverty. Industrialization, rising agricultural productivity, scientific progress, and, most important of all, a new respect for the rights of common men and women have each played a part in this transformation. Coincident with wider resource distribution, women's social power has increased proportionately. Although women are still handicapped in comparison with men, they are no longer thought of as property nor are they often sequestered.

Women now have the vote in all developed countries and have even held high offices in some of the democracies. Women are no longer excluded de jure from commerce, professions, or courts of law, and women now exercise some control in marriage and reproduction. Their rights over children are equivalent to the fathers'.

In the future, rising productivity, scientific and technical progress, and egalitarian mores, among other factors that promote the wider distribution of wealth, may provide ordinary people with better living standards and with more security than they have today. If this happens, the material conditions that favor male domination will have disappeared, and relations between men and women will be on a more equal footing. What changes in men's and women's behavior can be expected in light of the models described in chapter 5?

First, since women prefer control of resources to dependency on men, women in the future will choose to work outside the home. As ideological and practical barriers to women's employment drop, women will take full advantage of the resulting opportunities. They may take time off from work to care for young children, but they will not see child rearing as an alternative to paid employment. Not only resource control, but other benefits too, accrue to women who work. Data cited in chapter 3 concerning religious cults suggest that individuals need affiliations with larger-than-family groups. This need is readily related to mutualism, as defined in chapter 5. In any event, women fully involved in their places of work will not be cut off from others, as housewives are today. Women who have stopped working in order to raise their children report being more disturbed by loss of social contacts provided by employment than by the problems intrinsic to raising children.[2] Similar feelings are reported by men and women thrown out of work by economic factors.

Several issues have been raised concerning working women that are especially relevant to the argument of this book. First, a number of authors have asked whether women's innate interests, and consequently work affinities, differ from those of men in such a way as to relegate women to lower status or lower-paying jobs. Even women able to pursue university studies, for example, gravitate toward nontechnical disciplines that lead to less predictable and lower-paying work. Kate Millett, the noted feminist writer, considers these differences cultural: "[Patriarchal] educational institutions, segregated or co-educational, accept a cultural programing toward the generally operative division between 'masculine' and 'feminine' subject matter, assigning the humanities and certain social sciences (at least in their lower or marginal branches) to the female—and science and technology, the professions, business and engineering to the male."[3] The result, as Millett describes it, is that "while knowledge is fragmented even among the male population, collectively they could reconstruct any technological device. But in the absence of males, women's distance from technology today is sufficiently great that it is doubtful that they could replace or repair such machines on any significant scale."[4] Millett's lament may be less accurate today than it was when she wrote these words.

Lionel Tiger and Joseph Shepher, whose study of kibbutzim I cited in chapter 2, represent the viewpoint that these differences are innate.[5] Members of kibbutzim are given job assignments, which for ideological reasons are not expected to be typed according to sex. According to Tiger and Shepher, though, kibbutz women seek out jobs pertaining to food and child care, whereas kibbutz men seek out jobs involving mechanical work in the kibbutz factories. Men are also overrepresented in kibbutz political and administrative roles, apparently because of women's reluctance to take such positions. Referring to the fact that kibbutz job preferences cannot be accounted for by differences in physical strength, Tiger and Shepher conclude that: "women have no personal or social inclination to yield certain service tasks to men, and men are reluctant to yield certain production tasks to women. Even when technological development obviates one of the basic reasons for sexual division of labor, the division remains."[6] In contrast to

Millett, Tiger and Shepher conclude that these preferences, along with others of their findings, may reflect deeply rooted innate behavior patterns differing in the sexes and related to reproduction.

There seems to be no basis for deciding now whether the sexes differ in job affinities for innate reasons, and if so, to what extent they differ, but it does seem likely that whatever innate differences exist are exaggerated by data on current employment patterns. Women encouraged to pursue scientific and technical educations, and who fully expect to support themselves and their children after they finish their schooling, will certainly seek training and pursue careers in these fields more frequently than women of today. It is also important to keep in mind that a major reason that services traditionally performed by women are devalued is precisely because they were performed by women, and not because they are inherently less valuable. Child care and food services, areas dominated in the kibbutz by women, are as essential as factories to the kibbutz economy. In a society with different attitudes from those of our own, statistical differences in types of occupations chosen by men and women might not create invidious gender distinctions.

There is also a great difference between "public mothering," or work with children in a public setting recognized by one's social group, and mothering sequestered in the private home. The former leads to engagement in group life and confers rewards and independence as other jobs do. The latter leads to estrangement, loss of self-esteem, and dependence on one's mate. Kibbutz women who seek job assignments doing public mothering might well balk at the same work in a private setting. Tuula Gordon, a Finnish sociologist, interviewed feminist women in the United States, Britain, and Finland who had become mothers.[7] One of her informants, whose occupational choice was similar to those of women in the kibbutzim, referred to the importance of public mothering in discussing her reaction to having a daughter, Laura:

I had to make decisions about whether I was going back to work. . . . I had actually decided probably not to carry on working . . . and then when this job came up here, which was actually studying mothers' reactions to welfare clinics and child development in the under-ones, it brought together so many aspects of things that I have always been interested in and never been able to do that I applied and the whole thing came together. . . . It was another way of dealing with looking after Laura in a sense, except doing it in a public way and not doing it in a private way. . . . It is important for me in the long term in my relationship with Laura to see myself as more than just a mother to her.[8]

According to Gordon, other women interviewed also discussed public mothering.

Another issue relating to women's employment is whether working women will be handicapped by their desire to spend time with their children. Since women invest a greater proportion of their reproductive potential with each of their children than do men, evolutionary models predict that women, on the average, will be more concerned than men with their children's welfare. According to these models, women should be more willing than men to serve as attachment figures, which means maintaining proximity to and a close eye on children, and sacrificing one's interests in order to render assistance. Insofar as paid employment interferes with care of children, mothers more than fathers might experience some discomfiture. At least in our society, there is abundant evidence that working mothers are troubled in balancing work and children. Even the subjects interviewed by Gordon, who were ideologically committed to being more than mothers, reported great anxieties about their children's welfare when they were at work. The most striking of the findings reported by Tiger and Shepher was that kibbutz women resisted communal child care and had fought kibbutz ideology to care for their children in their homes, in spite of the fact that doing so entailed long hours after their work shifts ended. Kibbutz men, by contrast, were willing to accept completely communal care.

Whatever inherent problems women might face in balancing work and children are greatly compounded by today's working conditions. The modern-day workplace is still geared for men in traditional marriages, with wives who provide child care and manage family emergencies. As men with working wives share more of the burden of child care, and as employers become more dependent on women, the workplace ethos may change to accommodate working parents. More flexible hours, paid maternity and family sickness leave, and child care at work for parents of small children are among the obvious steps that would ease parents' minds and help working mothers in particular.[9] Subsidies for child care would also serve this purpose. Some parents may seek out communal living arrangements, which could provide for child care in place of the nuclear family.[10] Communal living arrangements could also help provide feelings of group solidarity many people are missing in today's society.

Finally, the emphasis modern attachment theory places on the mother-child relationship can be misconstrued to mean that children are harmed if their mothers work rather than caring for them on a full-time basis. For this reason, Tuula Gordon implied that Bowlby, who originated modern-day interest in attachment, purveyed patriarchal mores concerning the place of women.[11] In fact, given the opportunity, children form multiple attachments to adults and to older children, not just to their mothers, and this was probably commonplace in ancestral groups. Women in modern-day preagricultural tribes care for children cooperatively, once they are able to walk. Children form attachments to several women in the tribe, as well as to older youngsters.[12] Communally raised kibbutz children have also grown up normally, without apparent ill effects, and studies generally show no adverse effects of day care in our own society.[13] Having multiple attachment relationships may actually protect children from harm, should their principal attachment figure, who is likely to be the mother, be mentally or physically ill and therefore unavailable, or if desertion or divorce disrupts the family home. Women caring for young children in the private home suffer high rates of depression, which is thought to have severe effects on children's attachment behavior.[14]

Attachment theory does have some implications for the structure of public child care. To encourage children to form subsidiary attachments, child care arrangements should be long term and well staffed by permanent employees, and children of different ages should be cared for together. This type of child care is expensive, but if it seems prohibitive, it is only due to mores that devalue child care because it is done by women.

In chapter 5, I noted that male sexual arousal is rapid, visual, and conditionable to culture-specific signs of female sexual availability. Female sexual arousal is slower and more determined by emotional cues. Rapid male arousal promotes adherence to the male reproductive strategy, which is to maximize sexual access to women, and slower female arousal promotes adherence to the female reproductive strategy, which is to select mates with good genes or who are capable of giving paternal aid. Differences in sexual response between men and women may be determined by early hormone levels. There is evidence, for example, that women exposed in utero to high testosterone levels grow up to have more driven, appetitive sexual needs, contingent on visual stimuli, than do other women.[15] On the other hand, because it can lead to bonds of friendship and reciprocity, advantages can accrue from having sexual intercourse even if it serves no reproductive function. Therefore, insofar as women are able to raise children without paternal assistance, they might be less selective in their sexual activity. If, for example, women were less attentive to potential paternal aid and chose mates more on the basis of their genes, as these are reflected in bodily form and vigor, then their patterns of arousal might be more like the modern-day male's. Helen Fisher, a cultural anthropologist with the American Museum of Natural History, cites cross-cultural studies to show that economically independent women do have sexual appetites similar to men's.[16] According to Fisher, many cultures recognize that women's sexual needs can be as strong as men's.

Patricia Draper and Henry Harpending, whose work on somatization I cited in chapter 3, argued that a contingent cue affecting women's sexual selectivity, and specifically women's tendency to ensure paternal assistance before mating, is whether or not they were raised with their father's aid.[17] Women who were raised without assistance from fathers have thereby learned that children can be raised by mothers alone. Women who were raised with paternal aid believe they need fathers' assistance in order to rear their children. The former group of women will be the less selective. However, the evidence for this theory is weak. In our society, important social factors covary with fathers' presence—for instance, fathers tend to be present in upper- and middle-class families—and these other factors may affect daughters' sexual lives more strongly than fathers per se. In other societies, presence or absence of fathers varies with women's control of resources needed by children. If Draper and Harpending's theory does turn out to be true, today's high divorce rate may cause future women to be sexually less selective and more independent with respect to men.

Whatever its "natural" level, women's sexual selectivity is certainly increased by antisexual mores, and these will further erode as women gain social power. Once women are able to care for themselves and their children, if need be, men will no longer have means to control women's sexual lives. Parents who are confident that their daughters can earn a living and will not be left alone with children they cannot provide for will also be less anxious to indoctrinate their daughters with antisexual mores. Effective contraceptives, which offer protection from pregnancy at disadvantageous times, have probably already changed many parents' attitudes toward their daughters' sexual lives. In many families, rigid opposition to sexual activity has given way to pragmatic advice on possible risks.

Effective methods of birth control also permit women to complete their education and to work at jobs without interruptions because of unwanted pregnancies. Hence, they increase women's control of resources, which may in turn decrease their sexual selectivity, as noted above. Women may also be less selective if they know they cannot become pregnant, but decreased selectivity because of contraception per se may be hard to distinguish from decreased selectivity because of ideological and resource-control factors. Effective methods of birth control were obviously not available in the environment in which human behavior evolved. Hence, women may not have evolved so as to be directly influenced one way or another by newly acquired control over their fertility.

Future increases in women's sexual freedom may lead to increased male interests in uterine kin. Evolutionary models indicate that as so-called paternity certainty—a man's confidence that his nominal mate's children are also his own—drops, male resources that would otherwise be used to aid children are better directed toward uterine kin.[18] "Better," of course, refers only to inclusive fitness, not to moral or other considerations. Uterine kin, such as nieces and nephews born to a matrilineal sister, are definite genetic kin regardless of paternity. In directing aid to uterine kin, men in societies with low paternity certainty ensure that they adhere to a kin-altruistic strategy in their aid to youngsters. There are some modern societies in which paternity certainty is very low indeed. Being hunters, soldiers, or traveling merchants, men in these societies are unable to police their wives' sexuality, as men in the future may be unable to do for different reasons. In these societies, men aid in rearing uterine nephews and nieces. Kinship is matrilineal, and women need not choose their mates for paternal assistance.

Male domestic violence should also greatly diminish as women gain social power. Not needing men for subsistence for themselves or their children, women may not be willing to tolerate male violence. In modern American cities, incidents of domestic violence account for a large proportion of emergency calls to police.[19] These are the tip of the iceberg, since most such incidents currently go unreported. Domestic violence has been implicated as a cause of mental disorders, so decreases in such violence may improve the mental health of society as a whole and of women in particular. In chapter 4, I noted that child molestation, many cases of which are due to abusive fathers or stepfathers, may play a role in disorders dependent on role enactment. Depressives, too, often report having abusive fathers and home lives characterized by domestic violence.[20]

Finally, economically independent future women may expect something other than financial support from their mates. They may expect men to spend time with them and with their children and to contribute to household tasks such as cooking, shopping, cleaning, and household decoration, which are presently held in low esteem because they are done by women. Heretofore powerful mores limited women to household and men to public work. If women participate fully in the public domain, they may expect men to function in the private domain just as they do.

I have already mentioned the question of whether innate affinities for certain activities differ between the sexes in such a way as to lead to gender-related specialization of labor. Data like those gathered by Tiger and Shepher in their study of kibbutz labor patterns suggest that because of innate affinities men may resist performing some private tasks heretofore done by women, especially those tasks related to children. On the other hand, men might just perform these tasks in different ways than women. For example, if Tiger is correct in arguing that men innately like team sports more than women do, then men caring for children may spend more time teaching them sporting skills than women do.[21] Children cared for by both men and women would then be exposed to activities unfamiliar to children cared for by one sex alone. Also, the model of male behavior described in chapter 5 predicts that men will strive to do what women require as a condition of mating. They will even compete with each other in order to do it better, and thus to be more attractive to the opposite sex. Therefore, if women really are serious about demanding male involvement in domestic tasks, men will eventually find themselves wanting to comply.

Of course, domestic tasks will also be considerably eased by a decreased birthrate, which can be expected as women gain social power. Working women with reproductive choices have many fewer children than women who stay at home. In contrast to most populations in historic times, prehistoric populations apparently were stable.[22] Fertility was low and children were carefully nurtured, just as they are today in preagricultural tribes. As women gain social power, fertility is now falling in some industrialized countries, which are said to have undergone a "demographic transition." Women in these countries are bearing very few children, compared to fifty years ago, and in some cases not even enough to maintain existing numbers. Instead they devote their energy, or at least some of it, to nonreproductive activities distinct from their role as mothers.[23]

Japan, for example, is among the most highly industrialized of nations, and there fertility rates have fallen 27 percent in the last quarter century, to levels far below those needed to maintain the population.[24] This might seem advantageous, considering the population density of Japan, but it does foretell problems maintaining the labor pool needed for Japanese industry. Workers are already scarce enough that a number of companies have failed in recent years due to labor shortages. Labor-starved manufacturers have responded by hiring women in ever-larger numbers, so that women now comprise 40 percent of workers. Thus, falling fertility rates have led to women's employment, which undermines male dominance and leads to further declines in fertility rates. When workers are scarce, moreover, unions and other worker organizations become more powerful and wealth more widely distributed than in times of labor excess. Wider distribution of wealth undermines male dominance in the same way as women's employment does.

The Future of Women's Mental Health

Insofar as lack of social power adds to the risk of disorders that are more common in women, future women who exercise the same social power as men should be less likely to develop these illnesses. If women's greater risk is wholly due to their relative lack of social power, depression, anxiety, and the various disorders related to social roles cited in previous chapters may become equally common in future men and women.

Of course, women have already started to gain social power. For the last hundred years, each new generation of women has had more power than the one before. Hence, insofar as powerlessness causes women's increased risk for mental disorders, equalizing trends in the prevalence of these disorders may already be apparent. Four longitudinal studies reviewed by J. M. Murphy of Harvard Medical School indicate that men's and women's risks of depression and anxiety have, in fact, already begun to converge.[25] For example, the Lundby Study in Sweden studied a cohort born between 1908 and 1927 and another cohort born between 1918 and 1937. When they were studied in 1947, women in the first cohort had an incidence of depression eight times as great as the incidence for men. The ratio was even greater when the cohort was restudied in 1957. By contrast, in 1957 and again in 1972, men and women in the second cohort showed nearly identical incidence rates for depressive disorder. The equalization, unfortunately, resulted from rising rates in depression in male subjects, rather than from falling rates in female subjects, but nonetheless the sex difference was clearly disappearing. Other factors may be raising the risk of depression for the whole population. The Midtown Manhattan Study investigated a cohort born between 1895 and 1914 and another born between 1915 and 1934. When they were studied in 1954, women in the first cohort had twice the mental morbidity risk as men in the same cohort. Since self-reported "nervous breakdowns" and "nervousness" were heavily weighted in the classification scheme, acute depressive episodes and anxiety probably accounted for the gender difference in morbidity risk. Twenty years later, women in the second cohort showed lower morbidity risks, which were equivalent to men's. The U.S. National Study showed gender-related differences in psychological distress narrowing for all age groups between 1957 and 1976. The overall difference decreased by 38 percent in these twenty years. Twenty percent of the decrease in gender-related differences could be statistically shown to be caused by greater women's employment outside the home. Finally, the so-called Stirling County Study showed converging risks for aggregated depression and anxiety syndromes between men and women from 1952 to 1970, in a rural area of Canada. The Stirling County Study resembled the Lundby Study in that the convergence, which was most marked in subjects aged forty to sixty-nine, was generally attributed to rising risks in men. Future studies should show increasing equalization of risks for men and women.

Similar observations can be made for illness roles, in spite of the fact that precise data are not available. Cases described in chapter 3 show how nineteenth-century women developed hysteria when faced with pressing problems that they were otherwise powerless to solve. Few women today lack social power to the extent that these hysterics did, so comparable disorders should be rarer today than in the nineteenth century. The comparable disorders still diagnosed today are somatization disorder, which is essentially Briquet's hysteria, and multiple personality disorder. As noted in chapter 3, chronic fatigue syndrome may be the modern guise of neurasthenia, but neurasthenia was not limited to women. Instead, neurasthenia was considered respectable even for very successful men. Somatization disorder occurs in about one percent of American women and is even more rare in upper- and middle-class women.[26] In spite of the recent increase in the number of cases, multiple personality disorder is still distinctly uncommon, even in comparison with somatization disorder.[27] The hysterias, by contrast, were everyday matters for nineteenth-century doctors, even those who treated an upper-class clientele.[28] Hysteric patients, of course, were also depressed and anxious, and depression and anxiety are still common today. However, hysteric patients presented themselves with signs and symptoms not seen today as part of a mood disorder and which are best understood in terms of illness roles. These illness roles are seen less often than they were, despite the fact that mood disorders remain common.

Finally, although eating disorders were common one hundred years ago, the most severe eating disorders have seemingly increased in prevalence, even as women have generally gained social power (see chapter 4). Are eating disorders not really linked to power, or have other factors increased the prevalence of these disorders in spite of overall gains in women's social power? As described in chapter 4, changes in standards of women's ideal weight have certainly fueled the increase in eating disorders today. As some feminist authors have argued, increasingly unrealistic standards of feminine beauty represent a backlash against women's aspirations.[29] More and more unrealistic standards of feminine beauty are a defeat for women, regardless of gains they have made in other arenas. Also, many of the functions served by self-starvation, according to clinicians who specialize in eating disorders, relate to conflicts over women's changing roles.[30] That is, young women today, caught between changing expectations of their behavior, goals, values, and aspirations, sometimes use eating disorders—and consequent medical illnesses—to resolve their conflicts. Hence, the high incidence of eating disorders today may be a transitional, rather than a lasting, phenomenon.

Treatment and Research

Data in chapters 2 through 4 and the models of human behavior described in chapter 5 all point to social power, especially resource control, as a critical factor in mental health and behavior. Yet, trained in schools of thought that emphasize other factors, psychiatrists have not studied the mental health effects of resource control or power. At best they have studied effects of social variables, such as employment and number of young children, which indirectly affect power and resource control. Likewise, in clinical practice, psychiatrists and other practitioners have often been inattentive to issues of social power, which from the present viewpoint are especially important in treating women patients.

What types of studies might show effects of social power and resource control? One especially informative study would assess the extent to which mothers of young children believe they could maintain their own and their children's standard of living in the event of divorce. The viewpoint developed here predicts that such a measure of economic self-confidence would strongly predict risk of depressive disorder. A similar study might measure the effect of such confidence on the attachment needs of agoraphobic women or on the onset of illness-role behaviors. Another study might look at incomes and assets within families. When total family income is statistically controlled, married working women who make as much or more than their husbands should be less prone to illness than married working women who make much less than their husbands. The latter are more dependent on men for useful resources. Women who hold assets independently of their husbands and women living in states that offer better financial protection to divorced mothers should also be healthier, if this view is correct. A third type of study might look at job qualifications. Do women educated in practical fields, which prepare them for high-paying jobs, have lower risks of illness than women with education in other fields? Do women with job training do better than those without?

What kinds of clinical treatments follow from the emphasis placed here on social power? To begin with, if powerlessness contributes to risks of mental disorder, and if traditional women's roles lead to powerlessness, then a clinician treating women might do well to advise them to avoid traditional roles. In many cases, these roles are responsible for women's psychological problems, and in many more, they compound psychological problems resulting from other factors. As shown in chapter 2, unemployed housewife-mothers, who have the least social power, have the highest incidence of depressive disorders. Most agoraphobics are said to be unemployed housewives, perhaps because exposure contingent on employment works to reduce anxiety and avoidant behavior, but also because such women lack perceived social power, as that is defined in this book. The more traditional her marriage, the greater the chance that a woman acting as housewife-mother will have to resort to somatization disorder or other illness roles in order to be heard. Modern-day women with somatization disorder lack power in their families, as the case in chapter 3, from Phillip Slavney, indicates.[31]

In many cases, women come to therapists with conflicts concerning traditional roles. On the one hand they want to be wives and mothers; on the other hand, they want to have full-time careers. In large part, the conflict results from modern-day workplace customs, which were developed for men with wives who stayed at home and which make it unnecessarily difficult for working women to raise children (see chapter 5). In part, however, the conflict results from conflicting values and self-conceptions, which are appropriate on the one side to traditional women's roles and on the other side to roles of working men and women. A law student, S., for instance, became depressed shortly after moving in with her boyfriend. She found herself cleaning the house and doing most of the cooking in spite of the fact that her boyfriend, a businessman, had more time to spare than she had. He expressed no real interest in S.'s school or friends. S.'s mother, a writer, had given up her work when she married S.'s father and had since become bitter and disillusioned. She was more enraged than pleased by S.'s academic success. Discussion of these issues revealed that S. felt trapped. She felt she should sacrifice herself for her future husband and children, as her mother had done many years before—that is, she had internalized her mother's value system—but she wanted to be powerful and autonomous like her father. She moved out of the house and went on a trip to Europe. Her angry boyfriend broke off their relationship, but S.'s mood improved, and she threw herself into her studies. In therapy she discussed ways to have a relationship and eventually children without being trapped in a traditional role. She became more aware of how certain of her values, internalized from her mother, were discrepant with aspirations that she could not give up without risk to her mental health.

Another patient, L., had held a high-paying job in the same company as her fiancé. Because her long hours, as many as sixty per week, were incompatible with marriage and motherhood, L. quit her job to find less stressful work. Two months later, she started to get depressed and, for the first time, to feel anxious with others. Her fiancé seemed hesitant to set a date for marriage. She missed the excitement of her previous job and her many friends at work. She remained severely depressed for several years, when she finally obtained a position like that she had given up, but with more reasonable hours. She no longer felt she had to choose between work and motherhood.

J. dropped out of college in order to marry her husband. After the birth of three children over a five-year span, she began to get depressed and angry with those around her. She began to avoid public places, out of a sense of self-consciousness and fear of appearing ridiculous. She feared losing her temper and harming one of her children. She felt that her life was wasted. Her mood only improved when she returned to school and developed a reputation as a creative artist. Her mother, a compulsive, depressed, and anxious housewife, criticized J. for neglecting housework, and indeed, J.'s house was usually rather filthy, as if J. had chosen to illustrate her new priorities.

Many obvious conflicts related to women's roles are overlooked or misread by clinicians who assume that traditional roles meet women's deepest emotional needs. A clinician with such an assumption might conclude, for example, that S. is fleeing from intimacy, that L. is ambivalent about children (rather than about the one-sided sacrifices that children require in our society), and that J. is narcissistic or having an existential crisis. All of these things might be true, but the viewpoint developed here suggests they are incidental, or perhaps vulnerability factors. The central problem is that traditional women's roles do not meet women's needs for real social power and for participation in the real, economic life of their community. Women today are still pressured to accept such roles, in spite of the fact that alternatives roles have become available. Insofar as traditional gender roles are internalized, women are further handicapped in making healthy choices. The conflict is then intrapsychic, rather than out in the world.

Lack of social power may be even more harmful to women who have other risk factors for mental disorders discussed in the previous chapters. These include women who have strong family histories of depression, anxiety, or illness-role behavior, women who were mistreated as children, or women who fell ill at some earlier time. Pending the kinds of studies discussed above, which might clarify the interactions of risk factors, it seems only prudent to think that women with other risk factors would be especially well advised to avoid additional risk due to powerlessness. Thus, interventions aimed at increasing social power and especially resource control should be considered for this population.

Many women, of course, like traditional roles. Some women enjoy being full-time housewives and mothers, regardless of the disadvantages of that role, and would consequently not welcome advice to have a career. Some of these women belong to traditionally minded communities, such as religious groups, which reward women in certain ways for adhering to traditional roles. To change roles would entail losing a sense of community, as well as specific rewards for taking a woman's role. In chapter 2 I noted that in some cultural settings, traditional roles can even confer power on women, in comparison with the power they could have outside those roles. Women who truly enjoy their traditional roles are perhaps not likely to be mentally ill because of them. They are unlikely, in any event, to perceive themselves as powerless due to the roles they enjoy. Obviously, clinicians must respect patients' diversity, rather than try to fit everyone into a mold.

On the other hand, some women without power, or confidence in their power, feel threatened by change. To protect themselves from the need to change, they sometimes deny the reality of their lives and relationships. For example, women abused by their husbands sometimes make excuses for them and may even blame themselves for provoking violence. Some battered women admit that their husbands are dangerous only after they have been repeatedly injured. Women who really have very little security and who secretly worry about being left high and dry may nonetheless insist that they can rely on their husbands. One woman patient ignored her husband's philandering, or rather tried not to notice it, because she knew that she could not maintain her own and her children's standard of living if she obtained a divorce. Another, who saw marriage as a "shelter from the storm," managed to overlook the fact that her marriage was loveless and that her husband called her names and ridiculed her to others.

However, in being subject to patients' defensive efforts, gender roles are no different from other, more personal issues. Patients have trouble facing many troublesome aspects of their personal lives. Clinicians can only raise issues and then let events in therapy take the course they will. With some skill and with a good deal of luck, some patients will begin to comprehend how traditional roles contributed to their problems. Some will take action based on their new understanding, and others will use their new knowledge in more subtle ways. In either case the clinician's work is to point out factors patients themselves might not notice.

One of the slogans of the feminist movement—"the personal is political"—expresses the view that what appear to be personal problems often have political or sociocultural origins. In general, this brief exploration of evolved human nature, of the battle between the sexes, and of women's psychopathology has pointed us in this direction. Clinicians should stop assuming, however implicitly, that the social forms with which we are familiar manifest the human natures of their actors, or at least of all their actors, and instead should give serious thought to the ways in which these forms fail to meet some needs. While this injunction may be generally useful, and applicable in treating patients of both sexes, it is especially pertinent to women's traditional roles, which are implicated in stripping them of needed social power.

Another point made in previous chapters is that some disorders are really illness roles. This, too, has implications for research and practice. Regarding research, recognition of the importance of illness roles might lead to systematic study of role adoption in psychiatric settings. Data in chapters 3 and 4 indicate that early abuse and lack of present-day power lead to role malleability and that the tendency to adopt roles can be assessed by responsiveness to hypnotic suggestions. Individual cases and cross-cultural studies suggest that illness roles in particular attract those who cannot assert themselves. Could we develop a measure of proneness to illness roles? Illness roles, of course, are really collaborations between clinicians and patients. Thus, researchers might also ask, Why do clinicians encourage patients to take on illness roles? Linda Garfield, a psychiatrist at Stanford University, and I are currently studying therapists who frequently diagnose and treat satanic abuse, in the hope of identifying factors that distinguish these therapists from others.

Clinicians who are aware that some disorders are illness roles are loath to reify them, for fear of harming patients. First, when illness roles are taken too literally, they are likely to be treated with invasive or harmful methods. For example, believing that seizures and other hysterical symptoms resulted from disorders of women's genitals, late-nineteenth-century doctors performed dangerous operations on hysterical patients. Edward Shorter, a medical historian, observed that "nervous disorders" provided the bread and butter for early gynecologists, who started off, modestly enough, with cervical cauterizations and other relatively benign procedures.[32] Some cases of hysteria were attributed to uterine retroversion, which could be corrected with forceful manipulation or pessaries. In 1872, two surgeons unknown to each other—Alfred Hegar, professor of gynecology at the University of Freiburg, and Robert Battey, a practitioner in Rome, Georgia—performed the first oophorectomies (removal of ovaries), for nervous complaints. Because this was before the age of sterile surgery, Hegar's patient died from peritonitis several days after her operation. Battey's patient, a bedridden thirty-year-old, also developed a life-threatening postsurgical infection, but she went on to recover from her nervous disorder. Thereafter, hysterics were "Batteyized," as the procedure was called, up to World War I. By 1895, Robert Edes, a physician at the fifty-bed Adams Nervine Asylum, where Alice James was once treated, reported that twenty-seven recently admitted women had had oophorectomies for their nervous symptoms. According to Shorter, 51 percent of the articles on oophorectomies in the 1889 *Index Catalogue of the Library of the Surgeon-General's Office* concerned mental disorders. By 1907 the comparable figure was still 42 percent. Late-nineteenth-century American mental asylums employed staff gynecologists to operate on hysterics. The "pathology" in the ovaries removed by these physicians was thought to be too subtle to be seen with the eye or microscope.

As Shorter also showed, Richard Francis Burton was sorely misinformed in thinking that clitoridectomies he observed among Arab peoples were exotic enough to write home about. Even as Burton was traveling, clitoridectomies and clitoral cauterizations were being prescribed in Europe for treatment of nervous disorders, including hysteria. Early-nineteenth-century physicians performed these procedures in cases of nymphomania or chronic masturbation, but as the years passed, the indications for these procedures became more diffuse. According to nineteenth-century "reflex" theories of illness, local "irritations" could cause protean symptoms virtually anywhere in the body by activating reflex arcs involving spinal nerves. The male imagination could hardly find a more plausible site of irritation than the female organ analogous to the phallus. Moreover, extirpating the clitoris decreased sexual pleasure and hence increased virtue, without the certain sterility attendant on oophorectomy. Clitoridectomy became sufficiently common that, in 1866, a medical iconoclast wrote to an English journal:

It is well known that during the last few years many London Surgeons have been in the habit of amputating the clitoris for the cure of most of the imaginary ailments to which women are liable. To such an extent has this operation been performed that it will soon be somewhat rare to meet with a woman whose sexual organs are entire. Just as we commonly inquire of our female patients if the bowels act daily . . . so it will soon become necessary to ask, 'Has your clitoris been removed?'[33]

Clitoridectomy, though, was not just an English fashion; it was especially widespread in the United States, too. According to Shorter, right up until World War I *The American Journal of Obstetrics* printed numerous papers in favor of clitoridectomy.

Even when it does not lead to invasive treatments, reification of illness roles distracts attention from real problems inciting illness behavior, and it ratifies illness behavior that is not to the patient's advantage. Since the problems are never solved, and the patient's dysfunctional solutions are legitimized, the patient is likely to end up a chronic invalid of one kind or another. This happened with Alice James, whose illness was described in a previous chapter. As I noted earlier, Alice's problems were probably manifestations of her lack of meaningful opportunities and of the training she had received as a child. In spite of transient improvements induced by her various therapies, Alice spent most of her later years confined to her bed and sofa. In their rush to treat Alice's protean, apparently physical symptoms, which were variably attributed to deranged nerves, spinal asthenia, neurasthenia, or gouty diathesis, none of Alice's doctors considered it worthwhile to study her social setting or her feelings about it. Henry James, being a novelist and a keen observer of human nature, noticed how Alice's symptoms secured Katharine Loring's attention, and he apparently also intuited some of their other functions. For instance, after Alice's death, he wrote to his brother William that in light of her personality, Alice's "tragic health" was her "only solution" to "the practical problem of life."[34] But Alice's doctors would have scoffed at such observations, had they been apprised of them, and, misled by her physicians, Henry himself believed that Alice's illness was real. He never had the effrontery to approach her with his intuitions. Insights like Henry James's would have to wait for Janet, and really for Freud and his followers, to be considered relevant to psychosomatic disorders.

No one today is performing clitoridectomies for nervous complaints or intentionally removing ovaries for psychosomatic disorders. Today, patients with "nervous" complaints only undergo surgery if their imitations of illness are sufficiently skilled that they fool surgeons into thinking they need emergency treatment. Thus, the major risk of reification of illness roles now lies in the second realm: reification draws attention away from real problems even as it ratifies dysfunctional illness roles. The following case history, which may be more flagrant than most but differs from others only in degree, shows how this can happen even when the illness role is mental, not psychosomatic: P., a forty-five-year-old married mother of two, came to the psychiatry clinic of a major medical center with the fear that she had multiple personality disorder. Since her early twenties, she had had numerous undiagnosable somatic complaints, including headaches, but these had not reached the level of somatization disorder, and she had never been seen before in a mental health setting. One month before she presented herself to the psychiatry clinic, she had watched a television movie about a woman with multiple personality disorder. The movie had made her realize that she had been amnesic for periods in her own life and that she did not remember making important decisions. She did not remember her wedding, twenty-five years before, nor the births of her children, now eighteen and fifteen years old. She had clothes in her closet that she did not remember buying. In the subsequent weeks, she had tried to put this realization out of her mind, but she had begun having almost daily migrainous headaches and amnesic periods. She had decided to come to the clinic the week before after "waking up" in a motel with a strange man, with whom she had apparently spent the afternoon. She was terrified that she had caught AIDS or some other venereal disease. She worried about other things she feared she might start doing. When she was a teenager, P. was accused of shoplifting, but she had no memory of it.

P. was the youngest of three siblings and the only daughter in her family. Her mother was a housewife. Her father, who had since died, had been a severe alcoholic. He had been frequently unemployed, so he had spent long stretches of time at home. P. remembered that she and her older siblings had been afraid of their father, who had had a violent temper and had not liked to be disturbed, and she recalled that her eldest brother, now an alcoholic himself, had traded punches with her father on more than one occasion when he became a teenager. After graduating from high school, P. had taken a series of clerical jobs until she had married and had children. Her husband, a plumber with his own small business, was generally kind and considerate, and her two children, both girls, were doing well in school. Neither her husband nor her children had noticed her amnesias or thought her behavior remarkable. Her husband was not aware of her recent infidelity.

At the psychiatry clinic, P. was found to be highly hypnotizable. In a hypnotic trance, two alter personalities quickly emerged. One was an angry, foul-mouthed, teenage "vixen" who claimed to have been the person who arranged for P.'s infidelity. She claimed to have had numerous lovers for many years, but this was the first time she had let P. know what was happening. She knew that P. suspected what was going on, and she wanted to give her a good scare so she would "mind her business." She was thinking of killing P. "to get her out of my hair." The second was devoutly religious. She knew about the first alter's sexual liaisons, and she spent much of her time praying that God would forgive her. She worried about P.'s soul and tried to be nice to people, to make up for P.'s shortcomings. Later, more alters emerged, until there were twenty-three. When P.'s family was involved in her ongoing treatment, they began to meet her alters, who now emerged outside the hypnotic trance. After six months of therapy, a few of P.'s alters admitted that they had been molested by her drunken father. After describing such an experience, one of them tried to kill P. by cutting her wrists with a razor blade. Two other similar gestures followed on revelations of yet more severe abuse.

A review of P.'s case after eight months of treatment led to the realization that little or no effort had been made to obtain information about P.'s marriage or children or her current life. Just as with Alice James, P.'s real situation had not been considered pertinent to her disorder. According to the regnant theory, multiple personality disorder has its roots in childhood, not in current conditions. Thus, P. was thought to have had alter personalities most of her life; she was just unaware of them, as were her closest relatives. Perhaps by stirring up memories of her childhood traumas, the television movie that led to P.'s presentation was thought to have somehow "destabilized" P.'s system of personalities. The destabilized system could not be kept out of P.'s awareness or hidden from those around her.

However, if multiple personality disorder is an illness role, then P.'s current conditions were responsible for her disorder and should not have been neglected by those who purported to treat her. Why did she (unconsciously) decide to adopt an illness role at that particular time? What needs were met by her disorder that would not otherwise have been satisfied? What did specific "alters," such as the teenage vixen, tell us about P.'s feelings about her spouse and daughters? What changes might have been made in P.'s real situation to decrease P.'s need for illness roles, whether multiple personality disorder or psychosomatic illness? How could physicians have engaged P. in real treatment, without ratifying and hardening dysfunctional illness behavior? None of these questions, unfortunately, were ever addressed in P.'s case.

Sexual Equality

Some feminist authors believe that male dominance is wholly a cultural artifact, unrelated to real human nature. It follows from this view that sexual equality would automatically result if male-dominant culture could once be overthrown. Freed from the influence of patriarchal ideologies, the sexes would live in peace. Thus, in Marge Piercy's utopia, men and women hardly make gender distinctions at all.[35] They would no more imagine imposing the will of one sex on the other than they would imagine practicing human sacrifice. Sandra Bem envisions a similar genderless state.[36]

The view of human nature outlined in chapter 5 suggests a different view of the sexually just society. According to this view, women's social power depends on the wide distribution of resources needed by children. In most ecological settings, wide resource distribution, and consequently women's social power, can be undermined by male coalitions. Thus, in most ecological settings, women's social power will have to be defended, if it is to last. It is not enough to wipe clean the patriarchal slate; active safeguards are needed to keep it from being rewritten. Equality is a lull in the battle between the sexes, more akin to an armistice than to a real peace.

The argument of chapter 5 implies that a commitment to women's social power entails a commitment to economic productivity and equality. Women cannot become and remain powerful in a society with widespread poverty, in which many people lack the resources they need. This is not to say, as Lenin did, that women's issues cannot be separated from economic issues; it is only to say that for a society to be just to women, it also has to be able to meet its needs and it has to be economically just. Some feminists believe that American women have recently lost ground due to a backlash against their earlier victories.[37] Insofar as they are correct, it may not be merely coincidence that in the United States, the distribution of wealth is more unequal today than it was twenty years ago and that more people today seem to be threatened with poverty. Disproportionately many of the poverty-stricken are single mothers living with their children.

Notes

Notes to Chapter 1

1. In general, I will employ modern diagnostic terms, such as those defined in the American Psychiatric Association's *Diagnostic and Statistical Manual of Mental Disorders,* 3d ed., rev. (Washington, DC: American Psychiatric Association, 1987), but in discussing disorders that are mainly of historical interest, such as the various forms of hysteria, I will use terms like "hysteria," which are not in current usage. For the purposes of this book, the latter terms have sufficiently specific historical referents so as to be clear, regardless of the fact that they were not and are not well defined operationally. "Late luteal phase dysphoric disorder," the unfortunate current alternative to "premenstrual syndrome," is not used here for fear that many readers—unfamiliar with the American Psychiatric Association nomenclature—would not know what it refers to. Certain disorders, such as premenstrual syndrome and postpartum depression, are by definition limited to women, but these are peripheral to the theme of this study, which addresses disorders that can occur in either sex. Some abnormal personalities, or "Axis II" disorders, have also been said to be more common in women, but these will not be discussed at all. Abnormal

personality types are readily confused with gender roles and stereotypes; hence, their validity in this context is problematic. No one can say with confidence how their real incidence varies between the sexes. See, for example, M. Kaplan, "A woman's view of DSM-III," *American Psychologist* 38 (1983): 786, and P. Chodoff, "Hysteria and women," *American Journal of Psychiatry* 139 (1982): 545.

2. The history of grand hysteria in the Salpêtrière is found in G. F. Drinka, *The Birth of Neurosis: Myth, Malady, and the Victorians* (New York: Simon and Schuster, 1984).

3. B. Friedan, *The Feminine Mystique* (New York: W. W. Norton, 1963).

4. I will not address the issue of suicide in this book. First, although women attempt suicide, or make suicide gestures, more frequently than do men, completed suicides are much more common in men than in women. Eli Robins estimates that male suicides are three times as common as female suicides in the United States. Second, a considerable number of patients who commit suicide are depressed bipolars, rather than simply depressives, or they are alcoholics. In contrast to depression, bipolar affective disorder and alcoholism tend to occur in men at least as often as in women. Finally, insofar as the chance of suicide is affected by access to weapons and familiarity with them, suicide rates measure factors other than rates of illness. See E. Robins, "Suicide," in *Comprehensive Textbook of Psychiatry*, 4th ed., edited by H. I. Kaplan and B. J. Sadock (Baltimore: Williams and Wilkins, 1985). Some observers have noted that professional women, especially physicians and dentists, have suicide rates comparable to those of professional males and thus much higher than those of women in general. See, for example, C. G. Stefansson and S. Wicks, "Health care occupations and suicide in Sweden, 1961–1986," *Social Psychiatry and Psychiatric Epidemiology* 26 (1991): 259. This may seem to militate against the argument made in later chapters—that women's mental health is improved by their having professions—but such a conclusion would be premature. The base rates of mental disorders other than simply depression, such as bipolar disorder, have not been established in professional populations. Also, many of the women now active in such professions entered them many years ago, when women were penalized for pursuing ambitious careers. Hence, these individuals are highly self-selected and have suffered from disadvantages adventitious to professional work per se. For example, some of them may have been forced to forgo marriage

and children in order to have a career. Finally, health care professionals in particular have at their disposal a wide variety of lethal agents, and they are subject to subtle pressures against nonlethal self-injuries. After all, what could cast greater doubt on a physician's competence than a failed suicide attempt? On a related theme, Durkheim found that children decreased the risk of suicide among married women. See E. Durkheim, *Suicide* (London: Routledge and Kegan Paul, 1897). Georg Høyer and Eiliv Lund recently used Norwegian census data to confirm Durkheim's findings. The age-adjusted relative risk of suicide among married women declined as a linear function of the number of children they had borne in marriage. The lowest relative suicide rates were found in married women with six or more children. See G. Høyer and E. Lund, "Suicide among women related to number of children in marriage," *Archives of General Pyschiatry* 50 (1993): 134. In a later chapter, I cite evidence that women's risk of depression is increased by having young children at home. Once again, the apparent discrepancy between the suicide data and the data on depression—and Høyer and Lund's finding that never-married women had the highest suicide rate of all—may be due to women with diagnoses other than uncomplicated depression. For example, bipolar patients comprise a substantial proportion of those individuals at high risk for suicide. The differential assortment of bipolar women into the different marriage and parity groups could have accounted in part for Høyer and Lund's findings. Scandinavian studies found that bipolar individuals were less likely to be married than normal persons and were more likely to be divorced. Divorce, of course, militates against bearing large numbers of children in marriage. See M. M. Weissman and J. H. Boyd, "Affective disorders: Epidemiology," in *Comprehensive Textbook of Psychiatry,* 4th ed., edited by H. I. Kaplan and B. J. Sadock. Similar considerations apply to alcoholism, another major risk factor for suicide, and to schizophrenia.

5. J. B. Miller, *Toward a New Psychology of Women* (New York: Beacon Press, 1976).

6. For an example of how feminist authors have developed these themes, see J. Worell and P. Remer, *Feminist Perspectives in Therapy: An Empowerment Model for Women* (New York: John Wiley, 1992).

7. See, for example, S. Arieti and J. Bemporad, *Severe and Mild Depression: The Psychotherapeutic Approach* (New York: Basic Books, 1978); S. Arieti and J. Bemporad, "The psychological organization of depression," *American Journal of Psychiatry* 137 (1980): 1360. See also

M. M. Weissman and G. L. Klerman, "Sex differences and the epidemiology of depression," *Archives of General Psychiatry* 34 (1977): 98.

8. Research is needed to clarify how causal factors interact in depression. Brown and Harris made an early start in this direction by showing that early parental loss interacted with later premarital pregnancy to increase the risk of depressive disorder in women. See G. W. Brown and T. O. Harris, *The Social Origins of Depression: A Study of Psychiatric Disorder in Women* (London: Tavistock, 1978). More recently, Kendler and colleagues report an analysis of causal interactions responsible for depression in women. See K. S. Kendler, R. C. Kessler, M. C. Neale, et al., "The prediction of major depression in women: Toward an integrated etiologic model," *American Journal of Psychiatry* 150 (1993): 1139. Kendler and colleagues show how genetic and psychosocial factors might interact to increase the risk of depressive episodes. As I note in chapter 2, however, Kendler found no evidence for an effect of enduring environmental factors, or of environmental factors shared by twins. His findings are therefore at odds with much of the relevant literature, and they are also incompatible with the argument made here.

9. R. Morgan, *The Demon Lover: On the Sexuality of Terrorism* (New York: W. W. Norton, 1989), 336.

10. G. Lerner, *The Creation of Patriarchy* (Oxford: Oxford University Press, 1986).

11. C. F. Epstein, *Deceptive Distinctions: Sex, Gender, and the Social Order* (New Haven, CT: Yale University Press, 1988), 48.

12. S. L. Bem, *The Lenses of Gender: Transforming the Debate on Sexual Inequality* (New Haven, CT: Yale University Press, 1993).

13. M. Atwood, *The Handmaid's Tale* (New York: Ballantine Books, 1985).

14. Readers interested in the "level of selection" debate in evolutionary theory are referred to R. N. Brandon and R. M. Burian, eds., *Genes, Organisms, Populations: Controversies over the Units of Selection* (Cambridge, MA: MIT Press, 1984).

15. B. Friedan, *The Feminine Mystique.*

16. J. Ussher, *Women's Madness: Misogyny or Mental Illness?* (Amherst: University of Massachusetts Press, 1991).

17. P. Chesler, *Women and Madness* (New York: Harcourt Brace Jovanovich, 1989).

18. Ibid., 10.

19. M. Piercy, *Woman on the Edge of Time* (New York: Fawcett Crest, 1976).

20. M. Piercy, *Small Changes* (New York: Fawcett Crest, 1973), 506.

21. M. French, *The Women's Room* (New York: Ballantine Books, 1977).

22. K. Millett, *The Loony-Bin Trip* (New York: Simon and Schuster, 1990).

23. M. Daly, *Gyn/Ecology: The Metaethics of Radical Feminism* (London: Women's Press, 1979).

24. The political implications of the view that human nature is a tabula rasa are mentioned in B. Wenegrat, *Sociobiological Psychiatry: Normal Behavior and Psychopathology* (Lexington, MA.: Lexington Books, 1990). As I noted there, it is not entirely coincidental that psychologists and psychiatrists trained in an extreme social constructionist view of human nature were enlisted by the authorities to suppress political dissent in the late Soviet Union. Insofar as personality is wholly a social construction, the dissenter is by definition not only politically deviant, but mentally deviant too.

Notes to Chapter 2

1. S. Nolen-Hoeksema, "Sex differences in unipolar depression: Evidence and theory," *Psychological Bulletin* 101 (1987): 259.

2. Ibid.; M. M. Weissman and J. H. Boyd, "Affective disorders: Epidemiology," in *Comprehensive Textbook of Psychiatry,* 4th ed., edited by H. I. Kaplan and B. J. Sadock (Baltimore: Williams and Wilkins, 1985).

3. See R. S. Stangler and A. M. Printz, "DSM-III: Psychiatric diagnosis in a university population," *American Journal of Psychiatry* 137 (1980): 937.

4. See J. A. Egeland and A. M. Hostetter, "Amish study, I: Affective disorders among the Amish," *American Journal of Psychiatry* 140 (1983): 56.

5. See C. L. Hammen and C. A. Padesky, "Sex differences in the expression of depressive responses on the Beck Depression Inventory," *Journal of Abnormal Psychology* 86 (1977): 609.

6. J. Ussher, *Women's Madness: Misogyny or Mental Illness?* (Amherst: University of Massachusetts Press, 1991).

7. P. E. Bebbington, C. Tennant, and J. Hurry, "Adversity in groups

with an increased risk of minor affective disorder," *British Journal of Psychiatry* 158 (1991): 33.

8. See S. E. Bryson and D. J. Pilon, "Sex differences in depression and the method of administering the Beck Depression Inventory," *Journal of Clinical Psychology* 40 (1984): 529; D. A. King and A. M. Buchwald, "Sex differences in subclinical depression: Administration of the Beck Depression Inventory in public and private disclosure situations," *Journal of Personality and Social Psychology* 42 (1982): 963.

9. J. A. Egeland and A. M. Hostetter, "Amish study, I: Affective disorders among the Amish."

10. Overviews of Freud's and later psychoanalysts' views of women can be found in N. J. Chodorow, *Feminism and Psychoanalytic Theory* (New Haven: Yale University Press, 1989), and in E. Young-Bruehl, introduction to *Freud on Women: A Reader,* edited by E. Young-Bruehl (New York: W. W. Norton, 1990).

11. See C. F. Epstein, *Deceptive Distinctions: Sex, Gender, and the Social Order* (New Haven, CT: Yale University Press, 1988).

12. See, for example, J. B. Miller, *Toward a New Psychology of Women* (New York: Beacon Press, 1976); M. Scarf, *Unfinished Business: Pressure Points in the Lives of Women* (New York: Ballantine Books, 1980).

13. See S. Nolen-Hoeksema, "Sex differences in unipolar depression: Evidence and theory."

14. K. S. Kendler, M. C. Neale, R. C. Kessler, et al., "A population-based twin study of major depression in women: The impact of varying definitions of illness," *Archives of General Psychiatry* 49 (1992): 257; K. S. Kendler, R. C. Kessler, M. C. Neale, et al., "The prediction of major depression in women: Toward an integrated etiologic model," *American Journal of Psychiatry* 150 (1993): 1139; K. S. Kendler, M. C. Neale, R. C. Kessler, et al., "A longitudinal twin study of 1-year prevalence of major depression in women," *Archives of General Psychiatry* 50 (1993): 843; K. S. Kendler, M. C. Neale, R. C. Kessler, et al., "A longitudinal twin study of personality and major depression in women," *Archives of General Psychiatry* 50 (1993): 853; K. S. Kendler, M. C. Neale, R. C. Kessler, et al., "The lifetime history of major depression in women: Reliability of diagnosis and heritability," *Archives of General Psychiatry* 50 (1993): 863.

15. K. H. Bourdon, J. H. Boyd, D. S. Rae, et al., "Gender differences

in phobias: Results of the ECA Community Survey," *Journal of Anxiety Disorders* 2 (1988): 227; O. G. Cameron and E. Hill, "Women and Anxiety," *Psychiatric Clinics of North America* 12, no. 1 (1989): 175; R. M. Doctor, "Major results of a large-scale pretreatment survey of agoraphobics," in *Phobia: A Comprehensive Summary of Modern Treatments,* edited by R. L. Dupont (New York: Brunner/Mazel, 1982); W. W. Eaton and P. M. Keyl, "Risk factors for the onset of Diagnostic Interview Schedule/DSM-III agoraphobia in a prospective, population-based study," *Archives of General Psychiatry* 47 (1990): 819; T. P. S. Iei, K. Wanstall, and L. Evans, "Sex differences in panic disorder with agoraphobia," *Journal of Anxiety Disorders* 4 (1990): 317; M. M. Weissman and K. R. Merikangas, "The epidemiology of anxiety and panic disorders: An update," *Journal of Clinical Psychiatry* 47, no. 6 suppl. (1986): 11.

16. K. H. Bourdon, J. H. Boyd, D. S. Rae, et al., "Gender differences in phobias: Results of the ECA Community Survey."

17. M. Raskin, H. V. S. Peeke, W. Dickman, et al., "Panic and generalized anxiety disorders: Developmental antecedents and precipitants," *Archives of General Psychiatry* 39 (1982): 687.

18. A. Breier, D. S. Charney, and G. R. Heninger, "Major depression in patients with agoraphobia and panic disorder," *Archives of General Psychiatry* 41 (1984): 1129.

19. Much of the relevant literature is reviewed in A. Breier, D. S. Charney, and G. R. Heninger, "The diagnostic validity of anxiety disorders and their relationship to depressive illness," *American Journal of Psychiatry* 142 (1985): 787.

20. D. L. Chambless, "The relationship of severity of agoraphobia to associated psychopathology," *Behavior Research and Therapy* 23 (1985): 305.

21. K. Schapira, T. A. Kerr, and M. Roth, "Phobias and affective illness," *British Journal of Psychiatry* 117 (1970): 25.

22. R. C. Bowen and J. Kohout, "The relationship between agoraphobia and primary affective disorders," *Canadian Journal of Psychiatry* 24 (1979): 317.

23. D. J. Munjack and H. B. Moss, "Affective disorder and alcoholism in families of agoraphobics," *Archives of General Psychiatry* 38 (1981): 869.

24. R. C. Bowen and J. Kohout, "The relationship between agoraphobia and primary affective disorders."

25. J. F. Leckman, M. M. Weissman, K. R. Merikangas, et al., "Panic disorder increases risk of major depression, alcoholism, panic, and phobic disorders in affectively ill families," *Archives of General Psychiatry* 40 (1983): 1055.

26. A. Breier, D. S. Charney, and G. R. Heninger, "The diagnostic validity of anxiety disorders and their relationship to depressive illness."

27. A number of authors, for instance, have tried to relate anxiety to physiological changes women experience during the menstrual cycle. See, for example, M. B. Stein, P. J. Schmidt, D. R. Rubinow, et al., "Panic disorder and the menstrual cycle: Panic disorder patients, healthy control subjects, and patients with premenstrual syndrome," *American Journal of Psychiatry* 146 (1989): 1299; J. Gómez-Amor, J. M. Martínez-Selva, F. Román, et al., "Electrodermal activity, hormonal levels, and subjective experience during the menstrual cycle," *Biological Psychiatry* 30 (1990): 125.

28. K. S. Kendler, M. C. Neale, R. C. Kessler, et al., "Generalized anxiety disorder in women: A population-based twin study," *Archives of General Psychiatry* 49 (1992): 267; K. S. Kendler, M. C. Neale, R. C. Kessler, et al., "The genetic epidemiology of phobias in women: The interrelationship of agoraphobia, social phobia, situational phobia, and simple phobia," *Archives of General Psychiatry* 49 (1992): 273.

29. For example, see S. Arieti and J. Bemporad, *Severe and Mild Depression: The Psychotherapeutic Approach* (New York: Basic Books, 1978); S. Arieti and J. Bemporad, "The psychological organization of depression," *American Journal of Psychiatry* 137 (1980): 1360; G. L. Klerman, M. M. Weissman, B. J. Rounsaville, and E. S. Chevron, *Interpersonal Psychotherapy of Depression* (New York: Basic Books, 1984); M. M. Weissman and G. L. Klerman, "Sex differences and the epidemiology of depression," *Archives of General Psychiatry* 34 (1977): 98.

30. For the argument as it applies to humans, see J. Bowlby, *Attachment and Loss,* vols. 1, 2, and 3 (New York: Basic Books, 1969, 1973, 1980). For data on nonhuman primates, see W. T. McKinney, "Separation and depression: Biological markers," in *The Psychobiology of Attachment,* edited by M. Reite and T. Field (New York: Academic Press, 1985); W. T. McKinney, *Models of Mental Disorders: A New Comparative Psychiatry* (New York: Plenum, 1988).

31. J. Bowlby, *Attachment and Loss,* vol. 1.

32. Readers interested in the effects of parental loss, or parenting

styles, on the risks of psychopathology are referred to H. S. Akiskal and W. T. McKinney, "Overview of recent research in depression: Integration of ten conceptual models into a comprehensive clinical frame," *Archives of General Psychiatry* 32 (1975): 285; J. Birtchnell, "Depression and family relationships: A study of young, married women on a London housing estate," *British Journal of Psychiatry* 153 (1988): 758; G. W. Brown, "Early loss and depression," in *The Place of Attachment in Human Behavior,* edited by C. M. Parkes and J. Stevenson-Hinde (New York: Basic Books, 1982); G. W. Brown and T. O. Harris, *The Social Origins of Depression: A Study of Psychiatric Disorder in Women* (London: Tavistock, 1978); T. Crook and J. Eliot, "Parental death during childhood and adult depression: A critical review of the literature," *Psychological Bulletin* 87 (1980): 252; I. H. Gotlib, J. H. Mount, N. I. Cordy, et al., "Depression and perceptions of early parenting: A longitudinal investigation," *British Journal of Psychiatry* 152 (1988): 24; C. Lloyd, "Life events and depressive disorder reviewed," *Archives of General Psychiatry* 37 (1980): 529; G. Parker, "Parental characteristics in relation to depressive disorders," *British Journal of Psychiatry* 134 (1979): 138; G. Parker, "Parental reports of depressives: An investigation of several explanations," *Journal of Affective Disorder* 3 (1981): 131; G. Parker, "Parental 'affectionless control' as an antecedent to adult depression: A risk factor delineated," *Archives of General Psychiatry* 40 (1983): 956; B. Pfohl, D. D. Stangl, and M. T. Tsuang, "The association between early parental loss and diagnosis in the Iowa 500," *Archives of General Psychiatry* 40 (1983): 965; T. L. Rosenthal, H. S. Akiskal, A. Scott-Strauss, et al., "Familial and developmental factors in characterological depressions," *Journal of Affective Disorders* 3 (1981): 183; C. Tennant, P. Bebbington, and J. Hurry, "Parental death in childhood and risk of adult depressive disorders: A review," in *Psychological Medicine* 10 (1980): 289; C. Tennant, A. Smith, P. Bebbington, et al., "Parental loss in childhood," *Archives of General Psychiatry* 38 (1981): 309. See also J. Bowlby, *Attachment and Loss,* vols. 1, 2, and 3; I. Bretherton and E. Waters, eds., *Growing Points of Attachment Theory and Research,* Monographs of the Society for Research in Child Development, vol. 50, nos. 1–2 (Chicago: University of Chicago Press, 1985); C. M. Parkes and J. Stevenson-Hinde, eds., *The Place of Attachment in Human Behavior.*

33. J. Bowlby, *Attachment and Loss,* vols. 1, 2, and 3. Much of the research pertinent to this issue has been performed using the Ainsworth

Strange Situation Test, in which the young child is left by its mother in a strange playroom, with a stranger present. Originally designed to measure behavioral inhibition in the mother's absence, which is thought to reflect separation anxiety, the Strange Situation Test has been used primarily to study responses upon reunion. Some children show pleasure at the mother's return, but others show mostly angry or avoidant responses. Behaviors upon reunion are believed to reflect stable and general attachment styles, which are currently being studied as possible precursors of adult psychopathology. See, for example, M. D. Ainsworth, "Attachment: Retrospect and prospect," in *The Place of Attachment in Human Behavior*, edited by C. M. Parkes and J. Stevenson-Hinde; M. D. Ainsworth, M. C. Blehar, E. Waters, et al., *Patterns of Attachment: A Psychological Study of the Strange Situation* (Hillsdale, NJ: Lawrence Erlbaum Associates, 1978); I. Bretherton, "Attachment theory: Retrospect and prospect," in *Growing Points of Attachment Theory and Research*, edited by I. Bretherton and E. Waters.

34. S. F. Maier, M. E. P. Seligman, and R. L. Solomon, "Pavlovian fear conditioning and learned helplessness," in *Punishment and Aversive Behavior*, edited by B. A. Campbell and R. A. Church (New York: Appleton-Century-Crofts, 1969); M. E. P. Seligman, *Helplessness: On Depression, Development, and Death* (San Francisco: Freeman, 1975).

35. L. Y. Abramson, M. E. P. Seligman, and J. D. Teasdale, "Learned helplessness in humans: Critique and reformulation," *Journal of Abnormal Psychology* 87 (1978): 49; C. Peterson and M. E. P. Seligman, "Causal explanations as a risk factor for depression," *Psychological Review* 91 (1984): 347.

36. L. B. Alloy and L. Y. Abramson, "Depressive realism: Four theoretical perspectives," in *Cognitive Processes in Depression*, edited by L. B. Alloy (New York: Guilford Press, 1988); C. Hammen, "Depression and personal cognitions about personal stressful life events," in *Cognitive Processes in Depression*, edited by L. B. Alloy; L. P. Rehm, "Self-management and cognitive processes in depression," in *Cognitive Processes in Depression*, edited by L. B. Alloy.

37. See, for example, A. T. Beck, "Cognitive models of depression," *Journal of Cognitive Psychotherapy* 1 (1987): 5; I. M. Blackburn and K. Davidson, *Cognitive Therapy for Depression and Anxiety* (London: Blackwell, 1990); D. A. Clark and A. T. Beck, "Cognitive theory and therapy of anxiety and depression," in *Anxiety and Depression: Distinc-*

tive and Overlapping Features, edited by P. C. Kendall, and D. Watson (New York: Academic Press, 1989); R. E. McMullin, *Handbook of Cognitive Therapy Techniques* (New York: W. W. Norton, 1986).

38. See J. Price, "Hypothesis: The dominance hierarchy and the evolution of mental illness," *Lancet* 2 (1967): 243; J. Price, "The ritualization of agonistic behaviour as a determinant of variation along the neuroticism/stability dimension of personality," *Proceedings of the Royal Society of Medicine* 62 (1969): 1107; J. Price, "Genetic and phylogenetic aspects of mood variation," *International Journal of Mental Health* 1 (1972): 124; J. Price and L. Sloman, "The evolutionary model of psychiatric disorder," *Archives of General Psychiatry* 41 (1984): 211; R. Gardner, Jr., "Mechanisms in manic-depressive disorder," *Archives of General Psychiatry* 39 (1982): 1436; L. Sloman, "Intrafamilial struggles for power: An ethological perspective," *International Journal of Family Psychiatry* 2 (1981): 13; L. Sloman, "Inclusive fitness, altruism, and adaptation," *Canadian Journal of Psychiatry* 28 (1983): 18; L. Sloman, M. Konstantareas, and D. W. Dunham, "The adaptive role of maladaptive neurosis," *Biological Psychiatry* 14 (1979): 961.

39. Human dominance is discussed in I. Eibl-Eibesfeldt, *Human Ethology* (New York: Aldine de Gruyter, 1989). See also S. L. Ellyson and J. F. Dovidio, eds., *Power, Dominance, and Nonverbal Behavior* (New York: Springer-Verlag, 1985). Judgments of relative power are discussed in G. A. Parker, "Assessment strategy and the evolution of fighting behaviour," *Journal of Theoretical Biology* 47 (1974): 223, and in J. Maynard Smith, *Evolution and the Theory of Games* (Cambridge: Cambridge University Press, 1982).

40. P. Gilbert, *Depression: The Evolution of Powerlessness* (New York: Guilford Press, 1992).

41. See, for example, J. Bowlby, *Attachment and Loss,* vol. 2. A particularly important version of this argument, based in part on pharmacological response patterns, was presented by Donald Klein. See, for example, D. Klein, "Anxiety reconceptualized: Early experience with imipramine and anxiety," *Comprehensive Psychiatry* 21 (1980): 411.

42. See, for example, M. D. Ainsworth, "Attachment: Retrospect and prospect"; M. D. Ainsworth, M. C. Blehar, E. Waters, et al., *Patterns of Attachment: A Psychological Study of the Strange Situation;* M. D. Ainsworth and B. A. Wittig, "Attachment and the exploratory behavior of one-year-olds in a strange situation," in *Determinants of Infant Behav-*

iour, vol. 4, edited by B. M. Foss (London: Methuen, 1969); I. Bretherton, "Atttachment theory: Retrospect and prospect."

43. W. W. Eaton and P. M. Keyl, "Risk factors for the onset of Diagnostic Interview Schedule/DSM-III agoraphobia in a prospective, population-based study."

44. See, for example, W. A. Arrindell, P. M. Emmelkamp, A. Monsma, et al., "Perceived parental rearing practices in phobic disorders," *British Journal of Psychiatry* 143 (1983): 183; D. Buglass, J. Clarke, A. S. Henderson, et al., "A study of agoraphobic housewives," *Psychological Medicine* 7 (1977): 73; G. Parker, "Reported parental characteristics of agoraphobics and social phobics," *British Journal of Psychiatry* 135 (1979): 555; B. A. Thyer, R. M. Nesse, O. G. Cameron, et al., "Agoraphobia: A test of the separation anxiety hypothesis," *Behavior Research and Therapy* 23 (1985): 75.

45. M. E. P. Seligman, *Helplessness: On Depression, Development, and Death*.

46. For overviews of self-efficacy, see A. Bandura, "Self-efficacy: Toward a unifying theory of behavioral change," *Psychological Review* 84 (1977): 191; A. Bandura, *Social Foundations of Thought and Action: A Social Cognitive Theory* (Englewood Cliffs, NJ: Prentice-Hall, 1986); A. Bandura, "Self-efficacy conception of anxiety," *Anxiety Research* 1 (1988): 77; A. Bandura, "Perceived self-efficacy: Exercise of control through self-belief," in *Annual Series of European Research in Behavior Therapy*, vol. 2, edited by J. P. Dauwalder, M. Perrez, and V. Hobi (Lisse, Netherlands: Swets and Zeitlinger, 1988); A. Bandura, N. E. Adams, and J. Beyer, "Cognitive processes mediating behavioral change," *Journal of Personality and Social Psychology* 35 (1977): 125.

47. See, for example, C. F. Epstein, *Deceptive Distinctions: Sex, Gender, and the Social Order*, 48; S. Faludi, *Backlash: The Undeclared War against American Women* (New York: Crown Publishers, 1991); B. Friedan, *The Feminine Mystique* (New York: W. W. Norton, 1963); G. Lerner, *The Creation of Patriarchy* (Oxford: Oxford University Press, 1986).

48. See E. Chesler, *Woman of Valor: Margaret Sanger and the Birth Control Movement in America* (New York: Simon and Schuster, 1992); Elizabeth Badinter, *The Unopposite Sex: The End of the Gender Battle*, trans. B. Wright (New York: Harper and Row, 1989) also discussed this issue. Badinter observed that "When women first won the right to

contraception, men immediately lost all control over women's sexuality" (139).

49. B. R. Bergman, *The Economic Emergence of Women* (New York: Basic Books, 1986).

50. See, for example, C. Dweck, W. Davidson, S. Nelson, et al., "Sex differences in learned helplessness: II. The contingencies of evaluative feedback in the classroom" and "III. An experimental analysis," *Developmental Psychology* 14 (1978): 268; J. E. Parsons, C. Kaczala, and J. Meece, "Socialization of achievement attitudes and beliefs: Classroom influences," *Child Development* 53 (1982): 322; B. Sandler, *Project on the Education and Status of Women* (Washington, DC: U.S. Government Printing Office, 1982); L. A. Serbin, K. D. O'Leary, R. N. Kent, et al., "A comparison of teacher response to the preacademic and problem behavior of boys and girls," *Child Development* 44 (1973): 796.

51. See, for example, J. Worell and P. Remer, *Feminist Perspectives in Therapy: An Empowerment Model for Women* (New York: John Wiley, 1992).

52. B. B. Smuts, "Male aggression against women: An evolutionary perspective," *Human Nature* 3 (1992): 1. Marvin Harris's theory of male domination in warlike societies, which is discussed in chapter 5, dovetails closely with Smuts's argument. See M. Harris, "The evolution of human gender hierarchies: A trial formulation," in *Sex and Gender Hierarchies,* edited by B. D. Miller (Cambridge: Cambridge University Press, 1993).

53. For data on the prevalence of rape, see, for example, M. P. Koss, "The hidden rape victim: Personality, attitudinal, and situational characteristics," *Psychology of Women Quarterly* 9 (1985): 193; D. E. H. Russell and N. Howell, "The prevalence of rape in the United States revisited," *Signs* 8 (1983): 688. For data on violence in marriage, see, for example, G. Levinger, "Sources of marital dissatisfaction among applicants for divorce," *American Journal of Orthopsychiatry* 36 (1966): 803; M. A. Straus, "Wife beating: How common and why?" *Victimology* 2 (1978): 443.

54. For data on the sequelae of rape, see, for example, E. Frank and B. P. Anderson, "Psychiatric disorders in rape victims: Past history and current symptomatology," *Comprehensive Psychiatry* 28 (1987): 77; L. H. Gise and P. Paddison, "Rape, sexual abuse, and its victims," *Psychiatric Clinics of North America* 11, no. 4 (1988): 629; R. Janoff-Bulman, "The aftermath of victimization: Rebuilding shattered assumptions," in

Trauma and Its Wake: The Study and Treatment of Post-Traumatic Stress Disorder, edited by C. R. Figley (New York: Brunner/Mazel, 1985); D. G. Kilpatrick, P. A. Resick, and L. J. Veronen, "Effects of a rape experience: A longitudinal study," *Journal of Social Issues* 37 (1981): 105; D. G. Kilpatrick, L. J. Veronen, and C. L. Best, "Factors predicting psychological distress among rape victims," in *Trauma and Its Wake: The Study and Treatment of Post-Traumatic Stress Disorder,* edited by C. R. Figley; M. P. Koss and B. R. Burkhart, "A conceptual analysis of rape victimization: Long-term effects and implications for treatment," *Psychology of Women Quarterly* 13 (1989): 27; C. B. Meyer and S. E. Taylor, "Adjustment to rape," *Journal of Personality and Social Psychology* 50 (1986): 1226; R. Moscarello, "Psychological management of victims of sexual assault," *Canadian Journal of Psychiatry* 35 (1990): 25.

55. For instance, male crime was a major theme in *The Women's Room.* The protagonist of this novel dropped out of college and got married after barely escaping rape while socializing with male students. Another female character dropped out of college after being raped on the street by a man who was later sentenced to six months in jail. See M. French, *The Women's Room* (New York: Ballantine Books, 1977).

56. E. M. Ozer and A. Bandura, "Mechanisms governing empowerment effects: A self-efficacy analysis," *Journal of Personality and Social Psychology* 58 (1990): 472.

57. See F. S. Coles, "Forced to quit: Sexual harassment complaints and agency response," *Sex Roles* 14 (1986): 81. Susan Faludi *(Backlash: The Undeclared War against American Women)* also discusses harassment.

58. B. R. Bergman, *The Economic Emergence of Women.* See also M. N. Ozawa, ed., *Women's Life Cycle and Economic Insecurity: Problems and Proposals* (New York: Praeger, 1989).

59. V. R. Fuchs, *Women's Quest for Economic Equality* (Cambridge, MA: Harvard University Press, 1988).

60. Ibid., 147.

61. See, for example, G. W. Brown and T. O. Harris, *The Social Origins of Depression: A Study of Psychiatric Disorder in Women;* B. P. Dohrenwend and B. S. Dohrenwend, *Social Status and Psychological Disorder: A Causal Inquiry* (New York: John Wiley, 1969); P. G. Surtees, C. Dean, J. G. Ingham, et al., "Psychiatric disorder in women from an Edinburgh community: Associations with demographic factors," *British Journal of Psychiatry* 142 (1983): 238; E. H. Uhlenhuth, R. S. Lipmann,

M. B. Balter, et al., "Symptom intensity and life stress in the city," *Archives of General Psychiatry* 31 (1974): 759; G. J. Warheit, C. E. Holzer, and J. J. Schwab, "An analysis of social class and racial differences in depressive symptomatology: A community study," *Journal of Health and Social Behaviour* 14 (1973): 291.

62. J. A. Egeland and A. M. Hostetter, "Amish study, I: Affective disorders among the Amish."

63. C. G. Costello, "Fears and phobias in women: A community study," *Journal of Abnormal Psychology* 4 (1982): 280.

64. D. L. Chambless, "The relationship of severity of agoraphobia to associated psychopathology."

65. K. H. Bourdon, J. H. Boyd, D. S. Rae, et al., "Gender differences in phobias: Results of the ECA Community Survey."

66. G. L. Klerman, M. M. Weissman, R. Ouellette, et al., "Panic attacks in the community: Social morbidity and health care utilization," *Journal of the American Medical Association* 265 (1991): 742.

67. M. M. Weissman, J. K. Myers, and P. S. Harding, "Psychiatric disorders in a U.S. urban community," *American Journal of Psychiatry* 135 (1978): 459.

68. V. R. Fuchs, *Women's Quest for Economic Equality.* This point is graphically illustrated by Judith S. Wallerstein and Joan B. Kelly (*Surviving the Breakup: How Children and Parents Cope with Divorce* [New York: Basic Books, 1980]), who studied sixty divorced families in an affluent suburban county in the San Francisco Bay area. In spite of the fact that these families came from a higher social class and were less stressed in some respects than families that might be encountered in an urban setting, Wallerstein and Kelly found that only two-thirds of the fathers paid to support their children on a regular basis. One-fifth contributed irregularly, and over 10 percent failed to help at all. According to the authors, after their divorce one-third of the mothers became "enmeshed in a daily struggle for financial survival" (185).

69. N. Darnton, "Family: Mommy vs. mommy," in *Newsweek*, June 4, 1990.

70. M. French, *The Women's Room.*

71. S. Arieti and J. Bemporad, *Severe and Mild Depression: The Psychotherapeutic Approach.*

72. P. E. Bebbington, C. Dean, G. Der, et al., "Gender, parity, and the prevalence of minor affective disorder," *British Journal of Psychiatry* 158

(1991): 40; P. E. Bebbington, C. Tennant, and J. Hurry, "Adversity in groups with an increased risk of minor affective disorder."

73. See, for example, P. E. Bebbington, "Marital status and depression: A study of English national admission statistics," *Acta Psychiatrica Scandinavica* 75 (1987): 640; P. E. Bebbington, J. Hurry, C. Tennant, et al., "The epidemiology of mental disorders in Camberwell," *Psychological Medicine* 11 (1981): 561; P. E. Bebbington and M. Tansella, "Gender, marital status, and treated affective disorders in South Verona: A case-register study," *Journal of Affective Disorders* 17 (1989): 83; R. A. Gater, C. Dean, and J. Morris, "The contribution of child bearing to the sex difference in first admission rates for unipolar affective psychosis," *Psychological Medicine* 19 (1989): 719.

74. E. J. Costello, "Married with children: Predictors of mental and physical health in middle-aged women," *Psychiatry* 54 (1991): 292.

75. R. Cochrane and M. Stopes-Roe, "Women, marriage, employment, and mental health," *British Journal of Psychiatry* 139 (1981): 373.

76. These are C. L. Hammen and C. A. Padesky, "Sex differences in the expression of depressive responses on the Beck Depression Inventory"; R. S. Stangler and A. M. Printz, "DSM-III: Psychiatric diagnosis in a university population."

77. G. Parker, "Sex differences in non-clinical depression," *Australian and New Zealand Journal of Psychiatry* 13 (1979): 127.

78. See, for example, D. Blazer and C. D. Williams, "Epidemiology of dysphoria and depression in an elderly population," *American Journal of Psychiatry* 137 (1980): 439; W. M. Ensel, "The role of age in the relationship of gender and marital status to depression," *Journal of Nervous and Mental Disease* 170 (1982): 536.

79. See, for example, P. E. Bornstein, P. J. Clayton, J. A. Halikas, et al., "The depression of widowhood after 13 months," *British Journal of Pyschiatry* 122 (1973): 561; M. S. Stroebe and W. Stroebe, "Who suffers more? Sex differences in health risks of the widowed," *Psychological Bulletin* 93 (1983): 279. The data cited are from Bornstein et al.

80. R. Jenkins, "Sex differences in minor psychiatric morbidity," *Psychological Medicine Monograph Supplement* 7 (1985): 1.

81. Surtees's and Bancroft's data are found in T. Harris, P. Surtees, and J. Bancroft, "Is sex necessarily a risk factor to depression?" *British Journal of Psychiatry* 158 (1991): 708.

82. K. Wilhelm and G. Parker, "Is sex necessarily a risk factor to depression?" *Psychological Medicine* 19 (1989): 401.

83. G. Parker, "Sex differences in non-clinical depression."

84. S. E. Romans, V. A. Walton, B. McNoe, et al., "Otago women's health survey 30-month follow-up I: Onset patterns of non-psychotic psychiatric disorder," *British Journal of Psychiatry* 163 (1993): 733; S. E. Romans, V. A. Walton, B. McNoe, et al., "Otago women's health survey 30-month follow-up II: Remission patterns of non-psychotic psychiatric disorder," *British Journal of Psychiatry* 163 (1993): 739; S. E. Romans-Clarkson, V. A. Walton, G. P. Herbison, et al., "Psychiatric morbidity among women in urban and rural New Zealand: Psycho-social correlates," *British Journal of Psychiatry* 156 (1990): 84.

85. Y. A. Aderibigbe, O. Gureje, and O. Omigbodun, "Postnatal emotional disorders in Nigerian women: A study of antecedents and associations," *British Journal of Psychiatry* 163 (1993): 645.

86. Ibid., 648.

87. D. L. Chambless, "Characteristics of agoraphobics," in *Agoraphobia: Multiple Perspectives on Theory and Treatment,* edited by D. L. Chambless and A. J. Goldstein (New York: John Wiley, 1982).

88. Ibid.

89. C. G. Costello, "Fears and phobias in women: A community study."

90. D. Buglass, J. Clarke, A. S. Henderson, et al., "A study of agoraphobic housewives."

91. D. L. Chambless and J. Mason, "Sex, sex-role stereotyping, and agoraphobia," *Behavior Research and Therapy* 24 (1986): 231.

92. D. L. Chambless, "Characteristics of agoraphobics."

93. The attachment view of agoraphobia is stated in J. Bowlby, *Attachment and Loss,* vol. 2.

94. See, for example, D. Buglass, J. Clarke, A. S. Henderson, et al., "A study of agoraphobic housewives."

95. The difficulties faced by single mothers lacking adequate income are illustrated by J. S. Wallerstein and J. B. Kelly, *Surviving the Breakup: How Children and Parents Cope with Divorce.* See also L. A. Hall, D. N. Gurley, B. Sachs, et al., "Psychosocial predictors of maternal depressive symptoms, parenting attitudes, and child behavior in single-parent families," *Nursing Research* 40 (1991): 214.

96. See, for example, B. P. Dohrenwend and B. S. Dohrenwend, *Social Status and Psychological Disorder: A Causal Inquiry;* P. G. Surtees, C. Dean, J. G. Ingham, et al., "Psychiatric disorder in women from an Edinburgh community: Associations with demographic factors"; E. H. Uhlenhuth, R. S. Lipmann, M. B. Balter, et al., "Symptom intensity and life stress in the city"; G. J. Warheit, C. E. Holzer, and J. J. Schwab, "An analysis of social class and racial differences in depressive symptomatology: A community study." In our society, men retain their footing on the middle and lower steps of the social-class ladder by holding paid positions. Men who lose their positions are likely to be depressed. See, for example, D. I. Melville, D. Hope, D. Bennison, et al., "Depression among men made involuntarily redundant," *Psychological Medicine* 15 (1985): 789; S. D. Platt and J. A. Dyer, "Psychological correlates of unemployment among male parasuicides in Edinburgh," *British Journal of Psychiatry* 151 (1987): 27.

Notes to Chapter 3

1. For example, Alam and Merskey note that depressed mood was frequently cited in early accounts of patients with hysterical features. See C. N. Alam and H. Merskey, "The development of the hysterical personality," *History of Psychiatry* 3 (1992): 135. Depression is frequently cited in modern accounts as well. See, for example, P. R. Slavney, *Perspectives on "Hysteria"* (Baltimore: Johns Hopkins University Press, 1990).

2. For an introduction to role theory, see M. E. Shaw and P. R. Costanzo, *Theories of Social Psychology,* 2d ed. (New York: McGraw-Hill, 1982); or D. G. Myers, *Social Psychology,* 2d ed. (New York: McGraw-Hill, 1987). For a discussion of the effect of roles on social cognition, see S. T. Fiske and S. E. Taylor, *Social Cognition,* 2d ed. (New York: McGraw-Hill, 1991). The situationist position is described in L. Ross and R. E. Nisbett, *The Person and the Situation: Perspectives of Social Psychology* (New York: McGraw-Hill, 1991).

3. See P. G. Zimbardo, "A Pirandellian prison," *New York Times Magazine,* April 8, 1973, 38. An excellent videotape showing this study is also available (*Quiet Rage: The Stanford Prison Experiment* [HarperCollins College Publishers, 1992]).

4. M. Galanter, "The 'relief effect': A sociobiological model for neu-

rotic distress and large-group therapy," *American Journal of Psychiatry* 135 (1978): 588; M. Galanter, *Cults: Faith, Healing, and Coercion* (New York: Oxford University Press, 1989). See also B. Wenegrat, "Religious cult membership: A sociobiologic model," in *Cults and New Religious Movements: A Report of the American Psychiatric Association,* edited by M. Galanter (Washington, DC: American Psychiatric Press, 1989); B. Wenegrat, *The Divine Archetype: The Sociobiology and Psychology of Religion* (Lexington, MA: Lexington Books, 1990).

5. R. N. Bellah, R. Madsen, W. M. Sullivan, et al., *Habits of the Heart: Individualism and Commitment in American Life* (Berkeley: University of California Press, 1985).

6. J. Lofland and R. Stark, "Becoming a world-saver: A theory of conversion to a deviant perspective," *American Sociological Review* 30 (1965): 862.

7. S. V. Levine, "Role of psychiatry in the phenomenon of cults," *Canadian Journal of Psychiatry* 24 (1979): 593; S. V. Levine, "Alienated Jewish youth and religious seminaries: An alternative to cults?" in *Psychodynamic Perspectives on Religion, Sect, and Cult,* edited by D. A. Halperin (Boston: John Wright Press, 1983).

8. M. Galanter, "Psychological induction into the large group: Findings from a modern religious sect," *American Journal of Psychiatry* 137 (1980): 1574.

9. See, for example, B. Etemad, "Extrication from cultism," *Current Psychiatric Therapies* 18 (1978): 217; D. A. Halperin, "Group processes in cult affiliation and recruitment," in *Psychodynamic Perspectives on Religion, Sect, and Cult,* edited by D. A. Halperin; J. Lofland and R. Stark, "Becoming a world-saver: A theory of conversion to a deviant perspective."

10. M. Galanter, R. Rabkin, J. Rabkin, et al., "The 'Moonies': A psychological study of conversion and membership in a contemporary religious sect," *American Journal of Psychiatry* 136 (1979): 165.

11. T. E. Long and J. K. Hadden, "Religious conversion and the concept of socialization: Integrating the brainwashing and drift models," *Journal for the Scientific Study of Religion* 22 (1983): 1.

12. Ibid.

13. For a fascinating description of life in Rajneeshpuram, see J. S. Gordon, *The Golden Guru: The Strange Journey of the Bhagwan Shree Rajneesh* (Lexington, MA: Stephen Greene Press, 1987).

14. See, for example, J. G. Clark, "On the further study of destructive cultism," in *Psychodynamic Perspectives on Religion, Sect, and Cult,* edited by D. A. Halperin; M. F. Galper, "The atypical dissociative disorder: Some etiological, diagnostic, and treatment issues," in *Psychodynamic Perspectives on Religion, Sect, and Cult,* edited by D. A. Halperin; D. A. Halperin, "Group processes in cult affiliation and recruitment."

15. See T. Parsons, *Social Structure and Personality* (New York: Free Press, 1964); H. E. Sigerist, "The special position of the sick," in *Henry E. Sigerist on the Sociology of Medicine,* edited by M. I. Roemer, ed. (New York: MD Publications, 1960).

16. T. S. Szasz, *The Myth of Mental Illness: Foundations of a Theory of Personal Conduct,* rev. ed. (New York: Harper and Row, 1974).

17. This is the general point raised by Betty Friedan in *The Feminine Mystique* (New York: W. W. Norton, 1963) and by J. M. Masson in *The Assault on Truth: Freud's Suppression of the Seduction Theory* (New York: Farrar, Straus, and Giroux, 1984) and in J. M. Masson, "Freud and the seduction theory," *Atlantic Monthly,* February 1984.

18. J. Ussher, *Women's Madness: Misogyny or Mental Illness?* (Amherst: University of Massachusetts Press, 1991).

19. S. L. Bem, *The Lenses of Gender: Transforming the Debate on Sexual Inequality* (New Haven: Yale University Press, 1993).

20. Some extreme gender-role theorists (e.g., J. H. Pleck, *The Myth of Masculinity* [Cambridge, MA: MIT Press, 1981]) go so far as to claim that even sexual drives result from social training. By contrast, models of behavioral evolution imply that human sexual drives, and those of all other animals, are due to past selection and hence biologically based. For the argument here to hold up, the reproductive strategies described in chapter 5 must be innately determined, at least in large part.

21. The following material on grand hysteria, Charcot, Bernheim, and the Battle of the Schools is from G. F. Drinka, *The Birth of Neurosis: Myth, Malady, and the Victorians* (New York: Simon and Schuster, 1984).

22. E. R. Hilgard, *Divided Consciousness: Multiple Controls in Human Thought and Action,* expanded ed. (New York: John Wiley, 1986). For a thoughtful recent discussion of this issue, see F. H. Frankel, "Hypnotizability and dissociation," *American Journal of Psychiatry* 147 (1990): 823.

23. American Psychiatric Association, *Diagnostic and Statistical Manual of Mental Disorders,* 3d ed., rev. (Washington, DC: American Psychiatric Association, 1987).

24. For an overview of this research, see R. A. Baker, *They Call It Hypnosis* (Buffalo, NY: Prometheus Books, 1990); T. X. Barber, N. P. Spanos, and J. F. Chaves, *Hypnosis, Imagination, and Human Potentialities* (New York: Pergamon Press, 1974); J. F. Schumaker, ed., *Human Suggestibility: Advances in Theory, Research, and Application* (New York: Routledge and Kegan Paul, 1991); N. P. Spanos and J. F. Chaves, eds., *Hypnosis: The Cognitive-Behavioral Perspective* (Buffalo, NY: Prometheus Books, 1989).

25. H. Spiegel and D. Spiegel, *Trance and Treatment: Clinical Uses of Hypnosis* (New York: Basic Books, 1978).

26. D. Shapiro, *Neurotic Styles* (New York: Basic Books, 1965); M. Snyder, *Public Appearances, Private Realities: The Psychology of Self-Monitoring* (New York: W. H. Freeman, 1987); D. Riesman, *The Lonely Crowd* (New Haven, CT: Yale University Press, 1950).

27. S. J. Hirsch and M. H. Hollender, "Hysterical psychosis: Clarification of the concept," *American Journal of Psychiatry* 125 (1969): 909.

28. D. Spiegel and R. Fink, "Hysterical psychosis and hypnotisability," *American Journal of Psychiatry* 136 (1979): 777.

29. L. L. Langness, "Hysterical psychosis: The cross-cultural evidence," *American Journal of Psychiatry* 124 (1967): 47.

30. These case histories are summarized in G. F. Drinka, *The Birth of Neurosis: Myth, Malady, and the Victorians.*

31. Patients with so-called borderline personality disorder, which is thought to be caused in part by early emotional deprivation or maltreatment, frequently cut themselves, especially on the hands or wrists. See, for example, G. E. Vaillant and J. C. Perry, "Personality disorders," in *Comprehensive Textbook of Psychiatry,* 4th ed., edited by H. I. Kaplan and B. J. Sadock.

32. See, for example, J. Allison, "Adaptive regression and intense religious experiences," *Journal of Nervous and Mental Disease* 145 (1968): 452; D. G. Brown and W. L. Lowe, "Religious beliefs and personality characteristics of college students," *Journal of Social Psychology* 33 (1951): 103; A. Deutsch and M. J. Miller, "A clinical study of four Unification Church members," *American Journal of Psychiatry* 140 (1983): 767; J. P. Kildahl, "The personalities of sudden religious converts," *Pastoral Psychology* 16 (1965): 37; E. M. Pattison, N. A. Lapins, and H. A. Doerr, "Faith healing: A study of personality and function," *Journal of Nervous and Mental Disease* 157 (1973): 397.

33. J. Bowlby, *Charles Darwin: A New Life* (New York: W. W. Norton, 1990).

34. See, for example, J. J. Brumberg, *Fasting Girls: The History of Anorexia Nervosa* (New York: New American Library, 1988). For an analysis of the political role of the invalid woman, see D. P. Herndl, *Invalid Women: Figuring Feminine Illness in American Fiction and Culture, 1840–1940* (Chapel Hill: University of North Carolina Press, 1993).

35. T. Veblen, *The Theory of the Leisure Class* (1899; New York: Mentor, 1953).

36. S. Freud and J. Breuer, "Studies on Hysteria," in *The Standard Edition of the Complete Psychological Works of Sigmund Freud,* vol. 2, trans. J. Strachey (London: Hogarth Press, 1953–1974). See also L. Freeman, *The Story of Anna O.* (New York: Paragon House, 1990).

37. S. Freud and J. Breuer, "Studies on Hysteria," 21.

38. Quoted in L. Freeman, *The Story of Anna O.,* 156.

39. Dora's case is to be found in S. Freud, "Fragment of an analysis of a case of hysteria," in *The Standard Edition of the Complete Psychological Works of Sigmund Freud,* vol. 7. See also C. Bernheimer and C. Kahane, eds., *In Dora's Case: Freud-Hysteria-Feminism* (New York: Columbia University Press, 1985); S. R. Maddi, "The victimization of Dora," *Psychology Today,* September 1974, 91.

40. F. Deutsch, "A footnote to Freud's 'Fragment of an analysis of a case of hysteria,' " *Psychoanalytic Quarterly* 26 (1957): 159.

41. See T. R. Insel, "Obsessive-compulsive disorder," *Psychiatric Clinics of North America* 8 (1985): 105; I. M. Marks, "Genetics of fear and anxiety disorders," *British Journal of Psychiatry* 149 (1986): 406.

42. For information on Alice James, see G. F. Drinka, *The Birth of Neurosis: Myth, Malady, and the Victorians;* J. Strouse, *Alice James: A Biography* (Boston: Houghton Mifflin, 1980).

43. B. Dijkstra, *Idols of Perversity: Fantasies of Feminine Evil in Fin-de-Siècle Culture* (Oxford: Oxford University Press, 1986).

44. J. Strouse, *Alice James: A Biography.*

45. Ibid., 47.

46. See D. Goodwin and S. Guze, *Psychiatric Diagnosis,* 3d ed. (New York: Oxford University Press, 1984); J. C. Nemiah, "Somatoform disorders," in *Comprehensive Textbook of Psychiatry,* 4th ed., edited by H. I. Kaplan and B. J. Sadock.

47. American Psychiatric Association, *Diagnostic and Statistical Manual of Mental Disorders,* 3d ed., rev.

48. See, for example, M. Bohman, R Cloninger, A. L. Von Knorring, et al., "An adoption study of somatoform disorders: III. Cross-fostering analysis and genetic relationship to alcoholism and criminality," *Archives of General Psychiatry* 41 (1984): 872; D. Goodwin and S. Guze, *Psychiatric Diagnosis,* 3d ed.; R. Cloninger and S. Guze, "Psychiatric illness and female criminality: The role of sociopathy and hysteria in the antisocial woman," *American Journal of Psychiatry* 127 (1970): 79.

49. P. Draper and H. Harpending, "A sociobiological perspective on the development of human reproductive strategies," *Sociobiological Perspectives on Human Development,* edited by K. B. MacDonald (New York: Springer-Verlag, 1988).

50. P. R. Slavney, *Perspectives on "Hysteria."*

51. M. P. I. Weller, "Hysterical behaviour in patriarchal communities: Four cases, one with Ganser-like symptoms," *British Journal of Psychiatry* 152 (1988): 687.

52. S. E. Abbey and P. E. Garfinkel, "Neurasthenia and the chronic fatigue syndrome: The role of culture in the making of a diagnosis," *American Journal of Psychiatry* 148 (1991): 1638. Information on neurasthenia is also found in G. F. Drinka, *The Birth of Neurosis: Myth, Malady, and the Victorians,* and in E. Shorter, *From Paralysis to Fatigue: A History of Psychosomatic Illness in the Modern Era* (New York: Free Press, 1992).

53. S. E. Abbey and P. E. Garfinkel, "Neurasthenia and the chronic fatigue syndrome: The role of culture in the making of a diagnosis," 1644.

54. Neurasthenia is still commonly diagnosed in the People's Republic of China. Arthur and Joan Kleinman's sensitive case histories of neurasthenic patients in the People's Republic clearly illustrate how their somatic symptoms help them renegotiate work, living, and family arrangements they are otherwise powerless to change. See, for example, A. Kleinman, *Social Origins of Distress and Disease: Depression, Neurasthenia, and Pain in Modern China* (New Haven, CT: Yale University Press, 1986).

Notes to Chapter 4

1. Diagnostic criteria for multiple personality disorder are described in the American Psychiatric Association's *Diagnostic and Statistical Manual*

of Mental Disorders, 3d ed., rev. (Washington, DC: American Psychiatric Association, 1987). More detailed information and a proponent's view of the disorder can be found in F. W. Putnam, *Diagnosis and Treatment of Multiple Personality Disorder* (New York: Guilford Press, 1989). An excellent critical overview is presented in R. Aldridge-Morris, *Multiple Personality: An Exercise in Deception* (Hillsdale, NJ: Lawrence Erlbaum Associates, 1989).

2. F. W. Putnam, *Diagnosis and Treatment of Multiple Personality Disorder*.

3. The case of Eve is described in C. H. Thigpen and H. M. Cleckley, *The Three Faces of Eve* (New York: McGraw-Hill, 1957), and in C. C. Sizemore and E. S. Pittillo, *I'm Eve!* (Garden City, NJ: Doubleday, 1977). The case of Sybil is described in F. R. Schreiber, *Sybil* (Chicago: Regnery, 1973). Information about the Kenneth Bianchi case can be found in R. B. Allison, "Difficulties diagnosing the multiple personality syndrome in a death penalty case," *International Journal of Clinical and Experimental Hypnosis* 32 (1984): 102; in M. T. Orne, D. F. Dinges, and E. C. Orne, "On the differential diagnosis of multiple personality in the forensic context," *International Journal of Clinical and Experimental Hypnosis* 32 (1984): 118; and in J. G. Watkins, "The Bianchi (L.A. Hillside Strangler) case: Sociopath or multiple personality," *International Journal of Clinical and Experimental Hypnosis* 32 (1984): 67. The case of Billy Milligan is described in D. Keyes, *The Minds of Billy Milligan* (New York: Random House, 1981). The case of Trudi Chase is described in ("The Troops for") Trudi Chase, *When Rabbit Howls* (New York: Jove Books, 1987).

4. See H. Merskey, "The manufacture of personalities: The production of multiple personality disorder," *British Journal of Psychiatry* 160 (1992): 327.

5. Ibid.

6. R. L. Stevenson, *Dr. Jekyll and Mr. Hyde* (New York: Bantam Books, 1981).

7. Ibid., 79.

8. See, for example, F. W. Putnam, *Diagnosis and Treatment of Multiple Personality Disorder*.

9. See, for example, the discussion of hypnotic regression in R. A. Baker, *They Call It Hypnosis* (Buffalo, NY: Prometheus Books, 1990), 225–37; G. F. Wagstaff, "Forensic aspects of hypnosis," in *Hypnosis: The*

Cognitive-Behavioral Perspective, edited by N. P. Spanos and J. F. Chaves (Buffalo, NY: Prometheus Books, 1989).

10. See, for example, E. F. Loftus, "The reality of repressed memories," *American Psychologist* 48 (1993): 518.

11. J. S. Victor, *Satanic Panic: The Creation of a Contemporary Legend* (Chicago: Open Court, 1993); see also K. V. Lanning, "A law-enforcement perspective on allegations of ritual abuse," in *Out of Darkness: Exploring Satanism and Ritual Abuse,* edited by D. K. Sakheim and S. E. Devine (New York: Lexington Books, 1992).

12. K. V. Lanning, "A law-enforcement perspective on allegations of ritual abuse."

13. J. S. Gordon, "The UFO experience," *The Atlantic* 268, no. 2 (1991): 82; Gordon's book on the Rajneeshees is J. S. Gordon, *The Golden Guru: The Strange Journey of the Bhagwan Shree Rajneesh* (Lexington, MA: Stephen Greene Press, 1987).

14. The "classic" alien abduction account is described in great detail by D. M. Jacobs, in *Secret Life: Firsthand Accounts of UFO Abductions* (New York: Simon and Schuster, 1992). John Mack, a Harvard psychiatrist, wrote the introduction to this book. On page 12, Mack writes "For me and other investigators, abduction research has had a shattering impact on our views of the nature of the cosmos." He goes on to speculate that since "humankind has broken the harmony of being, aliens are placing Earth in a kind of receivership."

15. See R. A. Baker, *They Call It Hypnosis;* N. P. Spanos, "Past-life hypnotic regression: A critical review," *Skeptical Inquirer* 12, no. 2 (Winter 1987–88): 174.

16. See, for example, F. W. Putnam, *Diagnosis and Treatment of Multiple Personality Disorder;* F. W. Putnam, "Dissociation as a response to extreme trauma," in *Childhood Antecedents of Multiple Personality,* R. P. Kluft (Washington, DC: American Psychiatric Press, 1985).

17. F. W. Putnam, "Dissociation as a response to extreme trauma."

18. See, for example, J. B. Bryer, B. A. Nelson, J. B. Miller, et al., "Childhood sexual and physical abuse as factors in adult psychiatric illness," *American Journal of Psychiatry* 144 (1987): 1426; J. L. Herman, "Histories of violence in an outpatient population," *American Journal of Orthopsychiatry* 56 (1986): 137; J. L. Herman, J. C. Perry, and B. A. van der Kolk, "Childhood trauma in borderline personality disorder, *Ameri-*

can Journal of Psychiatry 146 (1989): 490; H. Sheldon, "Childhood sexual abuse in adult female psychotherapy referrals: Incidence and implications for treatment," *British Journal of Psychiatry* 152 (1988): 107.

19. F. W. Putnam, *Diagnosis and Treatment of Multiple Personality Disorder*.

20. For an excellent review of the long-term sequelae of child sexual abuse, see D. H. Schetky, "A review of the literature on the long-term effects of childhood sexual abuse," in *Incest-Related Syndromes of Adult Psychopathology*, edited by R. J. Kluft (Washington, DC: American Psychiatric Press, 1990).

21. For a review of this issue, see R. J. Loewenstein, "Somatoform disorders in victims of incest and child abuse," in *Incest-Related Syndromes of Adult Psychopathology*, edited by R. J. Kluft.

22. Freud stated the seduction theory in S. Freud, "The aetiology of hysteria," in *The Standard Edition of the Complete Psychological Works of Sigmund Freud*, vol. 3, trans. J. Strachey (London: Hogarth Press, 1953–1974). For information about the controversy, but not about Masson's position, see J. Malcolm, "Annals of scholarship: Trouble in the archives, Part I," *New Yorker Magazine*, December 5, 1983; J. Malcolm, "Annals of scholarship: Trouble in the archives, Part II," *New Yorker Magazine*, December 12, 1983. Masson presents his position in J. M. Masson, *The Assault on Truth: Freud's Suppression of the Seduction Theory* (New York: Farrar, Straus, and Giroux, 1984); and in J. M. Masson, "Freud and the seduction theory," *Atlantic Monthly*, February 1984.

23. See E. J. Frischholz, "The relationship among dissociation, hypnosis, and child abuse in the development of multiple personality disorder," in *Childhood Antecedents of Multiple Personality*, edited by R. P. Kluft; J. R. Hilgard, *Personality and Hypnosis: A Study of Imaginative Involvement* (Chicago: University of Chicago Press, 1970); M. R. Nash, S. J. Lynn, and D. L Givens, "Adult hypnotic susceptibility, childhood punishment, and child abuse: A brief communication," *International Journal of Clinical and Experimental Hypnosis* 32 (1984): 6.

24. R. Schultz, "Secrets of adolescence: Incest and developmental fixations," in *Incest-Related Syndromes of Adult Psychopathology*, edited by R. J. Kluft.

25. Ibid., 147.

26. R. J. Kluft, "Incest and subsequent revictimization: The case of

therapist-patient sexual exploitation, with a description of the sitting duck syndrome," in *Incest-Related Syndromes of Adult Psychopathology,* edited by R. J. Kluft.

27. R. J. Kluft, "On the apparent invisibility of incest: A personal reflection on things known and forgotten," in *Incest-Related Syndromes of Adult Psychopathology,* edited by R. J. Kluft, 25.

28. E. Carmen and P. P. Rieker, "A psychosocial model of the victim-to-patient process: Implications for treatment," *Psychiatric Clinics of North America* 12 (1989): 431; R. C. Summit, "The child sexual abuse accommodation syndrome," *Child Abuse and Neglect* 7 (1983): 177.

29. R. Aldridge-Morris, *Multiple Personality: An Exercise in Deception.*

30. B. G. Braun, "The transgenerational incidence of dissociation and multiple personality disorder: A preliminary report," in *Childhood Antecedents of Multiple Personality,* edited by R. P. Kluft.

31. R. P. Kluft, "Childhood multiple personality disorder: Predictors, clinical findings, and treatment results," in *Childhood Antecedents of Multiple Personality,* edited by R. P. Kluft.

32. G. W. Small, M. W. Propper, E. T. Randolph, et al., "Mass hysteria among student performers: Social relationship as a symptom predictor," *American Journal of Psychiatry* 148 (1991): 1200.

33. F. W. Putnam, *Diagnosis and Treatment of Multiple Personality Disorder.*

34. Ibid.

35. See, for example, the thoughtful discussion of this issue in J. T. Maltsberger and D. H. Buie, "Countertransference hate in the treatment of suicidal patients," *Archives of General Psychiatry* 30 (1974): 625.

36. R. Aldridge-Morris, *Multiple Personality: An Exercise in Deception.*

37. I. M. Lewis, *Ecstatic Religion: A Study of Shamanism and Spirit Possession,* 2d ed. (New York: Routledge and Kegan Paul, 1989).

38. L. B. Boyer, B. Klopfer, F. B. Brawer, et al., "Comparisons of the shamans and pseudoshamans of the Apaches of the Mescalero indian reservation: A Rorschach study," *Journal of Projective Techniques* 28 (1964): 173.

39. J. J. Brumberg, *Fasting Girls: The History of Anorexia Nervosa* (New York: New American Library, 1988). The historical material cited in the following pages also comes from Brumberg.

40. The opportunities available to women in the Church are described in B. S. Anderson and J. P. Zinsser, *A History of Their Own: Women in Europe from Prehistory to the Present,* vols. 1 and 2 (New York: Harper and Row, 1988).

41. Quoted in J. J. Brumberg, *Fasting Girls: The History of Anorexia Nervosa,* 69.

42. Ibid., 72.

43. S. L. Zimdars-Swartz, *Encountering Mary: Visions of Mary from La Salette to Medjugorje* (New York: Avon Books, 1991).

44. R. A. Gordon, *Anorexia and Bulimia: Anatomy of a Social Epidemic* (Cambridge, MA: Basil Blackwell, 1990).

45. Quoted in J. J. Brumberg, *Fasting Girls: The History of Anorexia Nervosa,* 183.

46. T. Veblen, *The Theory of the Leisure Class* (1899; New York: Mentor, 1953).

47. This figure is from M. Beck, K. Springen, L. Beachy, et al., "The losing formula," *Newsweek,* April 30, 1990.

48. The evidence for this hypothesis is presented in J. J. Brumberg, *Fasting Girls: The History of Anorexia Nervosa,* and in R. A. Gordon, *Anorexia and Bulimia: Anatomy of a Social Epidemic.*

49. R. A. Gordon, *Anorexia and Bulimia: Anatomy of a Social Epidemic.* In general, anorexics' families are often found to be preoccupied with thinness. In striving for abnormal weight loss, patients from such families are carrying their family value system to an extreme. See, for example, R. S. Kalucy, A. H. Crisp, and B. A. Harding, "A study of 56 families with anorexia nervosa," *British Journal of Medical Psychology* 50 (1977): 381.

50. See, for example, G. I. Szmukler and D. Tantum, "Anorexia nervosa: Starvation dependence," *British Journal of Medical Psychology* 57 (1984): 303; M. A. Marazzi and E. D. Luby, "An auto-addiction opioid model of chronic anorexia nervosa," *International Journal of Eating Disorders* 5 (1986): 191.

51. See, for example, H. Bruch, *Eating Disorders: Obesity, Anorexia Nervosa, and the Person Within* (New York: Basic Books, 1973); K. Chernin, *The Hungry Self: Women, Eating, and Identity* (New York: Harper and Row, 1985); A. H. Crisp, "The psychopathology of anorexia nervosa: Getting the 'heat' out of the system," in *Eating and Its Disorders,* edited by A. J. Stunkard and E. Stellar (New York: Raven Press, 1984);

D. M. Garner and P. E. Garfinkel, eds. *Handbook for the Psychotherapy of Anorexia Nervosa and Bulimia* (New York: Guilford Press, 1985); R. A. Gordon, *Anorexia and Bulimia: Anatomy of a Social Epidemic.*

52. See, for example, S. Brownmiller, *Femininity* (New York: Fawcett Columbine, 1984); S. Faludi, *Backlash: The Undeclared War against American Women* (New York: Crown Publishers, 1991).

53. R. A. Gordon, *Anorexia and Bulimia: Anatomy of a Social Epidemic.*

54. W. E. Buckley, C. E. Yesalis, K. E. Friedl, et al., "Estimated prevalence of anabolic steroid use among male high school seniors," *Journal of the American Medical Association* 260 (1988): 3441.

55. K. J. Brower, G. A. Eliopulos, F. C. Blow, et al., "Evidence for physical and psychological dependence on anabolic androgenic steroids in eight weight lifters," *American Journal of Psychiatry* 147 (1990): 510.

Notes to Chapter 5

1. For excellent overviews of sociobiology, see D. Barash, *Sociobiology: The Whisperings Within* (New York: Harper and Row, 1979); D. Barash, *Sociobiology and Behavior,* 2d ed. (New York: Elsevier, 1982); T. H. Clutton-Brock and P. H. Harvey, eds., *Readings in Sociobiology* (San Francisco: W. H. Freeman, 1978); R. Dawkins, *The Selfish Gene* (Oxford: Oxford University Press, 1976); R. L. Trivers, *Social Evolution* (Menlo Park, CA: Benjamin/Cummings, 1985); E. O. Wilson, *Sociobiology: The New Synthesis* (Cambridge, MA: Harvard University Press, 1975).

2. B. Wenegrat, *Sociobiology and Mental Disorder: A New View* (Menlo Park, CA: Addison-Wesley, 1984); B. Wenegrat, *Sociobiological Psychiatry: Normal Behavior and Psychopathology* (Lexington, MA: Lexington Books, 1990).

3. These strategies are described in D. Barash, *Sociobiology: The Whisperings Within;* in D. Barash, *Sociobiology and Behavior,* 2d ed.; in T. H. Clutton-Brock and P. H. Harvey, eds., *Readings in Sociobiology;* in R. Dawkins, *The Selfish Gene;* in R. L. Trivers, *Social Evolution;* and in E. O. Wilson, *Sociobiology: The New Synthesis.* Summaries can also be found in B. Wenegrat, *Sociobiological Psychiatry: Normal Behavior and Psychopathology.*

4. W. D. Hamilton, "The genetical evolution of social behavior," *Journal of Theoretical Biology* 7 (1964): 1.

5. Discussions of cross-cultural manifestations of kin altruism and of kinship systems in relation to sociobiology are to be found in R. D. Alexander, *Darwinism and Human Affairs* (Seattle: University of Washington Press, 1979); N. A. Chagnon, "Nepotism in tribal populations," *Current Problems in Sociobiology*, edited by King's College Sociobiology Group (Cambridge: Cambridge University Press, 1982); N. A. Chagnon and W. Irons, eds., *Evolutionary Biology and Human Social Behavior: An Anthropological Perspective* (North Scituate, MA: Duxbury Press, 1979); I. Eibl-Eibesfeldt, *Human Ethology* (New York: Aldine de Gruyter, 1989); R. Fox, *The Red Lamp of Incest* (New York: E. P. Dutton, 1980); N. W. Thornhill and R. Thornhill, "Evolutionary theory and rules of mating and marriage pertaining to relatives," in *Sociobiology and Psychology: Ideas, Issues, and Applications,* edited by C. Crawford, M. Smith, and D. Krebs (Hillsdale, NJ: Lawrence Erlbaum Associates, 1987); P. L. van den Berghe, "Human incest avoidance: Culture in nature," *Behavioral and Brain Sciences* 6 (1983): 91; P. L. van den Berghe, "Incest taboos and avoidance: Some African applications," in *Sociobiology and Psychology: Ideas, Issues, and Applications,* edited by C. Crawford, M. Smith, and D. Krebs.

6. Modern thinking on attachment is discussed in J. Bowlby, *Attachment and Loss,* vols. 1, 2, and 3 (New York: Basic Books, 1969, 1973, 1980); in C. M. Parkes and J. Stevenson-Hinde, eds., *The Place of Attachment in Human Behavior* (New York: Basic Books, 1982); and in articles in *Monographs of the Society for Research in Child Development,* vol. 50, nos. 1–2 (Chicago: University of Chicago Press, 1985).

7. For example, a number of studies indicate that postpartum contact between mother and child is needed to "prime" maternal warmth and caretaking behaviors. Diminished postpartum contact may impair later development of maternal behaviors or even lead to neglect. Presumably, the critical postpartum period is due to neuro-endocrine factors attendant on childbirth. See, for example, Z. Ali and M. Lowry, "Early maternal-child contact: Effects on later behaviour," *Developmental Medicine and Child Neurology* 23 (1981): 337; S. G. Carlsson, H. Faberberg, G. Horneman, et al., "Effects of amount of contact between mother and child on the mother's nursing behavior," *Developmental Psychobiology* 11 (1978): 143; P. DeChateau and B. Wiberg, "Long-term effect on mother-infant behaviour of extra contact during the first hour post-partum: I. First observations at 36 hours," *Acta Paediatrica Scandinavica* 66 (1977): 137; P. DeChateau and B. Wiberg, "Long-term effect on mother-infant behav-

iour of extra contact during the first hour post-partum: II. A follow-up at three months," *Acta Paediatrica Scandinavica* 66 (1977): 145; D. J. Hales, B. Lozoff, R. Sosa, et al., "Defining the limits of the maternal sensitive period," *Developmental Medicine and Child Neurology* 19 (1977): 454; M. H. Klaus, R. Jerauld, N. C. Kreger, et al., "Maternal attachment: Importance of the first post-partum days," *New England Journal of Medicine* 286 (1972):460; S. M. O'Connor, P. M. Vietze, J. B. Hopkins, et al., "Post-partum extended maternal-infant contact: Subsequent mothering and child health," in *Pediatric Research* 11 (1977): 380; J. Trowell, "Effects of obstetric management on the mother-child relationship," in *The Place of Attachment in Human Behavior,* edited by C. M. Parkes and J. Stevenson-Hinde.

8. The theory of reciprocal altruism was first developed in R. L. Trivers, "The evolution of reciprocal altruism," *Quarterly Review of Biology* 46 (1971): 35.

9. The importance of trading favors with others is obvious from our own experience, but A. Gouldner ("The norm of reciprocity: A preliminary statement," *American Sociological Review* 47 [1960]: 73) and I. Eibl-Eibesfeldt (*Human Ethology*) cite evidence that reciprocity is important in all cultures. Also, compare M. Mauss, *The Gift,* trans. I. Cunnison (London: Routledge and Kegan Paul, 1954), and C. Lévi-Strauss, *The Elementary Structures of Kinship* (Boston: Beacon Press, 1969). Mauss was specifically interested in why gifts compel the giving of other gifts in return. Lévi-Strauss turned Mauss's theory of gift-giving and receiving into a theory of relationships in general.

10. R. L. Trivers, "The evolution of reciprocal altruism."

11. The term "mutualism" as I am using it here is from R. W. Wrangham, "Mutualism, kinship, and social evolution," *Current Problems in Sociobiology,* edited by King's College Sociobiology Group. "Mutualism" has been used by ecologists to refer to mutually positive interactions between different species, which allows for a certain confusion when discussing a social strategy. See, for example, D. H. Boucher, ed., *The Biology of Mutualism: Ecology and Evolution* (New York: Oxford University Press, 1985). Other terms used in the evolutionary literature to refer to a social strategy like that described here are "synergistic selection," "weak altruism," and "indirect reciprocity." "Synergistic selection" is used by J. Maynard Smith, "The evolution of social behaviour—a classification of models," in *Current Problems in Sociobiology,* edited by

King's College Sociobiology Group. "Weak altruism" is used by D. S. Wilson, *The Natural Selection of Populations and Communities* (Menlo Park, CA: Benjamin/Cummings, 1980). "Indirect reciprocity" is used by R. D. Alexander, *The Biology of Moral Systems* (New York: Aldine De Gruyter, 1987). Mutualistic tendencies are no doubt closely related to the apparently universal human disposition to form cohesive in-groups, which treat out-group members invidiously. Wrangham uses the term "exclusive mutualism" to refer to mutualism that tends to harm outsiders. For studies and other evidence pertaining to group affiliations, in-group/out-group distinctions, and consensual realities within in-group, see P. L. Berger and T. Luckmann, *The Social Construction of Reality: A Treatise in the Sociology of Knowledge* (Garden City, NJ: Doubleday, 1966); M. Billig and H. Tajfel, "Social categorization and similarity in intergroup behaviour," *European Journal of Social Psychology* 3 (1973): 27; M. B. Brewer and M. Silver, "In-group bias as a function of task characteristics," *European Journal of Social Psychology* 8 (1978): 393; D. T. Campbell, "Social morality norms as evidence of conflict between biological human nature and social system requirements," in *Morality as a Biological Phenomenon*, edited by G. S. Stent (Berlin: Dahlem Konferenzen, 1978); I. Eibl-Eibesfeldt, *Human Ethology*; K. Lorenz, *On Aggression* (New York: Harcourt, Brace, and World, 1960); H. Tajfel, "Experiments in intergroup discrimination," *Scientific American*, November 1970, 96; H. Tajfel, "Social identity and intergroup behaviour," *Social Science Information* 13 (1974): 65; H. Tajfel, "Human intergroup conflict: Useful and less useful forms of analysis," in *Human Ethology: Claims and Limits of a New Discipline*, edited by M. von Cramach, K. Foppa, W. Lepenies, et al. (New York: Cambridge University Press, 1979); H. Tajfel, *Human Groups and Social Categories: Studies in Social Psychology* (London: Cambridge University Press, 1981); H. Tajfel, "Social psychology of intergroup relations," *Annual Review of Psychology* 33 (1982): 1; H. Tajfel and M. Billig, "Familiarity and categorization in intergroup behavior," *Journal of Experimental Social Psychology* 10 (1974): 159; L. Tiger, *Men in Groups*, 2d ed. (New York: Marion Boyars, 1984); L. Tiger and R. Fox, *The Imperial Animal* (Toronto: McLelland and Stewart, 1971). Well-known papers on conformity include S. E. Asch, "Studies of independence and conformity: I. A minority of one against a unanimous majority," *Psychological Monographs* 70, no. 9 (1956): 1; R. A. Crutchfield, "Conformity and character," *American Psychologist* 10 (1955): 191; R. C. Jacobs and D. T.

Campbell, "The perpetuation of an arbitrary tradition through several generations of a laboratory microculture," *Journal of Abnormal and Social Psychology* 62 (1961): 649; M. M. Sakurai, "Small group cohesiveness and detrimental conformity," *Sociometry* 38 (1975): 340; M. Sherif, "An experimental approach to the study of attitudes," *Sociometry* 1 (1937): 90.

12. For theoretical views of conflict strategies, see D. T. Bishop, C. Cannings, and J. Maynard Smith, "The war of attrition with random rewards," *Journal of Theoretical Biology* 74 (1978): 377; P. Hammerstein, "The role of symmetries in animal conflicts," *Animal Behaviour* 29 (1981): 193; J. Maynard Smith, "The theory of games and the evolution of animal conflicts," *Journal of Theoretical Biology* 47 (1974): 209; J. Maynard Smith, "Evolution and the theory of games," *American Scientist* 64 (1976): 41; J. Maynard Smith, *Evolution and the Theory of Games* (Cambridge: Cambridge University Press, 1982); J. Maynard Smith and G. A. Parker, "The logic of asymmetric contests," *Animal Behaviour* 24 (1976): 159; J. Maynard Smith and G. R. Price, "The logic of animal conflict," *Nature* (London) 246 (1973): 15; G. A. Parker, "Assessment strategy and the evolution of fighting behaviour," *Journal of Theoretical Biology* 47 (1974): 223; G. A. Parker, "Phenotype-limited evolutionarily stable strategies," in *Current Problems in Sociobiology,* edited by King's College Sociobiology Group.

13. C. Darwin, *The Descent of Man, and Selection in Relation to Sex* (London: John Murray, 1871).

14. Discussions of male and female reproductive strategies are found in D. Barash, *Sociobiology: The Whisperings Within;* in D. Barash, *Sociobiology and Behavior,* 2d ed.; in T. H. Clutton-Brock and P. H. Harvey, eds., *Readings in Sociobiology;* in R. Dawkins, *The Selfish Gene*; in R. L. Trivers, *Social Evolution;* and in E. O. Wilson, *Sociobiology: The New Synthesis.* A more complete treatment can be found in D. Symons, *The Evolution of Human Sexuality* (New York: Oxford University Press, 1979), and in D. M. Buss's recently published work, *The Evolution of Desire: Strategies of Human Mating* (New York: Basic Books, 1994).

15. See, for example, L. Festinger, "The social organization of early human groups," in *Changing Conceptions of Crowd, Mind, and Behavior,* edited by C. F. Graumann and S. Moscovici (New York: Springer-Verlag, 1986).

16. See, for example, I. Eibl-Eibesfeldt, *Human Ethology;* D. Symons,

The Evolution of Human Sexuality; D. M. Buss, "Sex Differences in human mate preferences: Evolutionary hypotheses test in 37 cultures," *Behavioral and Brain Sciences* 12 (1989): 1.

17. L. Tiger and J. Shepher, *Women in the Kibbutz* (New York: Harcourt Brace Jovanovich, 1975).

18. For a review of studies on differences in aggressiveness between the sexes, see E. E. Maccoby and C. N. Jacklin, *The Psychology of Sex Differences* (Palo Alto, CA: Stanford University Press, 1974). For ethnographic data on male and female violence, see V. K. Burbank, "Female aggressiveness in cross-cultural perspective," *Behavior Science Research* 21 (1987): 70. For a review of sex differences in criminality, see J. Q. Wilson and R. J. Herrnstein, *Crime and Human Nature* (New York: Simon and Schuster, 1985). Anne Campbell argues that differences in men's and women's aggressiveness results from differing conceptions of aggression. See A. Campbell, *Men, Women, and Aggression* (New York: Basic Books, 1993). Men, according to Campbell, see aggression instrumentally, as a means for controlling others, while women see aggression as a way of expressing emotion. Campbell's work belongs in the tradition of the so-called difference feminists and is subject to many of the same criticisms as are other difference feminist works. Campbell's view of men's aggression is consistent with the evolutionary models described in chapter 5, but her view of women's aggression portrays women as less interested in controlling others and less politically astute than the evolutionary models suggest they must be. If there are differences in the way men and women use aggression, these may simply reflect the power imbalance between them. Those who have social power can use instrumental aggression, while those who lack such power can use aggression only as a way of expressing emotion.

19. For example, T. H. Clutton-Brock and P. H. Harvey discuss sexual dimorphism in primate species in "Primate ecology and social organization," in *Readings in Sociobiology,* edited by T. H. Clutton-Brock and P. H. Harvey. See also R. L. Trivers, "Parental investment and sexual selection," in *Sexual Selection and the Descent of Man,* edited by B. Campbell (Chicago: Aldine, 1972).

20. B. S. Low, "Sex, coalitions, and politics in preindustrial societies," *Politics and the Life Sciences* 11, no. 1 (1992): 63. What Low describes is a form of mutualism aimed at obtaining women. Women's coalitions, according to Low's observations, are more often composed of kin and are

consequently more stable. They are built on enduring relationships, rather than on transiently confluent interests and are thus unlikely to end with the partners in opposition. Sarah Hrdy, a primate ethologist, has emphasized the importance to nonhuman primate groups of enduring female bonds, as opposed to fluctuating male alliances. See S. B. Hrdy, *The Women That Never Evolved* (Cambridge, MA: Harvard University Press, 1981). Carol Gilligan, Nancy Chodorow and others have recently written extensively about how women's relationships differ from those of men. According to these authors, women's relationships are deeper and less instrumental than those formed by men, a point that, if true, seems to be related to Low's observations. See, for example, C. Gilligan, *In a Different Voice: Psychological Theory and Women's Development* (Cambridge, MA: Harvard University Press, 1982); N. J. Chodorow, *Feminism and Psychoanalytic Theory* (New Haven: Yale University Press, 1989); C. Gilligan, A. G. Rogers, and D. L. Tolman, eds., *Women, Girls, and Psychotherapy: Reframing Resistance* (New York: Haworth Press, 1991).

21. See, for example, A. A. Ehrhardt and H. F. L. Meyer-Bahlburg, "Effects of prenatal sex hormones on gender-related behavior," *Science* 211 (1981): 1312; N. J. MacLusky and F. Naftolin, "Sexual differentiation of the central nervous system," *Science* 211 (1981): 1294; M. Schumacher and J. Balthazart, "Sexual differentiation is a biphasic process in mammals and birds," in *Neurobiology,* edited by R. Gilles and J. Balthazart (New York: Springer-Verlag, 1985); M. Schumacher, J. J. Legros, and J. Balthazart, "Steroid hormones, behavior, and sexual dimorphism in animals and men: The nature-nurture controversy," *Experimental and Clinical Endocrinology* 90 (1987): 129.

22. For discussions of differences in arousal patterns between men and women, see D. Symons, *The Evolution of Human Sexuality.*

23. Regarding hormone effects on aggressiveness, see A. A. Ehrhardt and H. F. L. Meyer-Bahlburg, "Effects of prenatal sex hormones on gender-related behavior"; H. F. L. Meyer-Bahlburg, J. F. Feldman, P. Cohen, et al., "Perinatal factors in the development of gender-related play behavior: Sex hormones versus pregnancy complications," *Psychiatry* 51 (1988): 260; D. Olweus, A. Mattsson, D. Schalling, et al., "Circulating testosterone levels and aggression in adolescent males: A causal analysis," *Psychosomatic Medicine* 50 (1988): 261; R. T. Rubin, J. M. Reinisch, and R. F. Haskett, "Postnatal gonadal steroid effects on human behavior," *Science* 211 (1981): 1318; M. Schumacher, J. J. Legros, and J. Balthazart,

"Steroid hormones, behavior, and sexual dimorphism in animals and men: The nature-nurture controversy." A recently published study showed that men administered a gonadotropin-releasing hormone antagonist, which decreased testosterone levels, experienced less outward-directed anger. See P. T. Loosen, S. E. Purdon, and S. N. Pavlou, "Effects on behavior of modulation of gonadal function in men with gonadotropin-releasing hormone antagonists," *American Journal of Psychiatry* 151 (1994): 271. Regarding hormone effects on nurturance, see C. A. Pedersen, "The psychiatric significance of oxytocin," in *Neuropeptides and Psychiatric Disorders,* edited by C. B. Nemeroff (Washington, DC: American Psychiatric Press, 1991); C. A. Pedersen, J. D. Caldwell, and G. F. Jirikowski, "Oxytocin and reproductive behaviors," in *Recent Progress in Posterior Pituitary Hormones,* edited by S. Yoshida and L. Share (Amsterdam: Elsevier, 1988). Cf. Anne Campbell's viewpoint in note 18, above.

24. G. Lerner, *The Creation of Patriarchy* (Oxford: Oxford University Press, 1986).

25. See, for example, B. R. Bergman, *The Economic Emergence of Women* (New York: Basic Books, 1986); V. R. Fuchs, *Women's Quest for Economic Equality* (Cambridge, MA: Harvard University Press, 1988); M. N. Ozawa, ed., *Women's Life Cycle and Economic Insecurity: Problems and Proposals* (New York: Praeger, 1989).

26. F. Engels, *The Origin of the Family, Private Property, and the State* (New York: International Publishers, 1972). Eleanor Leacock's introduction to this edition provides an excellent review of Engels's thesis in light of modern anthropological data.

27. For an overview of Soviet feminist history, see D. Meyer, *Sex and Power: The Rise of Women in America, Russia, Sweden, and Italy,* 2d ed. (Middletown, CT: Wesleyan University Press, 1989).

28. Ibid; see also H. Scott, *Does Socialism Liberate Women?* (Boston: Beacon Press, 1974).

29. T. Veblen, *The Theory of the Leisure Class* (1899; New York: Mentor, 1953).

30. Ibid., 34.

31. Ibid.

32. C. Lévi-Strauss, *The Elementary Structures of Kinship* (Boston: Beacon Press, 1969). Lévi-Strauss thought that the distinction between "our" and "other" women, the former being salable and the latter being marriageable, is deeply rooted in the male mind. From an evolutionary

point of view, exchange of female kin for women from other families allows powerful men to benefit reproductively from their female relatives without actually having to mate with them themselves. Children conceived from genetically inbred matings suffer from decreased vigor and from genetic diseases. See, for example, N. S. Adams and J. V. Neel, "Children of incest," *Pediatrics* 40 (1967): 50; C. O. Carter, "Risks to offspring of incest," Lancet 1 (1967): 436; E. Seemanova, "A study of children of incestuous matings," *Human Heredity* 21 (1971): 108; M. Yamaguchi, T. Yanase, H. Nagamo, et al., "Effect of inbreeding on mortality in Fukuoka population," *American Journal of Human Genetics* 22 (1970): 145. Edward Westermarck, a student of marriage customs in the early years of this century, was the first to suggest that humans, like other animals, innately avoid inbred matings, but his theory was overshadowed by findings by psychoanalysts. See E. A. Westermarck, *A Short History of Marriage* (New York: Macmillan, 1926); E. A. Westermarck, "Recent theories of exogamy," *Sociological Review* 26 (1934): 22. Psychoanalysts thought that incestuous lust was suppressed by cultural prohibitions. Robin Fox, an anthropologist, reviewed modern data pertinent to this issue and argued that Westermarck essentially was correct. Large-scale studies of Israeli kibbutzim and recent anthropological studies of Chinese marriages provide key findings in favor of Westermarck's theory, at least in modified form. Much of the high rate of incest reported in our society is actually nominal—step-fathers being the culprits—or due to alcoholism, a disease of modern times, comparatively speaking. See R. Fox, *The Red Lamp of Incest* (New York: E. P. Dutton, 1980). See also J. Shepher, *Incest: A Biosocial View* (New York: Academic Press, 1983); A. P. Wolf, "Childhood association, sexual attraction, and the incest taboo: A Chinese case," *American Anthropologist* 68 (1966): 883; A. P. Wolf, "Adopt a daughter-in-law, marry a sister: A Chinese solution to the problem of incest taboo," *American Anthropologist* 70 (1968): 864; A. P. Wolf, "Childhood association and sexual attraction: A further test of the Westermarck hypothesis," *American Anthropologist* 72 (1970): 503.

33. G. Lerner, *The Creation of Patriarchy.*

34. M. Harris, "The evolution of human gender hierarchies: A trial formulation," in *Sex and Gender Hierarchies,* edited by B. D. Miller (Cambridge: Cambridge University Press, 1993). Harris's theory, of course, dovetails with work by Barbara Smuts, which shows that male violence against women has evolutionary roots. See B. B. Smuts, "Male

aggression against women: An evolutionary perspective," *Human Nature* 3 (1992): 1. Harris, in effect, argues that weapons serve to amplify the advantage men have over women by virtue of their willingness to use force against them.

35. William H. Durham describes this scenario among the Mundurucú tribesmen in the Amazon in W. H. Durham, *Coevolution: Genes, Culture, and Human Diversity* (Stanford: Stanford University Press, 1991).

36. B. S. Low, "Sex, coalitions, and politics in preindustrial societies"; B. S. Low, "Sex, power, and resources: Ecological and social correlates of sex differences," *International Journal of Contemporary Sociology* 27, nos. 1–2 (1990): 49; B. S. Low, "Cross-cultural patterns in the training of children: An evolutionary perspective," *Journal of Comparative Psychology* 103 (1989): 311.

37. See, for example, D. Symons, *The Evolution of Human Sexuality*. Helen E. Fisher, an anthropologist with the American Museum of Natural History, argues that serial monogamy is a "natural" pattern for human mating arrangements. See H. E. Fisher, *Anatomy of Love: The Natural History of Monogamy, Adultery, and Divorce* (New York: W. W. Norton, 1992).

38. William H. Durham discussed polyandrous marriages among Tibetan serfs, who use such marriages to maintain the integrity of family land holdings. See W. H. Durham, *Coevolution: Genes, Culture, and Human Diversity*.

39. A. Schlegel and H. Barry III, "The cultural consequences of female contributions to subsistence," *American Anthropologist* 90 (1986): 142.

40. See N. A. Chagnon, *Yanomamö: The Fierce People* (New York: Holt, Rinehart, and Winston, 1968); N. A. Chagnon, "Mate competition, favoring close kin, and village fissioning among the Yanomämo indians," in *Evolutionary Biology and Human Social Behavior: An Anthropological Perspective*, edited by N. A. Chagnon and W. Irons (North Scituate, MA: Duxbury Press, 1979).

41. N. A. Chagnon, "Mate competition, favoring close kin, and village fissioning among the Yanomämo indians."

42. E. Rice, *Captain Sir Richard Francis Burton: The Secret Agent Who Made the Pilgrimage to Mecca, Discovered the Kama Sutra, and Brought the Arabian Nights to the West* (New York: HarperCollins, 1990).

43. For discussion of Bachofen's thesis, see G. Lerner, *The Creation of*

Patriarchy; J. J. Bachofen, *Myth, Religion, and Mother Right: Selected Writings of J. J. Bachofen,* trans. R. Manheim (Princeton, NJ: Princeton University Press, 1967).

44. See, for example, H. E. Fisher, *Anatomy of Love: The Natural History of Monogamy, Adultery, and Divorce;* M. Harris, "The evolution of human gender hierarchies: A trial formulation"; E. Leacock, "Social behavior, biology, and the double standard," in *Sociobiology: Beyond Nature/Nurture? Reports, Definitions, and Debate,* edited by G. W. Barlow and J. Silverberg (Washington, DC: American Association for the Advancement of Science, 1980); E. Leacock, "Ideologies of male dominance as divide and rule politics: An anthropologist's view," in *Woman's Nature,* edited by M. Lowe and R. Hubbard (New York: Pergamon Press, 1983). An especially vivid account of women's place in a hunter-gatherer group is found in M. Shostak, *Nisa: The Life and Words of a !Kung Woman* (Cambridge, MA: Harvard University Press, 1981).

45. Semiramis, Tamara, Caterina Sforza, Catherine the Great, and the Rani of Jhansi, among other notable women, are discussed in A. Fraser, *The Warrior Queens* (New York: Alfred A. Knopf, 1989).

46. Ibid.

47. G. Lerner, *The Creation of Patriarchy.*

48. General histories of the women's movement are found in M. Cohen, *The Sisterhood: The Inside Story of the Women's Movement and the Leaders Who Made It Happen* (New York: Fawcett Columbine, 1988); in F. Davis, *Moving the Mountain: The Women's Movement in America since 1960* (New York: Simon and Schuster, 1991); in D. Meyer, *Sex and Power: The Rise of Women in America, Russia, Sweden, and Italy,* 2d ed.; and in E. Badinter, *The Unopposite Sex: The End of the Gender Battle,* trans. B. Wright (New York: Harper and Row, 1989). S. Faludi, *Backlash: The Undeclared War against American Women* (New York: Crown Publishers, 1991), presents a more pessimistic view.

49. B. R. Bergman, *The Economic Emergence of Women.*

50. C. F. Epstein, *Deceptive Distinctions: Sex, Gender, and the Social Order* (New Haven: Yale University Press, 1988), 48.

51. I. M. Lewis, *Ecstatic Religion: A Study of Shamanism and Spirit Possession,* 2d ed. (New York: Routledge and Kegan Paul, 1989).

52. B. S. Low, "Cross-cultural patterns in the training of children: An evolutionary perspective." In one sense what girls are taught is not to be deferential, but that they lack social power, from which submissiveness

follows as a matter of self-preservation. Readers interested in how relative power shapes conflict-related decisions are referred to P. Hammerstein, "The role of asymmetries in animal conflicts"; J. Maynard Smith, "The theory of games and the evolution of animal conflicts"; J. Maynard Smith, "Evolution and the theory of games"; J. Maynard Smith, *Evolution and the Theory of Games;* J. Maynard Smith and G. A. Parker, "The logic of asymmetric contests"; G. A. Parker, "Assessment strategy and the evolution of fighting behaviour."

53. Eli Robins estimates that completed suicide is three times as frequent in men as in women, in spite of the fact that more women are depressed. According to Robins, the greatest risk for suicide in both men and women occurs after age forty-five. See E. Robins, "Suicide," in *Comprehensive Textbook of Psychiatry,* 4th ed., edited by H. I. Kaplan and B. J. Sadock (Baltimore: Williams and Wilkins, 1985). Women's suicide risk is discussed in note 4 to chapter 1.

Notes to Chapter 6

1. F. Engels, *The Origin of the Family, Private Property, and the State* (New York: International Publishers, 1972).

2. T. Gordon, *Feminist Mothers* (New York: New York University Press, 1990).

3. K. Millett, *Sexual Politics* (New York: Simon and Schuster, 1969), 42.

4. Ibid., 41.

5. L. Tiger and J. Shepher, *Women in the Kibbutz* (New York: Harcourt Brace Jovanovich, 1975).

6. Ibid., 264.

7. T. Gordon, *Feminist Mothers.*

8. Ibid., 107–8.

9. Felice Schwartz, a well-known business consultant, created an uproar in 1989 when she argued that many women in managerial positions would gladly trade career and financial advancement for better working hours, more consistent with the exigencies of child rearing. Schwartz later denied that she was advocating coercively shunting working women onto so-called mommy tracks, but some feminist authors feared that this might result. See F. Schwartz, "Management women and the new facts of life," *Harvard Business Review,* January–February 1989, 65; S. Faludi, *Back-*

lash: The Undeclared War against American Women (New York: Crown Publishers, 1991).

10. See T. Gordon, *Feminist Mothers.*

11. Ibid.

12. The existence of multiple attachments is discussed in J. Bowlby, *Attachment and Loss,* vol. 1 (New York: Basic Books, 1969). For anthropological data, see M. Konner, *The Tangled Wing: Biological Constraints on the Human Spirit* (New York: Harper and Row, 1982); R. LeVine, "Cross-cultural study in child psychology," in *Carmichael's Manual of Child Psychology,* edited by P. H. Mussen (New York: John Wiley, 1970).

13. The classic study of kibbutz-reared children is B. Bettelheim, *Children of the Dream* (New York: Macmillan, 1969). See also A Sagi, M. E. Lamb, K. S. Lewkowicz, et al., "Security of infant-mother, -father, and -metapelet attachments among Kibbutz-reared Israeli children," in *Growing Points of Attachment Theory and Research,* edited by I. Bretherton and E. Waters, Monographs of the Society for Research in Child Development, vol. 50, nos. 1–2, (Chicago: University of Chicago Press, 1985). A study by B. E. Andersson ("Effects of public day-care: A longitudinal study," *Child Development* 60 [1989]: 857) is representative of the type of work that has been done to ascertain effects of day care in our society. Full-time day care does seem to affect mother-infant attachment (see, for example, P. Schwartz, "Length of day-care attendance and attachment behavior in eighteen-month old infants," *Child Development* 54 [1983]: 1073), but the long-term significance of these changes are unknown. See also T. J. Gamble and E. Zigler, "Effects of infant day care: Another look at the evidence," *American Journal of Orthopsychiatry* 56 (1986): 26.

14. See, for example, A. Pound, "Attachment and maternal depression," in *The Place of Attachment in Human Behavior,* edited by C. M. Parkes and J. Stevenson-Hinde (New York: Basic Books, 1982).

15. For an overview of this research, see D. Symons, *The Evolution of Human Sexuality* (New York: Oxford University Press, 1979). See also data in A. A. Ehrhardt and H. F. L. Meyer-Bahlburg, "Effects of prenatal sex hormones on gender-related behavior," *Science* 211 (1981): 1312; N. J. MacLusky and F. Naftolin, "Sexual differentiation of the central nervous system," *Science* 211 (1981): 1294; M. Schumacher and J. Balthazart, "Sexual differentiation is a biphasic process in mammals and birds," in *Neurobiology,* edited by R. Gilles and J. Balthazart (New York: Springer-Verlag, 1985); M. Schumacher, J. J. Legros, and J. Balthazart,

"Steroid hormones, behavior, and sexual dimorphism in animals and men: The nature-nurture controversy," *Experimental and Clinical Endocrinology* 90 (1987): 129.

16. H. E. Fisher, *Anatomy of Love: The Natural History of Monogamy, Adultery, and Divorce* (New York: W. W. Norton, 1992). See also M. K. Whyte, *The Status of Women in Preindustrial Societies* (Princeton, NJ: Princeton University Press, 1978).

17. P. Draper and H. Harpending, "A sociobiological perspective on the development of human reproductive strategies," in *Sociobiological Perspectives on Human Development,* edited by K. B. MacDonald (New York: Springer-Verlag, 1988).

18. J. A. Kurland, "Paternity, mother's brother, and human sociality," in *Evolutionary Biology and Human Social Behavior: An Anthropological Perspective,* edited by N. A. Chagnon and W. Irons (North Scituate, MA: Duxbury Press, 1979).

19. Taking just one crime, for instance, Daly and Wilson showed that approximately 25 percent of all Detroit murder victims in 1972 were related to their killers. In two-thirds of these cases, the killer was their spouse. See M. Daly and M. Wilson, *Homicide* (New York: Aldine de Gruyter, 1988).

20. This is especially true for depressives with so-called borderline features, who are emotionally unstable, impulsive, and prone to self-mutilation or injury. Borderline personality is discussed in B. Wenegrat, *Sociobiological Psychiatry: Normal Behavior and Psychopathology* (Lexington, MA: Lexington Books, 1990).

21. L. Tiger, *Men in Groups,* 2d ed. (New York: Marion Boyars, 1984).

22. See, for example, M. N. Cohen, "Speculations on the evolution of density measurement and population regulation in *Homo Sapiens,*" in *Biosocial Mechanisms of Population Regulation,* edited by M. N. Cohen, R. S. Malpass, and H. Klein (New Haven, CT: Yale University Press, 1980); F. Hassan, "The growth and regulation of human population in pre-historic times," in *Biosocial Mechanisms of Population Regulation,* edited by M. N. Cohen, R. S. Malpass, and H. Klein.

23. It may seem paradoxical, from an evolutionary point of view, that women with more resources would bear fewer children, but women may have more than one strategy for maximizing reproductive success. One, which is more appropriate when resources are uncertain, is to bear the

maximum number of young and invest little in the care of each. The other, which is more appropriate when resources are predictably available, is to bear fewer young and invest heavily in each. Pretransition women may be following something like the first strategy, while posttransition women may be following the second. In any event, reproductive success is more than a matter of just having babies. Decisions have to be made about caring for them as well. See E. R. Pianka, "On r- and K- selection," *American Naturalist* 104 (1970): 592.

24. C. S. Manegold, B. Powell, and Y. Hoshiai, "Hang up the help-wanted sign," *Newsweek*, July 16, 1990.

25. J. M. Murphy, "Trends in depression and anxiety: Men and women," *Acta Psychiatrica Scandinavica* 73 (1986): 113.

26. American Psychiatric Association, *Diagnostic and Statistical Manual of Mental Disorders*, 3d ed., rev. (Washington, DC: American Psychiatric Association, 1987).

27. See, for example, R. Aldridge-Morris, *Multiple Personality: An Exercise in Deception* (Hillsdale, NJ: Lawrence Erlbaum Associates, 1989); F. W. Putnam, *Diagnosis and Treatment of Multiple Personality Disorder* (New York: Guilford Press, 1989).

28. See, for example, G. F. Drinka, *The Birth of Neurosis: Myth, Malady, and the Victorians* (New York: Simon and Schuster, 1984).

29. See, for example, S. Faludi, *Backlash: The Undeclared War against American Women.*

30. See, for example, H. Bruch, *Eating Disorders: Obesity, Anorexia Nervosa, and the Person Within* (New York: Basic Books, 1973); K. Chernin, *The Hungry Self: Women, Eating, and Identity* (New York: Harper and Row, 1985); A. H. Crisp, "The psychopathology of anorexia nervosa: Getting the 'heat' out of the system," in *Eating and Its Disorders*, edited by A. J. Stunkard and E. Stellar (New York: Raven Press, 1984); D. M. Garner and P. E. Garfinkel, eds. *Handbook for the Psychotherapy of Anorexia Nervosa and Bulimia* (New York: Guilford Press, 1985); R. A. Gordon, *Anorexia and Bulimia: Anatomy of a Social Epidemic* (Cambridge, MA: Basil Blackwell, 1990).

31. P. R. Slavney, *Perspectives on "Hysteria"* (Baltimore: Johns Hopkins University Press, 1990).

32. E. Shorter, *From Paralysis to Fatigue: A History of Psychosomatic Illness in the Modern Era* (New York: Free Press, 1992).

33. Ibid., 84.

34. Quoted in J. Strouse, *Alice James: A Biography* (Boston: Houghton Mifflin, 1980), 322.

35. M. Piercy, *Woman on the Edge of Time* (New York: Fawcett Crest, 1976).

36. S. L. Bem, *The Lenses of Gender: Transforming the Debate on Sexual Inequality* (New Haven, CT: Yale University Press, 1993).

37. S. Faludi, *Backlash: The Undeclared War against American Women.*

Index